The Reconstruction of
Family Policy

THE RECONSTRUCTION OF FAMILY POLICY

Edited by
Elaine A. Anderson
and
Richard C. Hula

Prepared under the auspices of the
Policy Studies Organization
Stuart S. Nagel, Publications Coordinator

CONTRIBUTIONS IN FAMILY STUDIES, NUMBER 15

GREENWOOD PRESS
New York • Westport, Connecticut • London

Library of Congress Cataloging-in-Publication Data

The Reconstruction of family policy / edited by Elaine A. Anderson and
    Richard C. Hula ; prepared under the auspices of the Policy Studies
    Organization.
        p.   cm.—(Contributions in family studies, ISSN 0147–1023 ;
    no. 15)
    Includes bibliographical references and index.
    ISBN 0–313–27899–7 (alk. paper)
    1. Family policy—United States. 2. United States—Social policy.
    I. Anderson, Elaine Adah. II. Hula, Richard C., 1947– .
    III. Policy Studies Organization. IV. Series.
    HQ536.R433   1991
    306.85'0973—dc20   91–46

British Library Cataloguing in Publication Data is available.

Library of Congress Catalog Card Number: 91–46
ISBN: 0–313–27899–7
ISSN: 0147–1023

First published in 1991

Greenwood Press, 88 Post Road West, Westport, CT 06881
An imprint of Greenwood Publishing Group, Inc.

Printed in the United States of America

The paper used in this book complies with the
Permanent Paper Standard issued by the National
Information Standards Organization (Z39.48–1984).

10 9 8 7 6 5 4 3 2 1

Contents

Tables and Figures

FIGURES

Acknowledgments

This work has been made possible by a grant from the College of Human Ecology, University of Maryland–College Park. Support given to each of the authors by the University of Maryland Curriculum Transformation Project provided the opportunity to explore many of the issues raised in this volume. A special thanks is due to the individual authors who worked so hard and faced long delays with good cheer. Finally, we would like to thank our own families who were often forced to share the pains of editorship.

The Reconstruction of
Family Policy

1

Introduction: Thinking About Family Policy

Richard C. Hula

During the decade of the 1980s, the appropriate role of government in society has been subjected to a near global reevaluation. Most often the result has been a public demand for a reduced public sector. Although the collapse of the socialist states in Eastern Europe is certainly the most dramatic example of this process, others can easily be cited. These include significant social experiments in privatization implemented in Great Britain and, to a lesser extent, throughout Western Europe (Pirie, 1988). In a number of Third World countries, traditionally strong central governments have implemented policies aimed at stimulating private sector development (Hanke, 1987). In the United States the very popular Reagan and Bush administrations have articulated an aggressive policy of government retrenchment.

An important element in this ongoing debate is the appropriate form and magnitude of public social welfare policy. The concrete political debate surrounding social programs centers around issues of who should be served, levels of funding, and program structure. Fundamental intellectual divisions regarding the nature of social organization and the role of the state in modern society underlie this policy debate. The chapters in this volume illustrate the impossibility of examining either concrete policy debates or fundamental theoretical issues in isolation of each other. Each needs to be considered in turn.

THE BASIS OF SOCIAL ORGANIZATION

Scholars have argued that an important source of confusion in the social welfare policy debate is the widely divergent assumptions brought to the discussion. Indeed, one can identify two broad, and largely incompatible, conceptions of society within the academic literature on social welfare policy. The first is derived from classical liberal theory in which society is conceptualized as a collection of individuals, each seeking to maximize his or her self-interest. Such maximization occurs most often within a free competitive market but can be expressed in a number of private sector institutions. The role of the state is largely to protect private property and act as an arbiter of private disputes. Central to this view is the essential neutrality of the state in resolving disputes among competing interests. In contrast to the individualism stressed by liberalism, Marxism argues that the basic units of societies are economic classes. Rather than a neutral arbiter, the state acts to protect the class interests of those who control economic capital.

Obviously the intellectual tradition one brings to the analysis of social welfare policy has a profound effect on how one describes and evaluates it. Liberal theorists claim that social welfare serves to mitigate the harshest aspects of individual competition. Such protection is typically targeted toward and restricted to those who are perceived as unable to compete successfully in the marketplace. Such limitations divide the objectively needy population into either the "deserving" or "nondeserving" poor. The politics surrounding social welfare policy serve to expand, reduce, or otherwise redefine these groups. Clearly U.S. social welfare policy is developed primarily within the parameters of this definition.

Marxist theory conceptualizes welfare in a quite different way. The welfare system is not to be understood in terms of benefits to individual recipients, but rather as a means to stabilize and protect the current economic order. Within the literature there is little consensus, however, as to whether or not such policies are likely to succeed. Some argue that social welfare is an integral element of the process of economic reproduction; others see it as a source of political instability that may ultimately threaten the economic order itself.[1]

THE ROLE OF FAMILY

It is striking to observe that the traditional nuclear family, and the social relations implied by it, spans both liberal and Marxist analysis of social welfare policy. Both cite a number of similar functional roles assumed by families and stress the importance of the family in social reproduction. Of particular importance are roles centering on child rearing and socialization. The assumption that traditional families are central to social organization, and are thus essential to the maintenance of the society, is clearly reflected in the concrete formulation of policy. Numerous authorities have pointed out the bias against persons with objective needs but who fail to fit traditional family patterns. The most obvious is the Aid to Families with Dependent Children (AFDC) program, which, in most states, has limited social aid to single women with children. There is no analog program for poor single women or men. After some reflection it is clear that this family metaphor is pervasive throughout a good deal of U.S. social policy. For example, consider municipal zoning. Students of local zoning have long noted the exclusionary impact of such policy. Less understood, however, is the importance of the traditional family as a model on which zoning decisions are made. Legislation that requires single family residences on large lots, isolated from all services and public transportation, seems to assume a family composed of a working husband, a stay-at-home mother, and children (Ritzdorf, 1986, 1990).

Given the importance of family in the framing of social welfare policy, it is hardly surprising that current political debate often focuses on the effects of social policy on the family. Demands for increased spending are justified as means of strengthening family values. Cuts in programs are presented as strengthening similar values. Thus, while it is apparent that the family is a symbol of fundamental importance in American politics, it is equally clear that it provides no clear guide to action.

Some scholars and policy makers have begun to argue the need to rethink a number of issues surrounding family policy. The most fundamental challenge has been the questioning of the traditional nuclear family as the guiding metaphor for social policy. Critics of current policy argue that since such families constitute only a small fraction of the population of the United States, it is not unreasonable to demand that policy be targeted to other, more common forms of families. These include, of course, dual working families and single-parent households.

While there is no doubt that the traditional family has become less common, it continues to have enormous normative power. That is, such families are seen as being the ideal, the model to which reasonable citizens strive. Such an argument underlies demands that social policy continue its traditional posture toward families even as its central model becomes a statistical rarity. Obviously the power of the traditional family as a symbol is not directly undermined by the fact that such families are no longer typical within the U.S. population. Criticism of the normative role of traditional families in social policy must necessarily proceed at a more theoretical level. Subject to particular scrutiny have been long unchallenged assumptions about the social arrangements implicit in traditional family relationships. Of particular importance is the traditional assignment of women to private, that is, unpaid, labor in the household, with men expected to provide major economic support for the family. The result is seen by some as forcing women into a marginal role in the paid labor force. From this emerging feminist perspective, family policy is seen as involving fundamental issues of social structure as well as practical issues of policy design.[2]

THE SEARCH FOR FAMILY POLICY

This volume seeks to stimulate the reconstruction of family policy in the United States. While individual chapters certainly differ in focus and approach, each is committed to rethinking fundamental elements of current policy debate surrounding family life. We begin with a set of chapters that explore some fundamental elements of family policy. John Scanzoni considers whether or not there is indeed an inherent conflict of interest between adults and children in fashioning social policy. Patricia Spakes, writing from a somewhat broader perspective, outlines the parameters of a feminist family policy. These chapters begin to sketch an alternative to conventional assumptions brought to the analysis of family policy.

Part II explores the linkage between ideology and action. Each of the chapters in this section shares two attributes. First, each provides useful descriptive information on concrete family policy over a range of specific issues. In addition, they share the common focus of trying to understand the process by which policy was designed and implemented. Such an analysis begins to provide an understanding of how broad ideological preferences are translated into concrete policy in the context of U.S. domestic politics.

This analysis begins at quite a general level in a chapter by Shirley L. Zimmerman. Zimmerman argues for a general link between state political culture and family policy. She reports support for this view in an analysis of family policy in three states with quite different political cultures. Stephen K. Wisensale's examination of state-level decision making in Connecticut stresses the importance of internal political leadership for family policy.

The link between ideology and political action can be quite complex. This complexity is revealed by Clifton P. Flynn and Hyman Rodman in an important discussion of the current debate on latchkey children. They note widespread feminist support for increased before- and after-school daycare. However, a number of arguments put forward to support public investment for such care are problematic. The terms of public debate often assume that children who are not cared for by stay-home parents are necessarily put at some measure of risk. The goal of before- and after-school care is to minimize this risk. The implication of such an argument is clear. An alternative to increasingly publicly provided child care is to have more parents (almost certainly mothers) stay at home with their children. Obviously this is not an outcome desired by most supporters of public daycare.

Issues of ideology also force the policy analyst to consider the relationship between abstract values and empirical facts. While it is obvious that facts seldom speak for themselves, it is equally clear that the real world data can serve to test empirical assertions imbedded in ideological positions. Two chapters show examples of how current policy fails such review. Doris E. Dinkins Ford argues that current policy toward caring for the nation's elderly seems based on a mythical past in which multigenerational households flourished. She provides data to suggest that such patterns were never really common and, even more important, that they are inconsistent with popular preferences today. As a result, current efforts to transfer a greater responsibility of elder care to families are likely to generate a number of unexpected negative effects. Gregory H. Wilmoth, Danielle Bussell, and Brian L. Wilcox provide a somewhat similar analysis to one of the most divisive debates in contemporary American politics: abortion. While there is little doubt that at the heart of the abortion debate are a set of nonempirical moral judgments, these authors document the lack of evidence for a number of specific empirical claims made by antiabortion advocates.

In the final chapter of Part II Jean Robinson presents a comparative example of family policy in the People's Republic of China. Robinson's chapter offers a powerful illustration of how traditional social values may impede the implementation of social policies that operate under alternative assumptions. Robinson suggests that for such policies actually to generate significant change, there needs to be a fundamental reordering of society.

Part III of this volume examines a number of specific policies and attempts to trace their impacts. Although ideology remains an important implicit issue, these chapters are more directly targeted to the question of concrete costs and benefits for specific programmatic efforts. These chapters express significant concern that retrenchment in social programs over the 1980s has had a significant and negative impact on low income families. For example, Theresa Funiciello and Sanford F. Schram review the economic effects of program cutbacks on AFDC recipients during the 1980s. Their analysis shows that in actual purchasing power, AFDC families have seen their subsidies significantly decrease. Deborah R. McFarlane documents a similar decline in family planning resources available to low income households. An analysis of child support payments by Andrea H. Beller and Seung Sin Chung documents that the economic risk of female-headed households is reinforced by a breakdown of the traditional child support system.

Several chapters describe alternative economic and social policy instruments. Sally Lubeck and Patricia Garrett, after reviewing shifts in family demography that generate a vastly increased demand for nonfamily-based care, outline a series of techniques by which that care might be provided. Clifton P. Flynn considers the potential of joint custody arrangements following divorce. Robert K. Leik, Mary Anne Chalkley, and Nancy J. Peterson cite evidence that Head Start continues to provide broad benefits to participants. While each of these chapters takes a relatively optimistic view of public action, each is careful to stress that there are no simple solutions to complex social issues. Not surprising, each of the specific reforms discussed is seen as having important limitations.

MAKING POLICY ANALYSIS RELEVANT TO POLICY

Both practitioners and scholars have expressed a commitment to having the development and implementation of public policy informed by evaluation and policy analysis. Indeed, a good deal of literature already exists exploring family policy. Often, however, specific efforts to create a policy analysis that links theory and practice are disappointing, breeding frustration and misunderstanding rather than enlightenment. Practitioners dismiss the works of academics as having little relevance to a world of limited resources, political constraints, and constant deadlines. Academic observers often see the work of practitioners as excessively narrow, with little appreciation for underlying intellectual issues. Unless this division is reduced, collections such as this are likely to have little impact on either the academic or policy world.

There are at least two broad strategies to mitigate this conflict. Examples of each can be found in this volume. The first is for the academic community to simply focus more clearly on concrete policy issues of direct concern to policy makers. In this way policy implications of analysis are clearly identified. Good examples include Leik and colleagues' exploration of the impact of a specific Head Start program and Flynn's discussion of concrete custody arrangements.

A second bridge between theory and practice involves a reassessment of policy analysis itself. Often, the goal of policy analysis seems to be the identification of the most efficient means to a given end. However, as noted above, an important theme in this book is that the metaphor of the traditional family, incorporated in so much family policy, must itself be reconsidered. Thus, successful policy analysis must be allowed to inform the ends as well as the means of social policy.

This aspect of policy analysis has been referred to as social learning (Stone, 1985). While one should certainly be interested in the substantive impact of concrete policies, it is essential to consider what policy outcomes tell us about society. For example, a number of cases reviewed in this volume suggest that some "failures" in family policy occurred, not so much because of poor design or implementation, but rather because of the nature of the world in which these policies exist. For example, Dinkins Ford shows clearly that a number of key assumptions that underlie policy for the elderly simply are incorrect. It is hardly surprising that policy resting on such assumptions will have, at best, a minimal positive effect.

Our belief that the current debate about family policy suffers from a variety of theoretical and empirical weaknesses has lead us to offer this collection. If these chapters spur further interest in reexamining the parameters of the debate on family policy, the effort to produce the volume will be well invested.

NOTES

1. For an excellent overview of these issues see M. P. Smith (1988).
2. For an overview of this literature see Abramovitz (1989) and Pascall (1986).

I
The Normative Context of Family Policy

2
Balancing the Policy Interests of Children and Adults

John Scanzoni

The argument has been made that a sharp distinction must be drawn between public policy and programmatic solutions (Scanzoni, 1983; 1989; Scanzoni and Arnett, 1987; Shehan and Scanzoni, 1988). Policy is defined in terms of broad, overarching objectives and goals—an image or vision of a desirable state of affairs (Naisbitt, 1984; Steiner, 1981). It is essentially a general philosophical framework from which specific programs and concrete aims can be derived, justified, and promulgated. Moreover, public policy is commonly linked to ideology; hence attempts to divorce family policy from value positions seem artificial at best. In a recent formulation of conservative family policy, Bauer (1986) sets forth several pivotal themes. Among these is the proposition that "the American family" is in serious decline owing largely to "abrasive experiments of two liberal decades" (p. 9). A second theme is found in the family's preoccupation with children's interests and virtual exclusion of the consideration of adult interests. Next, "a single set of standards" governing sexual as well as all other family/personal behaviors represents a third conservative family policy theme (p. 32). A fourth theme is the assertion that the family rests primarily on duty and obligation. Among these duties are: (1) the obligation to be chaste prior to legal marriage and monogamous afterwards; (2) the duty to have children and to bear them only in marriage; (3) the duty to live for the children and not to pursue interests (such as mother's employment) that might impact them negatively; and (4) that an additional duty is the requirement to maintain a permanent marriage so that the third obligation is not subverted.

In sum, the family policy of conservatives is focused on a structure or set of arrangements that are normatively ordered and highly predictable. Their vision or image is that the family is an organic system maintaining equilibrium in the face of societal vagaries and onslaughts. The foundation of this homeostatic perspective is adherence to duty based on a fixed and unchanging set of universal moral standards. Derived from this desirable state of affairs are particular programs that would, according to Bauer, "reverse the recent trend toward automatic divorce" (p. 21), place greater stress on the adoption option for pregnant teenagers (p. 47), refuse public schools the option of distributing contraceptives to adolescents (p. 39), allow "no Federal program [to] provide incentives for sexual activity by teens" (p. 41), restrict "the easy availability of welfare" (p. 34), and reverse increasing trends toward mothers' participation in the work force (p. 44).

Contrary to conservatives, progressives hold to an "evolving or process-oriented character of the world and human nature" (Francoeur, 1983, p. 381). Consequently one of their foundational themes is that families are not declining but instead are caught up in the continual evolution and transition that has been occurring since at least the Civil War and perhaps even earlier (Howard, 1981). "The family," for instance, has given way to the more comprehensive and variegated construct of *families* (Scanzoni, 1987; Scanzoni et al., 1989). Still more abstractly, we may say that the concept of "families" itself is essentially a lay or common-sense notion. A generalizing construct with greater scientific validity and utility (and thus of potentially greater policy/program significance) is *primary* or *close relationships* (Scanzoni, 1987; Scanzoni et al., 1989). A second and related progressive theme is that whatever uncertainties and stresses persons face with regard to contemporary relationships, those strains are not the result of forsaking the conservative vision. Instead, numerous stresses and strains emerge from the curious paradox of large numbers of citizens adhering to conservative family norms while at the same time actually behaving in nonconventional fashion (Francoeur, 1983). The contrast between expressed beliefs and reported behaviors pertaining to sexuality is one case in point (Ehrenreich et al., 1986). It follows that a third progressive theme is that rather than issuing inflexible fiats (e.g., telling adolescents to "say no to sex"), the progressive goal is to discover what works and what fails to work for varieties of citizens in numerous circumstantial permutations. Based on this pragmatic utilitarian approach the progressive goal is then to try to promote caring and responsible commitments among adults and between adults and offspring of all ages (Scanzoni, 1988). In short, progressives endorse the belief repudiated by Bauer: "there is no natural order of society and no inherently right patterns of living, loving, begetting and getting through life" (p. 30).

A fourth progressive policy theme becomes the prime focus of this chapter—the goal of balancing adult interests with children's interests.

Recall the conservative preoccupation with children's interests: "the divorce epidemic . . . has devastated children" (Bauer, 1986, p. 20). According to conservatives, the prime cause of children's devastation is said to be adult individualism because "the interests of children are secondary to our individual desire for career success or a new mate" (p. 31). Furthermore, Bauer cites Urie Bronfenbrenner that "somebody has got to be crazy about the kids," this being the "key ingredient" in child development (p. 31). Indeed there are a number of basic and applied professionals in addition to Bronfenbrenner who are not generally considered conservatives but who nonetheless express serious concern for the interests of contemporary and future children. Among these are J. Aldous (1987), A. Booth (1987), E. M. Levine (1987), R. S. Weiss (1987), and V. Gecas (1987), who conclude that "we must find ways to deal with the contemporary stresses on families, particularly in their capacity as agents of socialization, if the next generation is to have much of a chance. I thought it was tough growing up when I was a kid. It's much tougher now" (p. 436).

In contrast to those kinds of assessments, R. Rapoport et al. (1977) argue that the issue of the balance between children's and adults' interests is extraordinarily complicated. First they concur that the conservative value that families *should* be child-centered predominates as a cultural ideal in Western societies (p. 10). Second, they also concur with the conservative assessment that in actuality the realization of that notion is a "contemporary myth" (p. 10). However, Rapoport et al. part company with conservatives by asserting that "the child-centered, mother-focused paradigm is sorely in need of revision. The conditions which made the paradigm acceptable in the past are changing. But the issue now is how a more balanced formulation might be developed" (p. 11). The basis of a fresh formulation requires "an approach that clarifies the nature of the fit between parents' and children's lives. Children first, last and always is no longer a tenable maxim for family life" (p. 40). Whatever that new maxim is, it should be "based on an appreciation of how parents' preoccupations, needs, and requirements can be reconciled with those of children" (p. 14).

Unfortunately, the task of reconciliation is not easy because parents' and children's "needs are to varying degrees in opposition, imposing frustrations and sorrows and forcing mutual adaptation" (p. 16). For instance, Rapoport et al. observe that parenting may be seen as creating as well as interfering with life opportunities (p. 29) and that parenting is but "one set of interests among others" (p. 25). Moreover,

As families become more diverse in the patterns of relationships they contain—including "boyfriend," "girlfriend," stepparent, stepsibling and other combinations stemming from the increased tendency for divorce and remarriage, and more living together without marriage—it is important to recognize that different patterns of parenting may evolve and be legitimate in different contexts without necessarily being irresponsible or deviant (p. 21).

or harmful to children (Lamb, 1982).

The disjuncture between conservative and progressive policy on this particular balancing issue is neither academic or trivial. Recall Naisbitt's assertion that compelling practical programs as well as significant research questions are derived from an acute vision of desirable objectives. Program and research questions derived from policy suggesting that "in a healthy society, women and men who forego pleasures, delay purchases, foreclose options and commit most of their lives to the noblest undertaking of citizenship: raising children who, resting on the shoulders of the previous generation, see farther than we and reach higher" (Bauer, pp. 9–10) will be radically different in character than programs and research derived from the Rapoport et al. policy of mutual balance between child and adult interests. But before considering some programmatic and research issues, we need to flesh out certain aspects of the progressive mutual balance policy.

One of the premises on which this policy rests is that having children must be considered optional—not obligatory as Bauer argues. It must be plainly stated that some persons have neither the motivation nor the capabilities to balance the difficult demands of parenting with their own needs, goals, and interests. Alongside the zero option, the one-child option should also be endorsed. The once prevailing cultural notion that moral persons should have as many children as, but not more, than they can afford (Rainwater, 1965) has cost untold numbers of children and adults a great deal emotionally, physically, intellectually, and economically. The pronatalist bent of conventional policy (the notion that having children in and of itself is good) contrasts with progressive policy asserting that what matters is quality children defined not in the conservative sense of conformity to prescribed rules, roles, regulations, and standards. (For some persons "quality children" may mean not having any.) Instead, the term "quality children" in the progressive sense refers to their personal autonomy, self-direction, and problem-solving skills, as well as to their creative and imaginative capabilities. Thus fitted, they should be able to order their lives in conjunction with a fluid environment that influences them but which in turn they might also be able to influence (Turner, 1985).

In trying to account for "contemporary and projected low fertility" in the U.S., S. Nock argues that "motherhood, childbearing, and child-rearing are symbolic experiences with different meanings for women who endorse male-female equality and for those who do not" (1987, p. 373). Conservative policy is based on a symbolic meaning in which "women who hold motherhood as a sacred or natural consequence of their femininity . . . marry earlier than other women and . . . have earlier and higher fertility. . . . They . . . eschew educational or occupational pursuits as less rewarding than their roles as mothers" (p. 383; see also Scanzoni, 1975). In contrast, progressive policy endorses a different symbolic meaning of parenthood (not merely *motherhood*) in which women and men "focus more on their role as *consumers* of children" (competing with other potential life interests) instead of "focusing on their role as the producers of children" (Nock, 1987, p. 391).

A second premise of the mutual balance policy flows from the image of *feedforward* over time between children and their environment—particularly the adults in their milieu who do their parenting—irrespective of whether these adults and children are bonded by blood or by social ties. Rapoport et al. conclude that "the literature appears to assume that the child, encountering his parents' attitudes as he grows and changes, interacts with a fixed quantity—the adult. Yet parenthood itself is a developmental process. Not only do inner and societal forces effect changes in the parent; the child too has an influence on the adaptation and personality development of the parents" (1977, p. 18). In the progressive view, offspring must be seen as energetic actors significantly influencing the lives of their parents throughout the lifespan and not viewed merely in the conservative sense as fragile and passive reactors to the input of omnipotent adults (Lerner and Spanier, 1978). In short, the reality of feedforward over time is inseparable from the issue of mutual balance of interests because in large measure those continuing reciprocal influences either enhance or undermine the interests of both children and adults. Figure 2.1 graphically displays reciprocal influences among the developing child, the developing adult, the developing relationship between child and adult, and any developing paired relationships between adults in the child's milieu. Figure 2.1 addresses the charge often leveled against progressives that they endorse individual autonomy at the expense of group solidarity—autonomy over responsibility (Cherlin, 1983; 1984, p. 157). It meets the charge by implying that autonomy and responsibility may coexist in an ongoing, though uneasy balance.

Figure 2.1 places the developing child in a matrix interacting with three additional developmental realities that are equally significant both scientifically and practically. Based on this matrix, it is impossible to assert *a priori* that the developing child is of any greater consequence than the other forms of development. Quite the contrary—each one of them is inextricably enmeshed with the remaining three. Consequently, from a policy perspective, progressives reason that it is folly to seek to enhance one segment (e.g., child development) without simultaneously enhancing the additional segments as well. Hence, when Bronfenbren-

Figure 2.1
Ongoing Mutual Influences among the Developing Adult Primary
Relationship, the Developing Adult, the Developing Child, and the
Developing Child/Adult Relationships

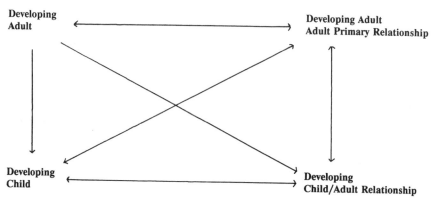

Source: Adapted from J. Scanzoni et al., *The sexual bond: Rethinking families and close relationships*, p. 168, copyright ©1989 by Sage Publications, Inc., Newbury Park, CA. Reprinted by permission of Sage Publications, Inc.

ner asserts, "Somebody has got to be crazy about the kids" (cited in Bauer, 1986, p. 31), the reality is that policy makers and applied professionals must be equally concerned about adults, adult primary relationships, and about child/adult relationships.

These feedforward influences are somewhat easier to grasp when considering the two lefthand segments of Figure 2.1. The child is continually changing and those ongoing changes are influencing and changing the parent figure(s), whether social or biological, in his or her life (Popenoe, 1987; Tanfer, 1987). As the adult is influenced and often changed by the child (as well as by other elements in Figure 2.1), those changes reciprocally impact on the child. Since it follows that the greater the well-being of the adult the greater the well-being of the child, policy (and thus programs) must be aimed at simultaneously enhancing the well-being of both, not merely the children. The empirical and policy realities become more complex when we take into account the upper right segment of Figure 2.1—any sexually based primary relationship(s) in which the adult(s) in the child's life are currently participating (Scanzoni et al., 1989). Subsumed under this rubric would be legal marriage, cohabitation, or partners maintaining separate households though experiencing physical proximity as a result of joint overnights. At any point in time the child may be living with adults in any of these three arrangements or, fourth, living with an adult not currently in any paired relationship. Assuming the existence of a relationship, Figure 2.1 suggests that the ongoing character of that adult relationship impacts on the developing child. Thus the well-being of that developing relationship influences the well-being of the child. Reciprocally, the well-being of the developing child influences the well-being of the ongoing adult relationship. These mutual influences occur at the same time that the individual adult(s) in the dynamic (not homeostatic) system is/are continually developing. Individual adult development impacts the adult relationship directly but also indirectly impacts on the child via that adult relationship. Finally, the lower right segment of Figure 2.1 indicates that the character of the ongoing relationship between the child and the adult(s) in his or her life is also developing continually and that it is reciprocally interconnected with the well-being of the developing child, the well-being of the developing adult, and the developing adult/ adult relationship of whatever sort that may be at any point in time.

Definitions of "well-being" are inevitably slippery. For children, well-being may be measured by intellectual, social, and emotional development among other factors. In addition, the well-being of adults, of children, and of primary relationships (child/adult, adult/adult) can in general terms be defined in K. E. Boulding's terms as "human betterment . . . described as a change in some system that is evaluated by one or more human beings as being 'for the better' " (1985, p. 37). More concretely, the literature makes a distinction between psychological well-being and social health. The former is "measured by exclusion, being inferred from the absence of symptoms of stress" (McDowell and Newell, 1987, p. 104). Thus we can say that the more an adult or child is free from stress symptoms, the greater the level of psychological well-being she or he is experiencing (Mirowsky and Ross, 1989). Furthermore, following Figure 2.1, we may assert that greater stress on the part of the adult produces greater stress in the child and vice versa; and conversely an adult characterized by greater well-being produces the same effect in the child and vice versa. Precisely the same logic applies to "social health . . . that dimension of an individual's well-being that concerns how he gets along with other people, how other people react to him, and how he interacts with social institutions and societal mores" (McDowell and Newell, 1987, p. 152). Social health of adults generates social health in children and vice versa. Consequently general policy and specific programs need to address the psychological and social well-being of adults as well as children if children (and adults) are ultimately to prosper as fully as possible.

Since public policy requires some sort of vision, Figure 2.1 supplies an image of the realities of contemporary families/close and primary relationships. Figure 2.1 rings far truer to the real world of today and tomorrow than does the usual textbook diagram of "the family" consisting of a static space containing neatly placed slots for mother, father, son, and daughter. Since the emerging vision is one of forms of development continually changing one another over time within the context of an ever-shifting milieu, the proposition that the interests of all elements of the vision or model must be equally addressed becomes self-evident and compelling. Children's interests do not stand alone, any more than do adult interests. By superordinating children's interests and simultaneously ignoring or downgrading adult interests, conservatives in actuality do damage to children's interests.

DERIVING RESEARCH QUESTIONS AND PROGRAM APPLICATIONS

Recently, a conservative family policy organization interpreted research findings in ways supporting its long-range goal of returning wives and mothers home from the paid work force. One set of studies showed that coital frequency is less among two-income than among husband-income marriages. The Family Research Council interpreters conclude these "findings have aroused concern among some experts who see the decline in sexual activity among two-income families as a symptom of a greater problem—too little time together" (1987, p. 3). To buttress the ominous nature of these trends they cite other researchers who "warn" that as " 'the number of dual-earner families increases, more spouses may be less able to sustain each other emotionally.' " A second essay in *Family research today* highlighted recent studies by J. Belsky suggesting that "infant daycare undermines a child's 'sense of trust, of security, of order in the world' " (1987, p. 3). Thus from the *Family research today* perspective the message is clear—"research demonstrates that employment of wives/mothers is harmful to marriages and especially to children." Consequently that message is utilized to reinforce their broader policy objective aimed at discouraging and substantially reducing the paid employment of women (Bauer, 1986).

The question arises as to how progressives would, from their policy of "mutual balance of child/adult interests," derive research questions and applied programs pertaining to the inextricably linked matters of daycare and women's employment. First, stimulated by Figure 2.1, progressives would emphasize the issue of adult interests arguing that if those interests are slighted, children's interests will also be slighted. Furthermore, the argument would be made (see Scanzoni, 1988) that contemporary (white) Western women are in effect losing the option that they have held for some 160 years—namely, the option *not* to be actively involved in the direct production of family resources. Just as it was incumbent on preindustrial women to labor for personal and household survival, so is paid labor incumbent on postindustrial women but for reasons more profound than survival. Belsky identifies two reasons for continuing increases in women's labor force participation: "personal fulfillment or economic need" (1985, p. 237). However those two widely accepted rationales tend to trivialize women's employment by implying that contemporary women do in fact retain the option *not* to work and that in any case their work motivation is different from men's. It is virtually impossible to find anywhere in the literature any assertion seeking to justify male employment primarily for reasons of economic need or personal fulfillment. Progressive policy seeks to explicate the goal that ultimately women are employed for precisely the same fundamental reason as are men—employment is the pathway to autonomy and control of one's destiny. The assumption is that it is in women's own best interests to be employed in precisely the same way it is for men.

Progressives acknowledge that the policy goal—women's employment justified in terms of autonomy and control—may sometimes clash with the short-range interests of children and of men (Rapoport et al., 1977). However, progressives contend that in the long run, it will be in the best interests of men and of children to justify women's employment in those terms. Thus, over time the greater common good will be better served. However, during the interim, concrete steps must be taken to try to reconcile the short-term interests of women, men, and children. To move in that direction, we must fit women's employment into the larger issues of health and well-being, whether mental, emotional, or social. The prime question becomes, what sets of employment-related factors promote the well-being of women (Thorne and Henley, 1975)? Recall that the answers affect children and men as much as women because the greater the well-being of women the greater the well-being of children and men. For instance, investigators might pose the heretofore unorthodox issue regarding the consequences for women's well-being (and thus children's/men's) due to women *not* being employed— or being *underemployed*. Similarly what are the effects on women's mental and emotional well-being of being located at reduced levels of job status and/or income as a result of dropping out of the labor force to attend to children or to husband? And what is the impact on the employed woman's well-being of having to cope with the prime responsibility for housework and child care along with her occupation? And, perhaps most significant of all, what are the effects on women's well-being (and thus children's) of never having wanted to be economically autonomous but nevertheless being thrust into having to provide for themselves and their children because a man is not, or never has been, around?

Unfortunately, current debates over women's employment and daycare seldom raise these sorts of research questions. Vastly more common is the reasoning followed by Belsky in his 1985 review of the research and politics of daycare: "The basic question for policymakers . . . [is] 'Is daycare bad for young children?' . . . If daycare proved detrimental to [children's] development, it would be hard to make the case that daycare was in the public's best interest, consequently, it would be difficult to endorse policies to promote, or even support, the group caring of young children beyond the confines of the family" (p. 239). In effect Belsky conforms to the assessment of Rapoport et al. (1977) that professionals tend not to take adult development and adult interests into account when considering whether daycare should be endorsed. Instead if current daycare arrangements are found to be harmful to children, *ipso facto* withdraw support for it. Nevertheless, later in this essay he concludes that "daycare is here to stay" irrespective of research results. Based on available data he then cautiously endorsed *quality* daycare (Belsky, 1985, pp. 250–251), owing to public pressure for it.

Belsky is quite correct in asserting that as a practical matter daycare is "here to stay," and so is women's employment, as he acknowledges. Given those realities, the task of reconciling the short-term competing interests of women, children, and men includes investigations into the positive and negative consequences on women's well-being of being employed or nonemployed—including the well-being of women and mothers who currently have no man with whom to share expenses. Very likely accumulating evidence from such studies of women would reveal the same bipolar tendencies as do studies of daycare and children (Lamb, 1982). Under certain conditions, *nonemployment* may have negative consequences for the well-being of wives and mothers (and their children), while under certain other conditions, it may not. Similarly, employment may impact on women (and children) sometimes adversely and sometimes positively. Examples of conditions mitigating her employment include the character of any male relationship she might currently have, as shown in Figure 2.1. What is the mitigating impact, for instance, on the well-being of her and her children of the degree of his participation with her in childcare as well as in routine household chores? What is the impact of the degree of his supportiveness of her employment efforts? A second set of conditions is also taken from Figure 2.1— namely, her own development as an adult. What, for instance, is the mitigating impact on her children/partner of the degree to which she is, or wishes to become, economically autonomous?

In any case, evidence of employment's negative consequences for women would hardly lead progressives to withdraw support for it, as Belsky suggests should be done for "group rearing of young children" in the event negative consequences flow from that. In actuality, as with all public policies and programs, the notion of reconciling children's and women's interests means dealing in terms of cost/benefit analyses (Katzner, 1979, p. 59; Dornbusch and Strober, 1988). Given that both women's employment and daycare are here to stay, and given that costs and benefits inevitably become attached to both, specific programs need to be devised that attempt to reduce costs and maximize benefits on both sides, not just on the children's side. Reinforcing that assertion is the win-win assumption underlying Figure 2.1. If the well-being of women is enhanced, children will be better off and vice versa. One step in that direction is to critique the studies alleging that today's children are suffering as a result of current trends in women's employment, divorce, and varieties of living arrangements. For example, in his critique of the methodologies of such studies, J. N. Edwards (1987) concludes that they often contain numerous critical flaws in both design and measurement. Consequently he argues that conclusions alleging that today's youth are in dire straits owing to women's employment or divorce per se are probably exaggerated and in any case need to be seriously reevaluated (see Polit, 1980).

In sum, the balance between child and adult interests will inevitably be delicate and uneasy, tipping sometimes to one side and then to the other. Programs aimed at reconciling these competing sets of interests can be informed by at least three overarching policy goals or guidelines. First is the policy goal described above: women's economic autonomy. It makes little sense to speak of the well-being of women and children (as well as of men) unless and until gender makes no difference with respect to adult economic autonomy. A second broad guideline is that men should expect to be efficient householders as well as effective parents if they choose to have children. The conventional family model relieves men of prime responsibilities to households and for children. That model is reflected at the programmatic level in part by child custody awards that generally go to women and also by the difficulties of collecting child support payments from men who sense minimal involvement in, and influence over, the offspring they have sired. The progressive model asserts that just as there are benefits (both extrinsic and intrinsic) and costs associated with women's economic autonomy, and that these benefits and costs should be equitably distributed, the same principle must apply to householding and especially to child care. It makes little sense for conservative family policy to argue that children are so extraordinarily vital and then to fail to assign shared parenting to men by retaining women as primary parenting agents.

A third policy guideline is a national commitment to high quality early childhood enrichment. Officials in and out of government have argued that the United States should make a policy commitment to land humans on the planet Mars during the 1990s. As laudable as that goal may be, it is surely no more compelling (though perhaps more costly) than the progressive policy of creating environments for U.S. children that are rich in learning and creative potentials. These opportunities would be available to all children regardless of the employment status of any parental figure(s) in their lives. Such opportunities would phase out and replace the often inadequate options currently available to many employed adults and their children. If children are indeed the nation's most valuable resource, then progressives espousing such a policy would in fact hold what G. Steiner (1981) calls the "high moral ground" by proposing it.

All three policy themes—women's economic autonomy, men's household and child-rearing involvement, and young children's enrichment—would contribute to the broader objective of balancing adults' and children's interests. Commitment to each of them would supply the bases for research and programs contributing to benefits for women, children, and men. Serious short-term, and perhaps intermediate-term, dislocations are certain to emerge in seeking to balance these competing interests. Nonetheless, a progressive article of faith is that in the long run, reasoning from a model such as that in Figure 2.1, children and adults developing under the rubric of these kinds of general policies and derived programs would be healthier, both as *individuals* and in terms of their relationships (child/adult, adult/adult) than they would be if the current confusion persists stemming from the predominance of conservative policies contradicted by vast numbers of citizens exploring non-conventional behavior patterns (Edwards, 1987).

Boulding observes that "conservatives . . . tend to know what they like, which is what they have now" (1985, p. 179). He also says that persons situated to the left of conservatives (i.e., progressives) "tend to have fairly clear views of what they do not like and move away from it, rather than knowing what they do like and moving toward it" (p. 178). The result, he says, is that rather than being "guided by a common love of some perceived good" (p. 179), progressives often clash and splinter over specific *program* interests and leave the *policy* field open to conservatives. The policy objectives and guidelines presented here represent certain directions progressives might choose to go. In any case some direction must be selected because it will no longer suffice merely to inveigh against conservative policy while simultaneously failing to develop an alternative vision and thus be "guided by a common love of some perceived good."

3

A Feminist Approach to National Family Policy

Patricia Spakes

Political rhetoric of the 1980s was remarkable in its idealization of family life and in its support of government action to strengthen families. Notable efforts were made on the part of the federal government to develop national family policy by implementing several specific family policy proposals. Welfare reform, of course, is intended to support families by providing alternatives to welfare and incentives for welfare mothers to work. Parental leave would give either parent (though certainly more often the mother) time off from work to care for children. However, the most popular support is for corporate daycare or for some form of federal subsidy for daycare, which is intended to help families afford the high cost of child care.

Although both parental leave and daycare are presented as family issues, in reality child care is still primarily women's responsibility (Ford Foundation, 1989). In fact, all the evidence suggests that even in dual-wage-earner families, women provide most of the child care and that, while more men now verbally espouse egalitarian relationships in the home, changes in their behavior have lagged behind changes in their professed beliefs (Googins and Burden, 1987).[1] The political idea that child care is a family issue, however, reflects the reality that it is more politically expedient in this society to sell a proposal in terms of its value to families rather than in terms of its value to women. It also reflects growing support for the ideology of a national family policy, support that is now coming from all parts of society—academicians, newspaper columnists, popular magazine editors, and some legislators, as well as feminists.

The idea of national family policy and what it seems to promise is in many ways seductive, particularly to working mothers. However, proposals that have been offered thus far have varied considerably. Earlier plans included controversial "liberal" programs such as guaranteed minimum income, nationalized health care, and public funding for daycare (Rice, 1977; Keniston, 1977). Such programs were aimed primarily at supporting low income families. Others have advocated tax reform measures and protections that favor the traditional nuclear family and promote conservative values (Family Protection Act, 1981). Still another approach has been to favor a "progressive policy," which is based on a set of "moral norms for contemporary families" and promotes negotiation based on equity, justice, and absence of exploitation (Scanzoni, 1981; 1982). S. Kamerman proposed that the United States adopt some of the family support programs currently offered in European and Scandinavian countries (Kamerman, 1979; 1984; Kamerman and Kahn, 1981), while G. Steiner (1981) argued the futility of national family policy and offered a single-issue, piecemeal approach.

As the decade of the 1980s closed, rhetoric shifted once more, with arguments centering on the need for national "child policy." Focusing on the needs of children and their future potential value to the labor market or, alternatively, their future potential cost to the economy has been perceived as an effective political tool (Denny, Poleka, Jackson, & Matava, 1989; Kamerman, 1989; Stipek and McCrosky, 1989). Child-centered family policy proposals are essentially the same proposals suggested by Kamerman and others earlier (i.e., subsidized child care, family and medical leave); however, they are presented as being intentionally supportive of children.

At this point, there is no shared vision of what American family policy can and should look like, nor of how it is to be implemented. Several possibilities for implementation have been offered, and these range from sweeping congressional action (Kamerman, 1979; 1984; Family Protection Act, 1981) to state action (Scanzoni, 1982) and to a single-issue advocacy approach (Steiner, 1981).

Among the various approaches, the one that appears to have generated the most popular support is probably that of Kamerman who suggests that the United States adopt reforms that emulate aspects of the family policies of several European and Scandinavian nations. Kamerman argues for changes in employment policies that permit greater part-time work, "parenting" or "child care benefits" that allow either parent to take unpaid but protected leave for child rearing, and expanded coverage in disability benefits and health insurance programs. Several bills currently in Congress would implement aspects of the Kamerman family policy proposal, while some state and even city governments are considering similar measures. What is *wrong* with these proposals, and why should feminists *not* support them, especially since it is obvious that, while they are purportedly aimed at families, it is primarily women who will benefit from them?

The answer to these questions requires: (1) an exploration of the fundamental, pronatalist value that forms the basis of all national family policy; (2) closer examination of the actual impact of Scandinavian family policies; (3) understanding of existing family policy in the United States; (4) exploration of how most current family-based policy proposals serve to maintain inequality rather than to promote equality both in society and in the home; and (5) determination of what the basic elements of a truly feminist family policy would look like.

FUNDAMENTAL PRONATALIST VALUES

Rationales offered in support of national family policies usually invoke images of the nuclear family as the "cornerstone of the nation"—the place where individual needs are met and children are produced and socialized. Since the future of the nation depends on having citizens— hopefully emotionally, physically healthy, and educated ones—the family is deemed to be of critical importance and worthy of support. Since there is evidence that the family is "at risk" (due to high rates of divorce, single parenting, and so forth), revised social policies are seen as critical to the family's survival.

One of the main reasons the family appears to be "at risk" relates to the influx of middle class mothers into the work force. Whether motivated by "need" or "greed" (both financial and personal), women are entering and staying in the work force in record numbers. The Women's Movement has been successful in its objective of freeing women from the confinements of the home, with the result that women are now convinced that they can and should have both a career and a family. A new generation of women has emerged who want both roles and are vocal in their demand for the social supports necessary to accomplish both goals. Kamerman's family policy proposals appear to offer the vehicles to obtain them. However, all family policy proposals have a hidden "catch." They are based upon pronatalist assumptions that women have little choice but to continue to have children, and they are accompanied by societal expectations that women will continue to provide the care for their children.

The coercive nature of American pronatalist policy has been described by J. Blake (1974), who pointed out that in American society, parenthood is universally prescribed. There are no legitimate or socially rewarded alternatives to the performance of parental roles, and, in fact, there are numerous social, psychological, and economic sanctions that are brought to bear on adults who choose not to have children (due to homosexuality, single status, or a choice to remain childfree). Blake's argument was further considered by M. E. Gimenez (1980), who pointed out that the Women's Movement has also taken pronatalism for granted. Her review of feminist writings evidenced several themes related to reproduction: (1) concern with current sex role definitions and expectations, with a vision, in most cases, of future androgyny; (2) critiques of marriage and the nuclear family with proposals that reflect egalitarian and/or androgynous relations and shared responsibility for child care and housework; and (3) a demand for nurseries and child care services crucial to the economic survival of working women.

Gimenez concluded that, while feminists have denounced the negative social, psychological, and economic consequences of socialization patterns that stress motherhood as the major social role for women, they have not questioned the pronatalist assumptions per se. (There are, of course, some exceptions, such as Firestone [1970]). Feminist advocacy for reproductive freedom has meant that women are given choices as to when to have children and how many to have but are not really free to choose *not* to have children at all. Thus, "pronatalist reward structures impel women and men marginally committed to parenthood to form families because that is the price to be paid for normalcy, respectability, credibility, and fulfillment of adult sex role expectations" (Gimenez, 1980, p. 227). She further notes that increases in illegitimacy, child abuse, spouse abuse, and divorce are a high price to pay for this societal proscription. Looked at in this way, the social programs advocated for the support of families are necessary precisely because of the broad pronatalist assumption that, for women, bases individual worth and the derivation of meaning in life on reproduction and mothering and offers no alternative.

Obviously, family policy proposals are based on support of the family unit, and, if we understand "family" to include children, they are by definition always pronatalistic. Although one might argue that the term "family" can be defined more openly and thus exclude children, this has not been the assumption upon which most current family policy proposals are based. In fact, family policies in the European and Scandinavian countries are specifically geared toward the support of children. They do not give people choices of whether or not to have children. They seek to provide supports for the *family* roles of women as mothers and men as fathers. Most of the European family policies that are held up as models were clearly designed to foster reproduction while still enabling women to participate in the labor force. The Scandinavian countries have added to that agenda the promotion of sexual equality by removing the obstacles that prevent women from doing their jobs in both the work place and the home.

SEXUAL EQUALITY AND FAMILY POLICY: THE SCANDINAVIAN EXPERIENCE

Is it possible to use national family policy to promote sexual equality in society? At least two of the family policy proposals for this country have the promotion of sex equity as either an implicit or explicit objective. This is an implicit goal of the Kamerman proposal, which argues for policies that will give women an opportunity to achieve equality by alleviating some of the burden upon them. It is explicit in the Scanzoni proposal, which seeks to promote changes in family structure, with a view toward promoting androgyny in spousal sex roles in the future. Thus, it should be instructive to examine the extent to which family policy has enabled the Scandinavian countries actually to achieve greater equality for women.

The Scandinavian nations have lived with their family policies for several decades and are now in a position to evaluate them. There, social scientists have recently begun to question why, in spite of the fact that the Scandinavian countries have extensive welfare systems that support women better than anywhere else in the world (to the envy and admiration of many Western women), "women still experience patterns of under-representation, discrimination, and subordination which are very similar to those elsewhere in the world" (Hernes, 1984, p. 26). (See also Sidel, 1986, p. 177; Wolfe, 1989, p. 20.) In other words, why has an extensive family policy failed to promote sexual equality?

Several analysts, who take a socialist feminist approach to understanding the Scandinavian problem, have pointed to the fundamental patriarchal nature of an industrial society as the cause of the continued inequality (see Holter, 1984). Patriarchal systems are based on a distinction between systems of production and reproduction. Money and power are distributed through the production system, which is dominated by men. Since most rights in society are tied to employment, and since women do not have equal access to employment (their ties being more tenuous), women are disadvantaged (Eisenstein, 1984b). Furthermore, the patriarchal bias provides a "housewife assumption," which forms the basis for laws, social programs, and income supports (Dahl, 1984). Women's rights and benefits are tied to the husband's employment record. Critics of Scandinavian family policy argue that, even though women there have entered the world of work in large numbers, the reproductive functions of these women have simply been moved into the paid economic sector (Waerness, 1984). Thus, women are found predominantly in child care, nursing, and other forms of "care giving work" in the public service sector, where their traditional reproductive roles continue. These jobs, of course, pay considerably less and are less valued than jobs in the production sector. Although many women are in the work force, their positions remain inferior, and they still lack access to money, power, and the decision-making system. According to Holter (1984), men in Scandinavian countries still control the decision making in both the government and corporate sectors and thus make the rules that "protect" women and children. It is also true, however, that Scandinavian women recognize the need for protection and view welfare programs as "woman friendly" (Hernes, cited in Wolfe, 1989, p. 17).

Social benefits in Scandinavia protect the reproductive function of women. Economic and social supports are provided for women with the assumptions that: (1) the woman has a husband who is the primary wage earner on whom she can depend; and (2) if she does not have a husband (due to death, divorce, or nonmarriage) she can depend on the government instead—as long as she is performing *maternal* functions. Such an approach replaces dependency on men with dependency on (male-dominated, paternalistic) government. This may not appear sexist until one reverses the words "women" and "men." While it is widely assumed that men and women are equally responsible for children, few would suggest that social policy should promote male dependency on either women or the state in order to protect their parenting functions.

What the Scandinavian experience has shown is that, while men and women may be equal under the Constitution, a woman's reproductive position puts her at a disadvantage. Formally, equal rights contribute to continued gender inequality because women still do not have true equality in the economic sphere of production, which is where benefits and rewards are obtained. Current Scandinavian family policies/welfare programs have helped women in the performance of their reproductive and care-giving functions in the home, but they have also served to maintain many of the structural deficiencies that promote inequality in the economy. The challenge for those countries now is to find ways to achieve true equality without jeopardizing public benefits to those who need them. The feminist challenge is to devise a social policy that gives women a real option *not* to have children (as well as to have children), thus making parenthood a genuine choice, and to find real alternatives and options for women to meet their identity needs.

CURRENT AMERICAN FAMILY POLICY: ITS IMPACT ON WOMEN

The argument over whether to have a national family policy in this country has no practical significance because it already exists. The only real argument is over its future direction and whether it should support a particular kind of existing family structure(s) or whether it should be more progressive and promote social change. However, before current proposals can be rationally evaluated, a better understanding of the existing policy is required.

In the United States, legal regulation of the family (and, subsequently, family policy) was fragmented and inconsistent as a result of the practice of federalism and a belief in the constitutionally protected right of state governments to regulate families in the interest of protecting the public welfare. While some inconsistency still exists, the judicial system in this country has provided a unifying force for the nationalization of family policy. While in other countries, national legislative bodies developed family policy, in the United States, the role of Congress has been limited, and much of the current family policy has been judicially developed. (For example, the Supreme Court has established national policy on marriage, divorce, contraception, abortion, and other related family issues.) The Supreme Court has been able to bring about consistency because it has the power of judicial review (which does not exist in other countries), and many constitutional challenges to state policies and laws have been resolved there (for a complete review, see Spakes, 1985).

The Supreme Court has responded on a case-by-case basis to public demands for greater individual freedom and increased consistency and has established the parameters of a national family policy. Out of the myriad decisions related to the family, there emerges a clear bias in favor of the traditional, legally defined nuclear family (and its extended family version, for which a long tradition of public support exists). This support can be discerned by reviewing a variety of decisions in cases related to the right to marriage, the rights of married couples to use contraception, the right to abortion, the right of parents to control the education of their children, and the rights of children against parents. In such cases, the primary issue concerns the existence of a family privacy right. The Supreme Court has said that such a right does exist and is constitutionally protected. However, once the Court concluded that there is a right to *family* privacy, it had to define what does and does not constitute a legally defined family. This came about through cases that tested whether extended families, foster families, and communal families shared the same constitutional right to privacy and whether unwed fathers, unwed mothers, illegitimate children, unwed couples, homosexual couples, and welfare families had the same rights as family members.

The philosophy that the Court has derived indicates that, in order for a family to exist, there must be a *legal marriage* between *two opposite sex persons*, and a *potential parent-child relationship* must exist. The marital couple and their offspring (biological or adopted) are a family, as are those extended families in which biological kinship ties exist. Cohabitation is not sufficient to qualify as a marital/family relationship; *permanence and formal commitment* are required. A biological relationship alone will not suffice to indicate familial relationship; in the case of unwed fathers, *psychological support and involvement* must be shown as well. However, cases involving the rights of foster parents show that, lacking the biological relationship, psychological support and involvement alone are insufficient. The homosexuality cases further suggest that psychological support and involvement are not the critical factor but that *moral fitness* of the parent is as important a criterion as the ability to nurture and support.

Thus, the Supreme Court has been extremely reluctant to extend family privacy rights and constitutional protection to any family type that does not fit the traditional nuclear model. Other families may be given protection for limited rights in certain situations. For example, certain unwed fathers who have demonstrated financial support and psychological involvement with their offspring have the right to be heard in court in cases involving the adoption of their offspring; however, the Court has not given all unwed fathers blanket protection of paternal rights. Similarly, illegitimate children have some rights in terms of the receipt of public benefits; however, the Court has upheld inheritance laws that discriminate in favor of legitimate children. The Court has concluded that families receiving welfare benefits do not have the same privacy rights as other families and therefore are not protected from state intrusion via mandatory home visits, and it has said that while single-parent families living in communal situations cannot be denied public benefits, they do not have the same privacy rights as other families.

Alternative family living arrangements (including communal families and foster families), unwed mothers, unwed fathers, illegitimate children, unmarried couples, and welfare families have not been granted rights equivalent to those of the traditional nuclear family. As a result, a dual family policy has been created and fostered. Legitimately constituted middle-class families are treated preferentially, while "illegitimate" and poor families are subjected to greater external regulation by the states. Meanwhile, judicially developed family policy is moving *all* families toward increased regulation by the courts (Spakes, 1985).

An analysis of the Supreme Court opinions that serve as a basis for judicially developed national family policy reveals the underlying values that shape the Court's decisions. First, the Supreme Court bases its decisions regarding constitutionally protected privacy rights on traditionally held values. Thus, the Court tends to be backward oriented in its reasoning. It does not promote social change; it follows social traditions. Second, current judicially developed national family policy reflects patriarchal notions of the family and paternalistic attitudes on the part of the justices. Third, the Supreme Court evidences strong concern for protection of the public purse. In an era of high individual freedom and movement away from legally constituted family relationships, the Court has sought to ensure that the government is not responsible for the care and welfare of children. Thus, many Supreme Court decisions protect the interests of the state or nation as opposed to the interests of either parents or children. This underlying policy goal is particularly detrimental for low income and minority families. Given trends toward the feminization of poverty and increases in the number of female-headed single-parent households, it is increasingly and primarily women and children who are subjected to greater regulation by the courts and the state under the guise of "protection."

The Courts and Sexual Equality

Although the courts have broadened their support of equal rights for women in recent years, most of the activity has taken place around the rights of women in the public rather than the private sphere (i.e., around issues of affirmative action in the workplace, disability benefits, and so on). In this context, an underlying earlier premise was that the special nature of women necessitated special protection by the Court. This position was articulated in *Muller v. Oregon* (208 U.S. 423, 1907), where the Supreme Court said:

Differentiated by these matters from the other sex, she [woman] is properly placed in a class by herself, and legislation designed for her protection may be sustained, even when like legislation is not necessary for men, and could not be sustained. It is impossible to close one's eyes to the fact that she still looks to her brother and depends on him. Even though all restrictions on political, personal, and contractual rights were taken away, and she stood, so far as statutes are concerned, upon an absolutely equal plane with him, it would still be true that she is so constituted that she will rest upon and look to him for protection: that her physical structure and a proper discharge of her maternal functions . . . justify legislation to protect her from the greed as well as the passion of man.

While the assumptions made in *Muller v. Oregon* may appear archaic, A. E. Freedman (1983) points out the difficulty judges have had in developing a theory of sexual equality that moves away from that assumption and differentiates "real" sex differences from those that are legally and socially created. Freedman argues that, while the courts have attempted to identify and condemn stereotypes regarding the proper roles and differential capacities of women and men, the issues have not been attacked as comprehensively as the problem demands. Furthermore, the courts have largely avoided dealing with the assumption of a dichotomous and separate "public realm of employment and politics, and a private realm of family and intimate relationships" (Freedman, 1983, p. 966).

The judicial system, which is a major source of family policy in this country, has not developed a clear, consistent understanding of gender differences, and it lacks an understanding of the interdependent relationship between the public and private sectors. Thus, equality for women is an issue to be dealt with primarily in the public employment and political sector, while the "family" is protected under a zone of constitutional privacy. The issue of the extent to which women need to be protected from men, require different treatment from men, or should be treated equally with men depends on the context, and the results are contradictory and confusing. Meanwhile, tradition continues to be a principal guidepost in the development of family policy, and the courts continue to weigh the interests of the state and the interests of the corporate sector against the interests of both women and families.

Legislative Family Policy and the Patriarchy

Current legislative family policy in the United States is also based on pronatalism, paternalism, and patriarchal notions of the family. In the past the government has sought to provide support and protection for the traditional, middle-class, nuclear family. Thus, social policies in this country reflect what M. Abramowitz (1985) calls a "family ethic." This is identical to the "homemaker ethic" described by social analysts in the Scandinavian countries. Here, too, it is assumed that women are dependent on men, that their primary place is in the home, and that their primary purpose is reproduction, which needs to be protected. Laws and social policies here have been made by men for the protection of women and children when there is no man available for their support. This is the underlying premise of social policies such as Social Security, unemployment compensation, and Aid to Families with Dependent Children (AFDC) (Abramowitz, 1985).

For middle income level, "legally constituted," traditional nuclear families in the United States, support for the family ethic has provided a variety of welfare programs directed toward providing security for families through the primary wage earner—the husband. For families that do not fit the traditional norm, the results have been destructive. This is particularly true for black and other minority families, who do not share the dominant "family ethic" but have their own family ethics that differ from the "norm." R. Staples (1973; 1989), E. Mizio (1974), H. P. Trader (1979), and K. S. Jewell (1988) have been justly critical of the impact of current family policies on minority families. For minority and low income families, for nontraditional families, current family policy has been disastrous.

AFDC provides an example. Originally intended to strengthen families by enabling mothers to remain in the home, this program in effect transfers the woman's dependency from a husband to the state. The program is clearly pronatalist. No forms of financial support are available in this country for low income women *without* children. Since alternative roles often do not appear to be available to young, poor women, and since having a child and becoming a mother is the one socially recognized and accepted way of securing identity and economic needs, AFDC encourages reproduction and dependency. At the same time, the welfare system seeks to discourage that dependency through punitive means—stigmatization, stringent and tedious application procedures, and mandatory work programs. Since women who do get off welfare generally enter the lowest paid, most tenuous positions in the service sector of employment, the only real alternative to dependency on the state is marriage or remarriage and dependency on a man. Policies and programs that are based on the middle-class, nuclear family ethic do not work well when they are applied to other groups.

There is, theoretically at least, a practical advantage and justification in the failure to design either legislative or judicial family policies and programs that meet the needs of nontraditional, low income, and minority families. The theory is that, if these families are given special treatment and protection, more people will be encouraged to enter their status. Thus, if unwed mothers have rights equivalent to wed mothers, more women will choose not to marry. If unwed women have the same protections and rights as married women, women will be discouraged from entering legally sanctioned relationships. If welfare mothers have the same rights as nonwelfare mothers, more women will go on welfare. Thus, current American family policy gives preferential treatment to some families at the expense of others, and it is quite often women who suffer from the dual policy the most.

A Critique of New Proposals

Recent family policy proposals are, for the most part, directed primarily at the upper-middle-class families that have always received preferential treatment in American family policy. (The proposals of K. Keniston [1977] and R. Rice [1977] are the exception and, in fact, gave preference to low income families; however, their proposals generated little support and are already almost forgotten in the debate.) The difference today is that the new proposals reflect a belief in the possibility of egalitarian marital roles and two choices for women: to have children and stay at home or to have children and work. In fact, the new proposals recognize that for many women, the only choice now, due to economic necessity, is to have children and work. Thus, current family policy proposals support the woman's right (and responsibility) to do both.

Yet, as women who do both can attest, trying to fulfill both sets of responsibilities often means doing neither job well. Doing both hampers women in career development, keeps attachment to the labor force tenuous, and often makes women feel guilty at the same time that they are not fulfilling the maternal responsibilities as well as they should. As a consequence, women have not gained the access to money, power, and status that feminists anticipated would come when women constituted over half the labor force. Nor have the social changes resulted in the ideal of equally shared parenting, which feminists hoped would accompany the increased employment of women. So, many women who are working now have been "liberated" and now have two jobs where once they had one. They have joined low income, single-parent, and minority women who have always held two jobs instead of one.

Current family policy proposals such as parental leave, employer-subsidized daycare, flexible work hours, and expanded disability benefits seek to alleviate the destructive impact of this situation by providing various forms of family support. These proposals are aimed especially at the revised middle-class family model—the dual-wage-earner, two-parent family—and at the single, working mother and her children. They are not particularly helpful and, in fact, are still potentially destructive for low income and alternative families. For example, corporate daycare and expanded disability benefits *only* help women who are firmly attached to the labor force in corporations or institutions large enough to support such programs. This family policy abandons the women who are most in need of subsidized daycare. Also, since small businesses are expected to be the largest source of new jobs in the future, these proposals, while they may be helpful to some well-educated and career-oriented women, may be described as "too little, too late" for everyone else. Corporate/private responsibility and income tax deductions for daycare may be easier to sell to the general public and legislatures, but they will, in all likelihood, block all chance for publicly subsidized daycare for the women who need it most. Corporations and middle-class taxpayers are unlikely to support programs for others that they are already subsidizing for themselves.

Current family policy proposals recognize the changing structural arrangements of families in the United States, but they are still protecting the reproductive function of women. They *allow* egalitarian relationships in families; however, they do not *promote* true equality in society. Current *family* policy proposals still limit the choices available to women. A woman in this country still has primarily one role open to her: that of wife/mother. The choices not to marry or to marry and not have children are still open to a relatively few (mostly upper-income-level, well-educated) women and are still socially sanctioned.

Women cannot compete on an equal basis with men in employment when they are handicapped by their responsibilities for children. In this patriarchal society, equal treatment does not produce equality, and, yet, protective policies do not produce equality either. What is required, therefore, is a social policy that provides women with real options. Poor young women need to see real alternatives to having babies as a way of getting their personal needs met. Women need training and educational opportunities that enable them to obtain meaningful employment. Women who choose the job of mothering need recognition for their work and ways to contribute to their own future security in their own right, rather than as dependents of men. Employment protection should be given to women who choose to mother and to work, not just to protect their reproductive functions but to enable all women to compete equally.

The last decade of discussion and experience with family policy formulation has demonstrated that it is possible to respond to the social and structural family changes that have occurred; that a variety of approaches are possible; and that, as in the past, each approach would help some families more than others. None, however, has offered real promise of addressing the needs of low income, minority, and "alternative" families, nor do any of the proposals address the causes of their distress. Most proposals are remedial in nature. Most would only contribute further to the confusion and disarray of existing family policy by adding a variety of new programs and policies targeted toward specific groups that have recently emerged as politically powerful families. Most would only exaggerate the dual nature of American family policy.

Only one of the current proposals is in any way truly "progressive" (Scanzoni, 1981; 1982) in the sense that it offers a future-oriented social agenda—in this case, a framework for future policy formulation that seeks to promote, or at least accommodate, sexual equity and justice in marriage. However, Scanzoni's proposal also has obvious class bias, and it provides the option for marital equity rather than promoting social equality. Perhaps the implicit assumption Scanzoni makes is that marital equity and androgynous sex roles in the family will eventually lead to social equality. However, such an assumption fails to take into account the effect of patriarchy outside the family.

FEMINIST FAMILY POLICY

How then do feminists resolve the contradictions and the dilemma that the apparently contradictory goals of national family policy and feminism create? First, the question needs to be framed differently and framed from a feminist perspective. The primary question then becomes, "How can we reach the goal of sexual equality?" and the corollary is, "How can we shape social policies that protect women immediately and still support the ultimate goal?" As Z. Eisenstein says:

The problem is delineating a politics that grasps this dilemma but does not support the patriarchal politics implied by it. A politics that attempts to create sexual equality must recognize this problem: that the politics of sex necessitates women's protection in and from patriarchal relations at the same time that it must move beyond protection and the notion of "difference" toward equality (1984a, p. 246).

Framing the problem in this way, whatever passes for family policy would need to have both short- and long-term objectives and a theoretical perspective in which it is grounded. Thus, the following assumptions would be made. First, the personal is indeed political. In reality, it is not possible to separate private and public spheres of life or of responsibility; the home and the state are integrally related and interdependent. Second, protection for women is necessary now and in the immediate future, but it is potentially dangerous. Protection—that is, being helped—is a double-edged sword because, while it does offer some people assistance and even solutions that they otherwise would not have, *people who require protection cannot be equal.*

As S. Firestone argued, "Day care centers buy women off. They ease the immediate pressure without asking why that pressure is on *women*" (1970, p. 233). While federal and corporate funding for daycare and other solutions are certainly necessary and helpful to women, they should be seen as a part of a transition stage.

A third assumption of feminist family policy is that, eventually, the family will have to change as will society. This does not necessarily mean having a "mother right" or matriarchal society that replaces the patriarchal society, with women gaining rights and responsibilities instead of men. The goal is not to pit women against children or to pit mothers and children against fathers. The goal is to include fathers. If this is the ultimate end, one cannot begin by accepting the assumption of innate differences between the sexes, which makes women better nurturers, or by accepting the assumption of women's "special sphere of influence." One need not necessarily assume that radical change is possible or even that it is desirable; however, it must be assumed above all else that the active promotion of sexual equality is a socially desirable goal for family policy.

A family policy can be developed that incorporates feminist assumptions and principles. It would, in fact, incorporate some of the specific policy proposals made by Kamerman and others but only as part of a more comprehensive national family policy that supports and advances sexual equality both in the family and in society, both in the courts and in the legislatures. Such a policy might, in fact, resemble Scanzoni's proposal for families of the future. The two approaches each offer partial solutions to the problems women face in families and might be successfully combined with additional specific policy proposals to develop a truly progressive and comprehensive strategy for reconciling the needs of women with the needs of families in our society. What follows is an attempt to begin to develop policy proposals that would need to be included in a feminist family policy. While the list is certainly not exhaustive, it is intended to suggest the direction in which feminists who support the development of national family policy should be moving.

Reproductive Choice and Freedom of Sexual Expression

For women to be truly equal to men, they must have control of their own bodies, which implies the freedom to choose whether and when they will bear children. The United States leads the industrialized world in its rates of teen pregnancy, teenage childbirth, and teenage abortion, although teens in the United States are no more sexually active than their European counterparts (Wattleton, 1989). A national agenda for promotion of sex education and teen pregnancy prevention are absolutely essential if women are to make informed choices regarding childbearing.

Complete freedom of reproductive choice also implies, however, that women would be free to enter alternative relationships. The parenting and family rights of gay men and lesbian women would have to be legislatively recognized and judicially protected.

Flexible Custody and Child Support

Many feminist critics of the judicial system have noted that the "tender years doctrine" has been a double bind for women. While it established an apparent "mother right" with regard to child custody, in reality women's incomes drop tremendously within a year after divorce. Thus, the spouse with the lower income and lower earning potential is left with the major responsibility for the children. Given the poor record of courts in awarding and of fathers in paying child support, women who win lose. On the other hand, P. Chesler (1986) and C. Brown (1986) point out that a maternal preference in child custody does not actually exist. When fathers seek custody, they usually get it, usually on the basis of greater ability to provide for children financially combined with the disadvantaged position of women in proving that they are equally fit as parents. Recent changes in child support enforcement are enforced now, primarily as a punishment for men's abandonment of their responsibilities. When fathers do not pay, welfare is not a viable, long-term solution since it transfers dependency onto the public patriarchy. As Brown (1986) points out, the existence of welfare, in fact, makes it easier for men to abandon their children along with their wives. In response, the state/public patriarchy tries to force the responsibility back onto the private patriarchy.

The solution to this, Brown suggests, is that women need to work for "mother right" in custody suits, that is, a true maternal preference. However, if shared responsibility and joint participation in childrearing is the ultimate goal, then flexible custody (as suggested by A. Sheppard [1982]) seems a more appropriate policy goal. As Sheppard points out, flexible custody is a scary thought to many women at the present time because, as society is currently structured, most women simply do not have equal resources and would not have equal status with their husbands as parents and in court. In addition, for flexible custody to work, women would have to have better wages, better access to education, and access to nontraditional employment opportunities. In the interim, the rights of mothers to retain custody must be protected in the courts, and the supports offered by child support enforcement, in combination with some form of welfare or family allowances, are necessary.

Education

A comprehensive feminist family policy, a genuine attack on the feminization of poverty, a national agenda to reduce teen pregnancy and welfare dependency—all these must be firmly based in education. The National Coalition for Women and Girls in Education (1989) has set forth a series of public policy recommendations that are intended to increase the access of women and girls to literacy programs.

Remedial efforts are important; however, there is extensive research evidence that confirms that classrooms in the country present a "chilly climate" for women. The Project on the Status and Education of Women of the Association of American Colleges has extensively documented inequities inside and outside of the classroom that discourage women and inhibit their learning (see Hall, 1982; Hall and Sandler, 1984; Sandler, 1986). Since success in the economic sphere depends on success in the educational sphere, it is imperative that teacher education programs throughout the nation develop a gender-balanced approach to the classroom and the curriculum. Young women, particularly low income and minority, need to be encouraged to stay in school, need opportunities to develop self-esteem, and need encouragement to enter technological, scientific, and nontraditional employment fields. Many policy analysts encourage job development for men as the best way to keep women and children out of poverty. However, education and training of women that enhances their independence is a more viable, long-term solution.

Work and Family

Feminists argue for caution regarding the rhetoric on integrating work and family. Job sharing and work at home, for example, too often mean that women do more work in less time, get paid less, receive fewer benefits, and, in the case of in-home work, are socially isolated. It is doubtful that, given foreign competition, corporations are actually going to expand benefits significantly to women. In fact, their arguments against mandating parental leave and disability benefits make that abundantly clear. Undoubtedly, family policy advocates will continue to work for parental leave, on-site child care, and flexible work hours; however, these will only be helpful if affirmative action, comparable worth, and full employment are also part of the national family policy agenda.

Welfare

In spite of "welfare reform," welfare is still a problem. As noted earlier, its patriarchal and paternalistic nature is incompatible with a policy approach that seeks to create real options for women. Nor have the family allowance systems of Scandinavian countries proven to be much more effective in creating opportunities and options for women. Yet, some system of welfare is a continuing necessity, even while advocates pursue the development of a more humane system that does not punish women and children (already the victims of society) but seeks to provide personal growth, education, training, and employment opportunities that do give women real choices.

The very fact that welfare policy is established by a legislative body that consists predominantly of middle- and upper-class, educated white men who have no experience with and little understanding of the problems that face low income women and their children is antifeminist. A feminist approach to solving the "welfare problem" would take as its starting point understanding of the problem from the point of view of the women who own it and would then proceed to develop policies and programs that are empowering for the women themselves. A feminist approach would understand that the problems welfare mothers face are much more complex than a willingness or reluctance to work and that these families often have faced a lifetime of hardship and degradation that, very early in life, damage self-esteem, erode self-confidence, and create personal problems that no coercive tactic or job program alone can overcome. It would recognize that multiple strategies are necessary for addressing such complex problems. However well intended, welfare reform that coerces women into employment while underfunding a program to place their children in an already inadequate system of child care, in the context of a job market where minimum wage jobs maintain families at a level well below poverty (all of which the Family Support Act of 1988 does), is a program that shows little hope of real success. Enforcement of child support obligations in those cases where fathers can afford to pay is important; however, it is only a partial, inadequate solution. As long as the public and private patriarchies continue to dispute whose responsibility it is to provide for women and for the children of two parents, they will be distracted from efforts to develop workable solutions that recognize the responsibility of both parents. A guaranteed family allowance for those women who are currently caught in the welfare trap, coupled with incentives for participation in education and training leading to employment, offers a temporary solution. Long-term solutions would enhance the ability of women to provide for children by incorporating recommendations regarding education, reproductive freedom, and child care.

Daycare and Health Care

Political rhetoric argues that daycare is a family (translated, woman's) responsibility. Similarly, health care is said to be a responsibility of the private sector. While the argument between the public and the private patriarchy continues, women are denied choices about whether and how to balance work and child care. Women who make up the "working poor" are particularly in need of health care for their families since minimum and near-minimum wage jobs in the service sectors seldom provide such benefits. Any feminist national family policy agenda would seek equal access to daycare and health care for every individual in society.

While business involvement in child care expands, feminist family policy advocates must remember that the majority of new jobs and jobs for women are being created in the service sector where corporate care is not feasible. Child care for low income families cannot simply be relegated to the private sector or to underfinanced federal programs. Popular mythology suggests that low income women prefer to find and use unregulated care provided by friends or relatives rather than regulated, center-based care. Research evidence contradicts this, however, and suggests that low income mothers are concerned for their children's safety and desire educational opportunities provided in centers (Brooks and Hurley, 1988). However, center-based care is often unavailable and/or costly, particularly in rural or inner-city areas.

To effectively meet the needs of low income and single-parent women, quality daycare should be available in a variety of forms, both home- and center-based. If the Scandinavian experience with daycare is suggestive, parents may, in fact, prefer home-based care for children under the age of three and educationally oriented, center-based care for preschool children (Huttenen and Tamminen, 1989). The recently expanded Finnish system allows parents to choose either home care support (with monetary remuneration) or publicly financed ("municipal") daycare. What is important is that a variety of options be available to both lower and higher income families, that low income women are empowered to make their own choices consistent with their own and their children's needs, and that federal financing be flexible enough to accommodate such choice.

CONCLUSION

A feminist analysis of current family policy proposals shows why they are, at worst, potentially counterproductive and at best, another set of conflicting, partial, temporary solutions offered to women in the context of the family. The proposals are potentially counterproductive to the extent that they support the status quo, fail to offer women real alternatives, reinforce assumptions regarding pronatalism and women's separate sphere of influence, and promote the continued dependency of women on either the private or the public patriarchy. At best, proposals for parental leave, daycare, and flexible work time are simply remedial in nature. They seek to undo the damage done to families by having women in the work force. They are certainly not proactive. Furthermore, current proposals fail to address the role of the judiciary in developing national family policy and the need for consistency in the assumptions and direction of both judicial and legislative family policy.

Family policy and feminism are not necessarily inconsistent and incompatible. Feminism seeks not to destroy the family and put an end to reproduction but to enable women to rearrange their family lives in ways that will give them real options and real equality. Feminists may support reactive family policy proposals because they could be immediately helpful for some women. Families today are under tremendous stress, but that stress falls disproportionately on women. Meanwhile, public policy proposals repeatedly suggest that the solution is to focus on expanding male employment and to provide temporary supports for women in their maternal functions—both on the basis of the explicit assumption that women and their children should be taken care of by spouses. Certainly, women will continue to choose to marry and to have children in the future, even as they continue also to strive toward an equitable society in which they are employed at equitable wages. For this reason, feminists *and* family policy advocates need to recognize the shortcomings in the proposed solutions and their dangers: the danger in thinking that they are universally applicable; the danger in believing that they are a panacea for the problems women face in the context of the family and the economic system; and the danger in expecting too much from them in terms of creating a just and humane society, which is the ultimate goal of feminist family policy.

NOTE

1. Data on the question of how much dual earner couples share child care and household responsibilities are inconsistent. G. Bird, G. Bird, and M. Scruggs

(1984) concluded that variance in the extent to which husbands participate in child care and other household responsibilities is related to the degree of status of the wife's employment and the husband's sex role orientation. E. Maret and B. Finlay (1984) observed "substantial variability" and some decrease in home responsibilities among women in dual-earner families. Variability was related to race (black women having lower levels of home responsibility than white women), wife's wages, and husband's income. To the extent that wives earned more and husbands less, women had lower levels of home responsibility. Such studies suggest that greater equity in household tasks and child care exists among black families, where sex role specialization has traditionally been lower, and among dual-career couples where the wife has higher employment status and greater career commitment (and thus higher marital power).

II
Linking Ideology to Action

4

The Policy Functions of Family Policies in Three States: A Comparative Analysis

Shirley L. Zimmerman

Such paired terms as explicit and implicit, manifest and latent, direct and indirect, intentional and unintentional are a part of the vocabulary of family policy (Kamerman and Kahn, 1978). These terms are used in discussing and analyzing the objectives and consequences of public policies for families. Thus, policies have been discussed in terms of their explicit and implicit family objectives, their direct and indirect effects on families, their manifest or latent family objectives and consequences, and their intentional and unintentional consequences for families. Family policies have not, however, been examined in terms of the functions they characterize, as outlined by T. J. Lowi (1964; 1970; 1972) and developed further by others (Tatalovich and Daynes, 1984; Salisbury, 1968; Spitzer, 1987; Jones, 1970; Kelman, 1978; and Wiggins and Browne, 1986), or that characterize them in different political cultures.

With this in mind, a comparative analysis was undertaken of the explicit/manifest family policies enacted by three states: Nevada, Minnesota, and South Carolina in 1979, 1982–1983, and 1985 in terms of the policy functions that typify them. In so doing, the analysis extended Lowi's typology of policy functions as applied to the business realm to the realm of family policy, comparing the functions that characterize family policies in the political cultures represented by these three states (Elazar, 1986). In effect, these three states represent a natural experiment in family policy. Is there a difference in the functions that characterize family policies in the political cultures represented by these three states?

LOWI'S TAXONOMY OF POLICY FUNCTIONS

Lowi (1964) classified policies related to business as distributive, re-distributive, and regulatory in function. Distributive policies are neutral with respect to the gains and losses they represent for particular groups or individuals, requiring little direct government intervention. Examples such as federal aid for highways and education come to mind (Spitzer, 1987). Regulatory policies, on the other hand, do require direct government intervention, restricting or limiting individual and institutional practices and behaviors through the imposition of penalties, sanctions, or prohibitions. Redistributive policies allocate or reallocate resources among broad classes of people, such as minorities, handicapped children, the disabled, the elderly, families with young children, gifted children, young or college-aged children, the wealthy, and so forth. Thus, they are *not* neutral with respect to the gains and losses they represent. Examples include the progressive income tax, minimum wage laws, general revenue sharing, antipoverty programs, educational scholarships, subsidies for families with mentally handicapped children or families who adopt hard-to-place children, and so forth. Actually, all governmental policies may be considered redistributive in that they invariably involve the allocation of resources for services and benefits that are more advantageous for some than for others (Jones, 1970) as well as the collection of revenues in the form of taxes and fees that inevitably are more burdensome for some than others.

Many who have worked with Lowi's scheme have observed that its categorical fit is better for some policies than for others. R. J. Spitzer (1985), for example, argued that policies most often represent a mix of functions. R. Tatalovich and B. W. Daynes (1984) focused their analysis on abortion policy as a case of regulatory policy, making a distinction between social and economic regulation, abortion being social in nature. Social regulation as defined by Tatalovich and Daynes refers to the use of government authority to modify individual and institutional practices and behaviors in ways that are legally proscribed. Examples specific to families include mandatory school attendance laws, marriage and divorce laws, school desegregation, abortion policies, Baby Doe legislation, home school laws, euthanasia laws, child abuse reporting laws, and so forth. Social regulation involving nonmarket behavior, however, also exists in the economic sphere (Kelman, 1978), affecting the behaviors and practices of businesses. Included in this category are environmental and consumer protection and equal employment opportunity laws, which represent a departure from narrow economic/market concerns.

C. W. Wiggins and W. P. Browne (1986) developed two additional categories in applying Lowi's typology to policy outputs in Iowa: structural and miscellaneous. They defined decisions as regulatory if they were primarily intended to restrain actions or limit the behaviors of a particular group. Distributive decisions were defined as awarding specific groups or potential users access to newly available political resources, and redistributive decisions, changing prior allocations of previously provided benefits or substituting rewards and/or beneficiaries. Decisions were defined as structural if they changed the procedural rules of the game for public institutions or modified their organization or responsibilities. They were defined as miscellaneous if their intent was so unclear that they could not be placed elsewhere. R. H. Salisbury (1968) also extended Lowi's categories to include structural policies, which he defined as decisions that involve the creation of units and guidelines for future allocations.

The analysis of policy outputs inevitably leads to the consideration of the inputs that go into the process in the first place (Jones, 1970). Wiggins and Browne (1986) examined, as inputs, the influence and position of interest groups and political figures with respect to policy outputs, following Lowi's typology with some modifications. T. Dye (1966) focused his analysis on institutional and economic factors associated with the policy outputs of the fifty states as measured by expenditures in such substantive areas as health, education, public welfare, highways, and so forth, concluding that economic, not political, variables were key. Later analysis of such expenditures revealed that attitudes toward such spending also are key (Zimmerman, 1987b; 1988), particularly in the case of spending for public welfare, the funding source for many programs that directly affect families. Such attitudes in part are cultural and could be reflected in the family policies of different states as measured by the functions that characterize them. The ways in which such policies might be reflective of the political cultures of different states is the question that prompted the research.

METHODOLOGY

The States and Reasons for Selecting Them

To answer the research question, summaries of the explicit/manifest family legislation enacted by three states—Nevada, Minnesota, and South Carolina—were content analyzed. The selection of these three states was based on an analysis that D. Elazar (1986) undertook of the political cultures of the fifty states in which he identified Nevada as being individualistic, Minnesota moralistic, and South Carolina traditionalistic. Although most states represent a mix of political cultures, he identified these three states as being singular in their cultural orientation with respect to attitudes toward government, state/market relationships, and politics.

In states where an individualistic political culture prevails, government that governs least is viewed as best. Except for promoting private initiatives and assuring broad access to the marketplace, its role is to keep the market in good working order by not intervening in private activities. Viewed as a necessary although dirty business, politics in this culture is "businesslike" rather than ideological, a matter for career politicians rather than citizens at large. Emphasizing private rather than public concerns, the culture nurtures government leaders who tend not to initiate new programs or open up new areas of public activity unless the demand is overwhelming that they do so.

In contrast, in states in which a moralistic political culture prevails, government that promotes and protects the public's welfare is viewed as best. Its role as protector and promoter of the public good justifies its intervening in private activities and tempering strains of individualism. In contrast to the individualistic culture, politics in a moralistic culture is viewed as the means by which a civil society deals with issues and problems that confront it. Hence politics is regarded important for every citizen, not just those who make it their career, public issues setting the tone for political discourse.

The third type of political culture identified by Elazar is rooted in an ambivalent attitude toward the marketplace coupled with a paternalistic and elitist conception of the commonwealth. In states characterized as traditionalistic, the culture supports a substantially hierarchical society as part of the natural order. While government is viewed in a positive light, it is largely limited to the maintenance of the existing social arrangements. While traditional patterns can be adjusted to respond to changing conditions, such adjustments are to be achieved in ways that do not disturb these patterns too much. In states where the traditional political culture is dominant, political leaders play a conservative and custodial role unless pressured by outside forces to do otherwise.

Thus in terms of attitudes toward government, the market, and politics, the three states of Nevada, Minnesota, and South Carolina are very different in the political cultures they represent.

The Years and Reasons for Selecting Them

The years selected for the analysis—1979, 1982–1983, and 1985—are important because they represent a period of raised public consciousness with respect to the family effects of public policies and of shifted responsibility for funding social programs from federal to state governments. The year 1979 was the year prior to the 1980 White House Conference on Families, the forum that served to heighten public awareness of the implications of public policies for families. The year 1982 not only followed the Conference but also the 1981 Omnibus Budget Reconciliation Act, the legislation that provided the framework for the shift that occurred in federal-state relationships. This legislation also gave states increased discretion as to the services they would provide and for whom. Because its legislature did not meet in 1982, 1983 was substituted for 1982 in the case of Nevada. Extending the analysis to include 1985 permitted conclusions to be drawn about the functions that characterize the family policies enacted by Nevada, Minnesota, and South Carolina over a longer term.

The Data Sources and Analysis

The data sources for the analysis were the summaries of the legislation enacted and published by each of the three states subsequent to their legislative session. Obtained from the governors' offices, these publications provide summary descriptions of all of the legislation the states enact in a given year. To make the task more manageable, the analysis was confined to only those bills that were explicit as to their family content or whose family content was manifest or obvious. Thus, unless they met the study criterion, many legislative items that had direct implications for families were not included in the analysis.

After identifying all of the bills each of the states enacted with explicit/manifest family content for the study period, individual legislative items were classified according to the policy functions they represented—distributive/redistributive, regulatory, structural, and definitional—drawing on Lowi's framework, the work of Wiggins and Browne (1986), and following the data themselves. The classification developed for the present analysis departs from Lowi's and Wiggins and Browne's typologies in at least four ways. Following C. O. Jones (1970), who said that all policies may be considered redistributive, policies that were distributive and redistributive in function were combined into a single category because of problems in trying to distinguish between these functions when classifying individual policies. Although some might have been considered distributive, most addressed families in particular situations and, hence, on the surface, were more redistributive than distributive. By combining the two categories, distributive and redistributive, ambiguities surrounding their distinctions were considerably diminished, thus increasing the reliability of the analysis.

Further, elaborations were made in Lowi's regulatory category to reflect the empirical data. These data revealed that the restraint of action or behaviors of particular groups involved not only the protection of individual family members and the larger society, as in the case of mandatory seat belt use and mandatory child abuse reporting, but also the rights of family members and the roles and obligations of the state and families in relation to each other. Examples of the latter include bills that mandate adoption agencies to inform prospective adoptive persons of their rights, child protection agencies to provide placement services for children whose mothers are incarcerated, and those who incur the costs of establishing paternity for children born out of wedlock to pay them.

Also, because so much of the regulatory legislation enacted by the states was procedural in nature, a separate category was created to capture this distinction. Examples include procedural provisions or arrangements for joint custody, the registration of adoptions, separate waiting rooms in court cases involving family members as defendants or witnesses, and contracts for services with agencies serving handicapped children. While such procedural legislation probably could have been classified as structural to be consistent with Wiggins and Browne's classification, this latter category was reserved for those instances in which actual structures were established to study problems related to families and make recommendations for action about them, in the manner suggested by Salisbury (1968). Examples include legislation creating a Brain Impairment Task Force to assess the needs of brain impaired persons and their families and a state planning council to examine the needs of mentally ill persons and their families, both Minnesota items, and a displaced homemakers center in Nevada.

A separate category was created for a few items that seemed to be purely definitional in character and thus did not seem to fit into the other categories, such as changing the definition of an American Indian child as it pertained to education, defining school age for mentally handicapped children, defining the age of a child with reference to juvenile court, defining children's shelters, and defining a delinquent child. This classification scheme then became the basis for identifying the policy functions that characterized the family policies the three states enacted and assessing whether one type of function was characteristic of one state more than another and, hence, reflective of the political cultures these states represented. The application of this classification scheme to family policies enacted in 1979, 1982–1983, and 1985 also allowed assessments to be made as to whether the policy functions of the family legislation enacted by these states changed over time.

WHAT THE DATA SHOW

Primary Policy Functions of Explicit Family Legislation Enacted by Nevada

How can the family legislation the three states enacted be characterized in terms of the policy functions outlined earlier? With respect to Nevada, taking the three years as a whole, Table 4.1 shows that most of the family legislation Nevada enacted during the study period was

Table 4.1
Primary Policy Function(s) of Explicit/Manifest Family Policies Enacted by Nevada in 1979, 1983, and 1985 (frequencies and percent*)

	1979	1983	1985	Total	Percent
Distributive/redistributive					
Economic, i.e., child support, tax retirement benefits, AFDC, funding					
of services. Percent of enacted family legislation, by year	6	7	5	18	.35
	.26	.47	.35		
Social provision, i.e., social services, health, education, housing, etc.	3	2	1	6	.11
Percent of enacted family legislation, by year	.13	.13	.07		
Regulatory					
Protection, i.e., family abuse, legal, health, safety. Percent of enacted	4	5	4	13	.25
family legislation, by year	.17	.33	.29		
Procedural, agency, and interagency.	5	3	2	10	.19
Percent of enacted family legislation, by year	.22	.20	.14		
Rights of family members/clarification, expansion, restriction.	6	0	3	9	.17
Percent of enacted family legislation, by year	.26	.00	.21		
Roles, responsibilities/State and families.	14	5	7	26	.50
Percent of enacted family legislation, by year	.60	.33	.50		
Structural					
i.e., board membership, creation of advisory committees.	3	0	0	3	.05
Percent of enacted family legislation, by year	.13	.00	.00		
Definitional					
Percent of enacted family legislation, by year	0	1	3	4	.07
	.00	.06	.21		
Total family legislation by year and for all years	—	—	—		
	23	15	14	52	

*Because legislation often represents a mix of policy functions, frequencies exceed number of bills enacted with explicit/manifest family content. Hence percentages exceed 100.

regulatory in function. Because individual policies were counted more than once if they fit into more than one category, the four regulatory categories yield percentages of over 100 percent when they are added together. This contrasts with the 46 percent of the family legislation Nevada enacted that was distributive/redistributive in nature, adding the percentages for legislation pertaining to economic and social provisions. Although it enacted more of this latter type of legislation in 1983 than in the other years of the analysis, the N was only 15 that year.

Table 4.1 also shows that most of the regulatory legislation that Nevada enacted pertained to the roles and obligations of the state and family to each other, which probably is related to the distinction that Nevada holds in having the highest marriage and divorce rates in the country. Indeed such regulatory policies constituted the largest percentage of the family legislation that Nevada enacted over the study period (50 percent), although this varied with the year. The next class of regulatory legislation that Nevada enacted with greatest frequency, constituting 25 percent of its family legislation, was protective in function: child and family abuse and health and safety measures. Interestingly, the smallest share of the regulatory legislation that Nevada enacted pertained to the rights of family members.

Nevada did not enact much family legislation of a definitional or structural function, only 5 percent and 7 percent respectively for the three years as a whole. Because it enacted less family legislation each succeeding year of the analysis, percentages are based on lower frequencies for 1983 and 1985 and, hence, for some categories are higher for those years than for 1979.

Primary Policy Functions of Explicit Family Legislation Enacted by Minnesota

Table 4.2 shows the frequency distribution of the policy functions of the family legislation that Minnesota enacted. As can be seen, adding the percentages for economic and social provisions, almost 75 percent of the family legislation enacted by Minnesota was distributive/redistributive in function.

A large percentage of Minnesota's family legislation also was regulatory in nature, and, like Nevada, most legislation of this type pertained to the roles and obligations of the state and families vis-à-vis the other. However, in Minnesota, this characterized only about one-third of the family legislation enacted, whereas in Nevada it constituted one-half. Relatively speaking, Minnesota enacted about the same amount of protective legislation as Nevada: 25 percent for the three years as a whole. Percentages for the other regulatory categories—procedural and rights— also hovered around 25 percent over the three years. Like Nevada, Minnesota did not enact many family policies that were structural or definitional in nature, each constituting only 5 percent of the family policies Minnesota enacted over the three years.

Year-to-year analysis shows that Minnesota enacted a larger percentage of distributive/redistributive family legislation in 1979 than in succeeding years, although in terms of social provision as opposed to economic provision, percentages were the same in 1979 and 1985. In 1979, a larger percentage of the regulatory family legislation that Minnesota enacted involved the rights of family members and the roles and obligations of the state and families relative to each other than is true for the succeeding years. However, in 1985 the frequency with which

Table 4.2
Primary Policy Function(s) of Explicit/Manifest Family Policies Enacted by Minnesota in 1979, 1982, and 1985 (frequencies and percents*)

	1979	1982	1985	Total	Percent
Distributive/redistributive					
Economic, i.e., child support, AFDC, tax, insurance and retirement benefits, adoption subsidies, funding and financing provisions of service, foster care payments, etc.	17	15	20	52	.47
Percent of enacted family legislation, by year	.68	.43	.46		
Social provision, i.e., health, housing, social services, education, etc.	7	6	14	27	.25
Percent of enacted family legislation, by year	.28	.17	.28		
Regulatory					
Protection, i.e., abuse, legal, employment, health.	8	7	12	27	.25
Percent of enacted family legislation, by year	.32	.20	.24		
Procedural, agency, and interagency.	6	9	15	30	.27
Percent of enacted family legislation, by year	.24	.26	.30		
Rights of family members/clarification, expansion or restriction.	10	11	8	29	.26
Percent of enacted family legislation, by year	.40	.31	.16		
Roles, responsibilities/state and families.	9	12	14	35	.32
Percent of enacted family legislation, by year	.36	.34	.28		
Structural					
i.e., board membership and creation of advisory committees.	0	1	4	5	.05
Percent of enacted family legislation, by year	.00	.03	.08		
Definitional					
	1	3	3	7	.05
Percent of enacted family legislation, by year	.04	.09	.06		
Total family legislation by year and for all years	25	35	50	110	

*Because legislation often represents a mix of policy functions, frequencies exceed number of bills enacted with explicit/manifest family content and percentages exceed 100.

it enacted the latter type of legislation was greater, as was its enactment of family policies of a procedural nature in both absolute and relative terms.

Primary Policy Functions of Explicit Family Legislation Enacted by South Carolina

Table 4.3 shows the frequency distribution of the policy functions for the family legislation that South Carolina enacted during this period. Two-thirds of the family legislation that South Carolina enacted had a distributive/redistributive function, almost three-fifths of which was economic in nature, many fewer items pertaining to social provision than

Table 4.3
Primary Policy Function(s) of Explicit/Manifest Family Policies Enacted by South Carolina in 1979, 1982, and 1985 (frequencies and percents*)

	1979	1982	1985	Total	Percent
<u>Distributive/redistributive</u>					
Economic, i.e., child support, tax, insurance, unemployment compensation, retirement benefits, AFDC funding and financing of services, service costs, fees, loans, tuition rates, disaster grants, etc.	9	2	15	26	.59
Percent of family legislation enacted by year	.56	.50	.62		
Social provision,i.e., social services, health, education, housing, etc.	0	0	2	2	.05
Percent of family legislation enacted by year	.00	.00	.08		
<u>Regulatory</u>					
Protection, i.e., family abuse, legal, health, safety.	2	1	5	8	.18
Percent of family legislation enacted by year	.13	.25	.21		
Procedural, agency, and interagency.	2	0	5	7	.16
Percent of family legislation enacted by year	.13	.00	.21		
Rights of family members, clarification, expansion, or restriction.	5	2	8	15	.34
Percent of family legislation enacted by year	.31	.50	.33		
Roles, responsibilities/state and families.	10	1	16	27	.61
Percent of family legislation enacted by year	.62	.25	.67		
<u>Structural</u>					
i.e., board membership, creation of advisory committees.	4	0	1	5	.11
Percent of family legislation enacted by year	.40	.00	.04		
<u>Definitional</u>					
	1	1	0	2	.05
Percent of family legislation enacted by year	.06	.25	.00		
Total family legislation by year and for all years	16	4	24	44	

*Because legislation often represents a mix of policy functions, frequencies exceed the number of bills enacted with explicit/manifest family content. Hence, percentages exceed 100.

was the case for Minnesota. Relative to other types of legislation, the family policies that South Carolina enacted were classified into more regulatory categories than was the case for Minnesota and Nevada, as can be seen by adding the percentages of each of the regulatory categories over the three years.

Like Nevada and Minnesota, most of the regulatory legislation South Carolina enacted during this period pertained to the roles and obligations of the state and families vis-à-vis the other—60 percent for the three years, considerably more than Minnesota and somewhat more than Nevada—as a comparison of the tables shows. Constituting one-third of the regulatory legislation that it enacted, South Carolina also enacted more legislation that pertained to the rights of family members than

Nevada and Minnesota, but fewer regulatory policies of a procedural or protective nature. That South Carolina did not enact more of the latter legislation, especially as it pertains to child and spouse abuse, as the other states did probably reflects its cultural traditions regarding family privacy and the separate spheres of family and government. Although South Carolina, like the other states, did not enact many items that were structural or definitional in function, relatively speaking, it enacted more of such legislation, 11 percent and 5 percent respectively. Again, note should be taken of the small Ns to which these percentages pertain.

Comparing 1979 to 1985, Table 4.3 shows that unlike Minnesota, which decreased the percentage of its distributive/redistributive legislative output, South Carolina, like Nevada, increased its output of this type, although again the frequencies on which these percentages are based are much smaller than Minnesota's. In 1982, South Carolina was so legislatively lethargic that 1982 probably should not be used as a basis of comparison with the other years. While its output of protective or procedural regulatory policy for the three years as a whole was small, both types showed an increase in 1985. This also pertains to the other two types of regulatory policies: the rights of family members and the roles and obligations of the state and families relative to each other. However, in 1985 its output of structural family legislation was smaller, and, if one and zero count, there was also less definitional legislation than in 1979.

CONCLUSION

What conclusions can be drawn from the above analysis concerning the policy approach that best characterizes Nevada, Minnesota, and South Carolina in relation to families? If sheer quantity of enacted explicit/manifest family legislation is a criterion, it is clear that Minnesota's policy approach to families is more family oriented than Nevada's and South Carolina's. While each of the three states enacted the same percentage of explicit/manifest family legislation in 1979, only 7 percent, this percentage dropped even further for both Nevada and South Carolina in 1982–1983. For Minnesota, however, it increased, and in 1985 it was double the output of 1979. Although South Carolina's output of such legislation increased sixfold in 1985 over 1982, this was only because its output in 1982 was so very low (N = 4). Taking the three years as a whole, Minnesota enacted almost two and a half times more explicit family legislation than Nevada and one and a half times more than South Carolina. Thus, in terms of quantity of enacted family legislation, Minnesota was the leader.

Of the three states, Minnesota also enacted the most legislation of a distributive/redistributive nature, considerably more in 1979 than in the years that followed. Even so, its output of such family legislation increased in 1985 over 1982, mostly in the category of social as opposed to economic provision. A similar shift occurred in the regulatory legislation it enacted over the study period, in that such legislation became increasingly procedural in nature and decreasingly dealt with the rights of family members and the roles and obligations of the state and families relative to the other. Thus, while Minnesota increased its output of family legislation over the study period, the nature of it changed in both the distributive/redistributive and regulatory categories.

Just as Elazar labeled Minnesota a moralistic state based on his analysis of the political cultures of the 50 states, the present analysis identifies Minnesota as a state that distributes and redistributes goods, services, and other benefits to families more than it regulates them. Indeed, of the 110 separate legislative items that Minnesota enacted over the study period, 20 represented new initiatives of some modest expansion of existing services and benefits, such as a sliding fee scale for daycare, preschool health screening programs, smoking intervention programs in the schools, community family life education programs, funding for maternal and child health programs, and so forth. These items represented 18 percent of Minnesota's total family legislative output in contrast to Nevada's (N = 6) and South Carolina's (N = 5) 11 percent. Thus even in the face of federal cutbacks and uncertain times, Minnesota moved ahead in support of families. This also is reflected in census data that show an increase in Minnesota's expenditures for public welfare, education, and mental health over these years (Council of State Governments, 1982; U.S. Bureau of Census, 1983a; 1983b; 1984; 1986b), which consistently were higher than Nevada's and South Carolina's.

Given its political culture (Elazar, 1986), Minnesota's leadership in this area should not be surprising. Indeed, Minnesota is the only one of the three states that had a Governor's Council on Families prior to the 1980 White House Conferences on Families (Zimmerman, 1987a). Still, although greater than the other states, its output of explicit family legislation relative to all the legislation it enacted over the study period cannot be considered high (18 percent). In this regard, it was surprising to find that Nevada enacted more legislation overall than either Minnesota or South Carolina, given its predilection toward individualism and minimum government intervention, in fact almost twice as much legislation as these two states over the years of the analysis. More in keeping with Nevada's proclivities in this regard was its decreased output of family legislation on such private matters as family planning, abortion, and Baby Doe cases. Indeed, Nevada mirrors the present federal government in other ways as well, particularly by not doing more to support families in their economic functioning.

True to its cultural traditions, the family policies that South Carolina enacted represent a mix of functions, distributive/redistributive and regulatory, with a bias toward the latter, its output of family policies representing *all* types of both functions increasing over the study period: economic and social provisions as well as protective and procedural rights, roles, and obligations of the state and families in relation to each other. This reflects the fact that more than the other states, South Carolina seems to have enacted family policies that are distributive/redistributive and regulatory in function along several dimensions simultaneously.

Because individual family policies were counted more than once if they applied to more than one functional category, some may wonder what the results would have been if the classification had been reduced to only the four main types—distributive/redistributive, regulatory, structural, and definitional—and each item were counted only once. To answer this question, such an analysis was undertaken. While certainly less complex and much faster, the essence of the findings remains essentially the same: Minnesota's policy approach to families may be characterized as largely distributive/redistributive in function. Nevada's as regulatory, and South Carolina's as a mix of the two, leaning toward the latter. Such a simplified typology, however, does not capture the multiple dimensions of individual family policies. While the additions to Lowi's taxonomy increased the complexity of the analysis, they also identified dimensions that may be unique to policy in the family realm.

Although the findings of this analysis cannot be generalized to states other than those to which they apply, the application of Lowi's policy typology in conjunction with Elazar's typology of the political cultures that characterize different states was useful in analyzing family policies enacted under different cultural conditions. From this it may be hypothesized that family policies enacted by states whose political culture is moralistic are likely to be more distributive/redistributive than regulatory in function; family policies enacted by states whose political culture is individualistic are likely to be more regulatory than distributive/redistributive in function; and family policies enacted by states whose political culture is traditionalistic are likely to represent a mix of the two functions with a bias toward the regulatory. Because most states represent a mix of political cultures—individualist/moralistic, moralistic/traditionalistic, traditionalistic/individualistic, and individualistic/moralistic/traditionalistic—the combination of functions that might characterize their family policies can only be known by extending the research to other states. This is a task in which other family policy researchers may wish to join, as well as in the further development and refinement of a typology of functions that characterize family policies in general

and those of different states in particular. Such analysis provides yet
another way for understanding family policies and their complexities,
and the cultural influences that shape them.

NOTE

The research in this chapter was made possible by a grant from the University
of Minnesota, Agricultural Experiment Station, St. Paul, Minnesota. The author
wishes to express her appreciation to Phyllis Owens for her assistance in the
research.

5

State Initiatives in Family Policy

Steven K. Wisensale

Since the 1980 White House Conference on Families, there has been almost a constant flow of policy-oriented literature on the family. A. Cherlin (1989), J. Dempsey (1981), I. Diamond (1983), R. Genovese (1984), D. Moynihan (1986), R. Moroney (1986), J. Noble and M. Sussman (1987), J. Peden and F. Glahe (1986), G. Steiner (1981), and S. L. Zimmerman (1988) have all produced works that have at least three messages in common.

First, the family is changing rapidly. Single-parent households grew by 69 percent from 1970 to 1983, and the so-called typical nuclear family, in which the father works and the mother stays home, now accounts for less than 10 percent of all households. In addition, nearly 70 percent of women of childbearing age are in the work force, thus creating a need for daycare and parental leave policies.

A second message states that families—especially single-parent households—are in trouble economically. More than 20 percent of all children in the United States live in poverty; among black children it is 47 percent. But poverty is not confined to the young. About 10.5 percent of the elderly over 65 live in poverty. For black elderly it is 32 percent, for black women over 65 living alone it is 56 percent, and for all elderly over 85, almost 26 percent live in poverty.

Third, the family is being squeezed between two generations. Not only is child care in great demand due to two-earner couples and single-parent households, but so too is elder care. Almost 62 percent of all women between the ages of 45 and 54 now work, as do 42 percent of those who fall in the 55–64 age bracket. It is precisely these two groups of middle-aged families who are most likely to provide the necessary care to the disabled parent or spouse. Today, one out of every ten people 65 years and older has a child at least 65 years of age (Brody, 1986). As a result, and for the first time in American history, the average American couple has more parents than children.

In addition to a growing body of literature and the large volume of demographic information it has spawned, there is also evidence of major policy initiatives being undertaken at both the federal and state levels. Passage of the Family Support Act of 1988 brought with it the first successful attempt at welfare reform in fifty-three years. Although legislative efforts to increase the minimum wage as well as provide both parental leave and daycare failed, proponents remain optimistic about their eventual enactment in the not too distant future.

While most family-policy initiatives have originated within the Democratic party, the Reagan administration's publication of a special report in 1986, *The Family: Preserving America's Future*, and Orrin Hatch's public conversion concerning his opposition to a federally funded daycare program are indicative of both the bipartisan nature of the issue as well as its political volatility. These facts are further substantiated by reports that dozens of family-oriented position papers were distributed by candidates from both parties during the 1987 presidential primaries (Johnson, 1987).

Both in terms of political initiatives taken and in the volume of family policy literature produced, the focus has been primarily on Washington and what it has or has not done for families. Recent works by J. Scanzoni (1989) as well as S. Kamerman and A. Kahn (1989) continue this tradition by discussing family policy from a national perspective. Scanzoni, for example, utilizes the Reagan administration's document (*The Family: Preserving America's Future*) for raising critical issues. What are the consequences of ignoring "varieties" in families and focusing policy instead on the Reagan administration's "benchmark family"—two heterosexual adults legally married and residing together with their own natural children? Should policy focus on workable immediate programs, or should it be a product of a broader long-term vision? In short, can the family afford the traditional incremental approach to policymaking? Why not identify the needs of citizens first and then design programs to meet them? Is there time, and can we agree on the term "need"? Finally, in designing family policy, can we separate the interests of adults from those of children? Whatever the answer, what is the price, and are we willing to pay it?

Kamerman and Kahn also address family policy from a national perspective. Common characteristics present in European family policy such as child allowances, maternity and parenting policies, child support laws, and child care services are identified. Significant factors involved in formulating family policy are also discussed. These include the importance of economic resources, demographic patterns such as a low fertility rate, a high female labor force participation, an ongoing quest for sexual equality, and a commitment to redistributive social welfare policies. But perhaps most important is the authors' analysis of specific gaps in U.S. family policy (no universal child care) and the conscious decisions of policy makers to choose "small ticket items" (parental leave but unpaid) over "big ticket items" (child allowances and a commitment to child health care).

Clearly, the discussion on family policy remains primarily at the national level. Except for studies by S. Zimmerman and P. Owens (1989) and S. Wisensale (1990), state efforts have been largely ignored in the literature. This is in spite of the fact that the states have a long history of involvement in family issues, including the regulation of marriage and divorce; the establishment of parental authority and responsibility; the regulation of child support, custody, and adoption; the creation and enforcement of tax laws that affect family economic status and behavior; and even the recognition of local zoning ordinances that restrict a large portion of our living space to "one-family residential" uses. In short, family policy is not new to state legislators.

The purpose of this chapter, therefore, is threefold: first, to examine the efforts of one state (Connecticut) to design and pass the first comprehensive family policy in the nation; second, to present an overview of important family policy initiatives passed in other states during 1987; and third, to examine the future of family policy, particularly at the state level, in light of the impact of Reagan's New Federalism and the likelihood of George Bush pursuing a similar strategy.

THE CONNECTICUT INITIATIVE

In January 1987 the Connecticut General Assembly introduced a total of thirty-five proposals in the form of a legislative package specifically designed to "assist and stabilize" the state's families. The original proposals were combined into twenty-six bills and funneled into the Select Committee on Families and the Workplace. Consisting of twenty-six members (fifteen Democrats and eleven Republicans), it was this specially created joint committee that was to divide the package of proposals into five categories and guide its passage through both houses.

The first attempt by a state to pass a comprehensive family policy resulted in sixteen of twenty-six bills being passed at a cost of $34,499,400. The five major categories covered in the legislation included: (1) economic self-sufficiency, which focused on job training and other efforts to reduce the welfare rolls; (2) supportive services, which included such work and family issues as daycare and parental leave; (3) preparing families for the future, which concentrated on maternal and child health as well as the problem of teen pregnancy; (4) housing, which addressed the issue of homelessness and the need for both emergency and transitional shelter; and (5) family stability, which identified so-called families at risk and called for specific interventions and counseling programs.

The major accomplishments included passage of a parental and medical leave bill for state employees, an adjustment in eligibility criteria that improved access to daycare for low and moderate income families, and creation of a pilot program for displaced homemakers. The major disappointments came in failing to pass any of the proposed legislation directed at inadequate maternal and child health care and the problem of teenage pregnancy. Wisensale (1989) completed a more detailed analysis of Connecticut's family policy initiative and thus examines each of the five categories outlined above more closely.

Clearly, the Connecticut General Assembly chose 1987 to be the Year of the Family. However, amidst a flurry of activity that brought with it both success and failure emerges a series of questions that need to be addressed. For example, how successfully will the legislation be implemented? What will succeed, what will fail, and why? Where should Connecticut go from here? What should be the objectives of future legislative sessions? Does such a huge undertaking by a state give the federal government a reason to do less? If so, how could that in turn impact on states that are without a budget surplus and lack the political chemistry so crucial in addressing controversial family issues? These represent but a few concerns that demand further exploration.

Since 1987 the Connecticut legislature has extended parental leave into the private sector, created three family resource centers as demonstration projects in three public schools, and increased the financial commitment made to the newly established displaced homemakers program. The committee also oversaw the work of three task forces that were established by the legislature to investigate a variety of family and work place issues. Finally, several bills that failed in 1987 involving child health and teen pregnancy were restructured and passed between 1989 and 1990.

How and why Connecticut succeeded in passing a large portion of its family policy package is one thing. Whether or not other states should undertake similar initiatives is quite another matter. In reviewing the Connecticut experience, it can be concluded that at least four dominant themes converged at the very heart of the family policy agenda: (1) political power; (2) party leadership; (3) economic resources; and (4) comprehensive legislative proposals. Before political leaders, interest groups, and service providers in other states choose to pursue a similar path, they may first want to consider the following themes in greater detail.

First, with respect to political power, the 1986 election year witnessed the relatively easy reelection of a Democratic governor and a return of Democratic majorities to both houses of the General Assembly. With the Democratic return to power for the first time in six years coupled with the steady decline in President Reagan's popularity that was obviously impacting on Republicans at the state level, the time was right for aggressive legislative action. As a result, there was relatively little Republican opposition to the proposed family policy package and even the most hotly debated bill (parental and medical leave) resulted in only two negative votes in the House and one in the Senate.

The second dominant theme concerned the role of party leadership. In the end it was the Democratic party leadership (Senate President Pro Tempore and the Chairman of the Appropriations Committee) that created the Family and Workplace Committee and then introduced, supported, and escorted the family package through the legislature. The governor was supportive but did not play a direct role. In short, it was policymaking at the top trickling down rather than grassroots lobbying bubbling up that pressured legislators into taking action. Although interest groups became involved and testified at public hearings for specific bills, their role and impact was limited. Most of the testimony presented came from administrative heads of agencies that would inherit particular programs if enacted and from representatives of state commissions such as the Permanent Commission on the Status of Women and the Commission on Children.

The third theme centered on economic resources. Particularly during the 1980s, Connecticut became one of the most prosperous states in the nation. In 1986–1987 it ranked first in both defense contracting and per capita income, and its unemployment rate of 3.2 percent was one of the lowest in the country. In addition, a substantial budget surplus in the vicinity of $140 million was established, some of which was set aside specifically for human service programs. So without question, Connecticut was sufficiently strong economically to push forward with major family policy legislation.

The fourth and final major theme associated with the family policy package concerned the comprehensiveness and thus broad appeal of the legislative proposals. From the beginning, the strategy of the Democratic party leadership was to make the package as comprehensive as possible and sufficiently appealing to rural/suburban conservative legislators, the anticipated opposition. There was a deliberate attempt to play down the "welfare image" and play up parental and medical leave as well as the displaced homemaker programs. Both of these bills impact on all income groups.

Not surprisingly, early in the process the Democratic leadership had to fight off two interest groups in particular that sought greater influence over the legislation: the AFL-CIO (American Federation of Labor–Congress of Industrial Organizations) and a statewide welfare rights organization. The leadership was especially sensitive about considering labor-oriented legislation that would be more appropriate for the collective bargaining table. Of equal concern was that the family policy package would be incorrectly viewed as welfare reform and perhaps employed by the Republican opposition. Therefore, a demand by the welfare rights organization that $50 million be budgeted to cover increased AFDC rates was promptly dismissed.

In addition to the four themes identified and discussed above, there are at least four important lessons that emerged from this case study. First, when the party leadership openly supports a legislative package, it is going to pass regardless if there is grassroots support or not. Therefore, even in states where there is strong support for a family policy package, much time and energy must be devoted to lobbying key leaders in both parties. In short, leaders need to be identified, accessed, educated, and monitored throughout the legislative session.

Second, although it may not be mandatory, the creation of a special committee to introduce and oversee family-policy legislation may facilitate the political process. Connecticut's Family and Workplace Committee became the focal point for information, debate, and legislative initiatives concerning the family. Such a process coincides with Scanzoni's (1989) suggestion of first identifying the needs of citizens and then designing programs to meet those needs. Other states could create similar committees with comparable objectives.

Third, it is important to remember that family policy may be both explicit and implicit as well as both object and vehicle. It is imperative, therefore, that proposals be sufficiently comprehensive in substance and appeal so as not to confuse family policy with welfare policy or to allow it to be used as a political Trojan horse by a particular interest group. So while the Democratic leadership proposed legislation designed to appeal to the middle class, it also spent time fighting off the state's largest welfare rights organization and the AFL-CIO, both of which saw the family policy package as a vehicle to satisfy their own self-interests. The former wanted increased benefits, and the latter wanted parental leave extended to the private sector, thus removing the issue from the private negotiating table. Other states proposing family policy will need to address similar situations and be capable of differentiating between object and vehicle.

Fourth, timing appears to be crucial. The time must be ripe both politically and economically. Not only must the party in power exhibit strong support for a family policy agenda, but the economy must be strong enough to support such political initiatives. However, and despite these two attributes, Connecticut clearly chose a more cautious, incremental path. Thus, the focus was primarily on the "small ticket items" (daycare services for the working poor and unpaid parental leave that is limited to state employees) as opposed to the "big ticket items" (child allowances and child health care). The latter category fell short, Kamerman and Kahn (1989) would argue, because Connecticut policy makers chose to center the "debate on what is wrong with families rather than on how to do better by children." Similar sentiments have been echoed recently by D. Moynihan (1986) and H. Rodgers (1986) in addressing the need for a national family policy.

But perhaps the most outstanding characteristic of the Connecticut family policy package lies in the fact that it was initiated by liberal Democrats and thus stands in sharp contrast to Kamerman and Kahn (1989) who argue that "much of new family policy has been generated by conservatives." In short, it appears that, perhaps for the first time since the 1980 White House Conference on Families, the Democrats have developed at least one alternative to what Scanzoni (1989) refers to as the "Reagan White House Family" and, in doing so, have captured in at least one state what G. Steiner (1981) refers to as "the higher moral ground." Whether or not the policies enacted ultimately work and become political assets instead of liabilities remains to be seen, but at least there is a model in place for future reference.

FAMILY POLICY INITIATIVES IN OTHER STATES

Although Connecticut was the first and only state to put forth a family policy package, there was much family-oriented legislation passed throughout the country between 1987 and 1990. Based on a study by Wisensale (1990) and data gathered by the National Conference of State Legislatures (1987), these initiatives included child care and early education legislation, custody and visitation rights, child support enforcement laws, domestic violence, maternal and child health, child welfare, kidnapped and missing children laws, teen pregnancy, parental leave, and family preservation and prevention legislation.

Most of the states' activity focused more on children and child welfare legislation than on the family as a whole. For example, forty-seven states passed more stringent child abuse and neglect laws, forty-one states passed stronger child support enforcement bills, and thirty-three states passed child care and early education legislation. Two other areas in which there was much legislative activity were family preservation and prevention services (ten states passed seventeen laws) and family leave (twenty-eight states introduced and four passed such bills). Each of these five areas is discussed in greater detail below.

Child Abuse and Neglect

In response to parental concerns over growing reports of child abuse in daycare facilities, eleven states passed bills that require security checks prior to the hiring of employees and the issuing of licenses. The Virginia statute (Chapter 130), for example, prohibits licensed child care institutions or child care centers from hiring compensated or volunteer employees who have been convicted of certain offenses including murder, abduction for immoral purposes, sexual assault, certain obscenity offenses, and other similar violations. Both Nevada (Chapter 534) and Nebraska (L.G. 386) extended security checks to foster care homes.

At least twenty-three states passed legislation that clarified court procedures concerning child abuse and more clearly defined such activity so as to include both psychological and sexual abuse. Michigan (Public Acts 46 and 47), for example, defined psychological abuse as an injury to a child's mental condition or welfare that is not necessarily permanent but results in substantial mental distress. Both North Dakota (Chapter 166) and Washington (Chapter 187) addressed the issue of death caused by abuse. The former defined murder of an unborn child (excluding abortion and medical malpractice), and the latter defined the death of a child under 16 due to "extreme indifference to human life" as homicide.

Other pieces of legislation concerning child abuse and neglect included the creation of special trust funds (Maryland and Georgia) for innovative prevention, treatment, education, and support programs for both offenders and victims; the development of specific guidelines and procedures for reporting and investigating child abuse in the community (Colorado, Illinois, and Massachusetts expanded their lists of mandatory reporters); and special laws to protect victims and their witnesses in reporting such crimes were also passed. Texas was particularly active in this area, having passed five separate bills.

Child Support Enforcement

Perhaps the most popular family-oriented issue in 1987 at the state level was that concerning child support enforcement laws. While much activity was directed toward compliance with newly enacted federal legislation, other areas included the administration and collection process, staffing procedures, specific enforcement techniques, and measures to enhance interstate cooperation.

Five states in particular focused on the administration of child support laws. Illinois (P.A. 85–114), for example, provided access to State Board of Elections data to locate parents. Iowa (Chapter 234) appropriated special funds for the child support clearinghouse. Massachusetts (Chapter 310) transferred its entire division of child support enforcement to the Department of Revenue. A North Carolina law (Chapter 591) requires an employer to provide the state parent location unit with specific employee information, and Wisconsin's Act 57 initiates a child support supplement program as an alternative to AFDC.

A key to successful enforcement is adequate staffing. At least three states took special steps to increase the number of employees assigned to support obligation cases. New Mexico (Chapter 340) appropriated funds to the human services department for fifty-three additional child support enforcement employees. Iowa (Chapter 234) appropriated additional funds to cover twenty-eight full-time employees to operate the state's newly created child support clearinghouse. Also, Massachusetts (Chapter 310) established a child support trust fund under the state treasury than can be tapped for the future hiring of enforcement officers.

Concerning enforcement techniques, there was much variation across the states. California, in passing three bills under this category, was especially stringent in its approach. Property may be seized by the state if enforcement orders are ignored (Chapter 473); certain obligors are required to deposit assets worth one year's support to secure future payments (Chapter 1389); and, beginning in 1990, the state may offset delinquent child support payments with state income tax refunds (Chapter 473).

Actions by other states included the following: Illinois (P.A. 85–219) requires an obligor, upon failure to appear in court, to post property worth at least 20 percent of the amount owed. A Wisconsin law (Act 27) allows disclosure of support debts to consumer credit agencies. At least five other states (Colorado, New Mexico, North Carolina, Texas, and Wyoming) passed wage garnishment laws in 1987. One state (Delaware, Volume 66, Chapter 7), concerned about discriminatory practices directed toward child support delinquents, passed a bill that penalizes employers $200 for discrimination against child support obligors.

Finally, several states enacted laws designed to enhance interstate cooperation and enforcement of child support statutes. Kansas (Chapter 121), Louisiana (P.A. 637), and Utah (Chapter 35) all passed laws that require that interstate support orders be treated the same as instate orders for enforcement purposes. A Connecticut Act (P.A. 483) created a wage garnishment process to enforce interstate support, and a Massachusetts bill (Chapter 310) established an interstate wage information sharing program.

Child Care and Early Childhood Education

The rapid increase in two-earner couples and single parents has inflated the demand for adequate daycare facilities. This in turn has created a concern on the part of families about the quality of such care. In response to this concern, in 1987, 33 states passed 124 bills that focused on child care and early childhood education.

The major issues covered in the legislation included the administration and licensing of daycare centers, employer support of child care, low income child care, resource and referral programs, services for special needs children, and work training programs. In addition, nine states created special commissions or task forces to explore these issues more deeply, and eleven other states passed legislation designed to expand their existing programs.

With respect to licensing and administration, Connecticut (P.A. 110) chose to focus much of its attention on quality of care by replacing optional preregistration inspections with mandatory inspections and by increasing unannounced visits to registered homes from 10 percent to 33 percent of such homes per year. Similarly, Alabama (Act 459) toughened its standards by encouraging local district attorneys to give priority to the enforcement of laws regarding the operation of unlicensed or out-of-compliance child care facilities. One state (Kansas, Chapter 233) passed a bill to protect family daycare home operators and workers who have committed acts of abuse and neglect. The law requires and defines the validation of such acts and allows the continuation of operation or employment if the perpetrator completes a correction action plan.

Seven states passed laws to encourage employers to support child care. Oregon (Chapter 682), for example, created a 50 percent employer tax credit for child care assistance paid for or provided to an employee. The bill also provides tax credits to employers who improve property for use as a child care facility. Rhode Island (Chapter 477) established a 30 percent tax credit for employers who provide licensed child care services for employees and for landlords who provide licensed child care services for employees of their commercial tenants. Texas (Chapter 944) introduced a salary reduction agreement that allows certain public employees to have an amount set aside from their gross earnings for payment of child care expenses.

Finally, six states passed special bills geared to the daycare needs of low income families, four states passed enabling legislation to either create or maintain resource and referral programs, four states passed bills to address daycare requirements of special needs children, seven states created work training programs, and eight states established special commissions and task forces to examine daycare needs.

Two daycare bills that had particularly unique features were California's SR 23 and Minnesota's Chapter 290. The California act created a special Senate Task Force on Child Care to conduct a twelve-month study on the feasibility of establishing a social insurance program funded by employee and employer contributions to provide affordable child care. The Minnesota bill, on the other hand, focused on the problem of low wages. It requires child care providers to pay more than 110 percent of the county average wage for child care workers in order to secure maximum reimbursement for subsidized child care.

Family Preservation and Prevention Services

Ten states passed seventeen laws designed to preserve and protect the family unit. Five states were particularly active in this area: California, New York, Washington, Iowa, and Minnesota.

California (Chapter 1260) created a special advisory committee to assist the state's lead agency on children and youth in the development of day treatment services as an alternative to foster care.

New York's legislation (Chapter 465) authorizes and sets state reimbursement levels for community preventive services to avert foster care placement, reunify foster children with their families, and reduce foster care recidivism. It also authorizes demonstration programs and eases administrative requirements for developing innovative approaches.

Washington passed two laws that addressed the issue of family preservation and prevention services. Chapter 434 created a Family Independence Program to provide training and job placement activities, remedial education, child care, and medical benefits for welfare recipients who enter designated job training programs. Chapter 518, on the other hand, established Project Even Start to provide adult literacy programs for eligible parents of at-risk children. It also authorized various support services that include child care and family counseling.

Iowa, under Chapter 234, created a three-year pilot family preservation services program to address the needs of at-risk families. The act limited caseload size, reduced duration of service provision, required the development of a performance-based payment system for providers based on outcome measures, and required the evaluation of the program to determine its cost-effectiveness.

Lastly, Minnesota's Indian Family Preservation Act (Chapter 403, Article 2) authorized specially focused state grants for certain Indian tribes and organizations for independent living skills programs, child abuse and neglect, teenage pregnancy, and other child welfare services.

Family Leave

During 1987 twenty-eight states introduced parental and family leave legislation. Each of these terms are to be distinguished from each other and from pregnancy leave. Parental leave constitutes an absence from work for the purposes of caring for a newborn, sick, or adopted child. In contrast, family leave refers to that broader category of leaves that

Table 5.1
Parental and Family Leave by State, 1987

State	Type	Gender	Length	Employer	Status
AK	parental	neutral	18 wks	15+	in comm.: no action
AZ	parental	mothers	16 wks	not spec.	died in committee
CA	parental	neutral	16 wks	25+	passed: gov. veto
CO	parental	neutral	26 wks	15+	died in committee
CT	family	neutral	24 wks	state	enacted into law
FL	parental	mothers	16 wks	25+	died in committee
IL	family	neutral	18 wks	15+	died in committee
MA	parental	neutral	18 wks	6+	died in committee
MD	family	neutral	18 wks	public	died in committee
MI	family	neutral	18 wks	not spec.	in comm: no action
MN	parental	neutral	6 wks	21+	enacted into law
MO	parental	mothers	16 wks	not spec.	in comm.: no action
NJ	family	neutral	12 wks	25+	passed Senate
NY	parental	neutral	18/52 wks	15+	in comm.: no action
OR	parental	neutral	12 wks	25+	enacted into law
PA	parental	neutral	16 wks	not spec.	in comm.: no action
RI	parental	neutral	13 wks	50+	enacted into law
TN	parental	mothers	16 wks	100+	enacted into law
VA	parental	neutral	18 wks	15+	died in committee
WA	family	neutral	18 wks	25+	in comm.: no action
WI	family	neutral	20 wks	15+	passed Senate

Other legislation associated with pregnancy/disability leaves, but not properly parental/family leave:

GA: related to maintaining seniority and benefits for teachers who take disability/pregnancy leave; carried to next session.

IA: provides for 8 weeks disability leave due to pregnancy; enacted.

KY: prevents employers with eight or more employees to deny pregnancy disability leave to female employees. Withdrawn.

LA: prevents discrimination against women due to pregnancy, childbirth and related disability leaves; enacted.

SC: precludes denial of benefits to persons having taken unpaid maternity (parental leave); in committee: no action.

TX: Would provide maternity benefits for mothers of adopted children. Died in committee.

VT: precludes discrimination due to pregnancy; requires employers to provide pregnancy/disability leave; passed House.

extend beyond parents of children to include dependent care of other family members such as a spouse or elderly parent.

Table 5.1 illustrates the twenty-eight states and the respective bills that they introduced during the 1987 session. The specific type (parental or family), gender base, length of leave, size of employer to which it applies, and each bill's status at the conclusion of the session are presented for twenty-one states. The other seven states introduced legislation that related more to pregnancy/disability leaves than to parental/family leave. Therefore, their characteristics and status are presented at the bottom of the table.

Of the twenty-eight states that introduced parental/family leave legislation in 1987, only four (Connecticut, Rhode Island, Oregon, and Minnesota) enacted such laws, and only one (Connecticut) broadened its bill sufficiently to include elderly parent care, thus qualifying as a family leave package. Few of the remaining states saw their proposals move beyond legislative committees. However, at least four states (California, Massachusetts, New Jersey, and Wisconsin), though unsuccessful in their attempts, put forth significant initiatives that are worthy of further exploration. What follows is a brief analysis of the four successful efforts as well as a review of four unsuccessful attempts to enact parental/family leave legislation at the state level.

In summarizing the four family leave bills that passed in 1987, the following points should be emphasized. First, they were all produced by Democratically controlled governments at the state level, not by private initiatives or by federal action. In addition, each bill passed fairly easily and eventually relied on Republican support for final adoption. Second, all leaves are unpaid. Third, all are gender neutral. Fourth, only Connecticut included a provision for caregivers of the elderly; the others did not. But Connecticut was also the only state not to apply its policy to the private sector. Finally, there was much variation among the states regarding specific provisions of their bills. The length of leave ranged from six weeks (Oregon) to twenty-four (Connecticut), the size of companies to which the leave applied ranged from twenty-one employees (Minnesota) to fifty (Rhode Island), and some states included health insurance coverage during leave while others did not.

With respect to four big states that were unsuccessful in their attempts to establish family and parental leave policies, the following points should be emphasized. In general terms, all four proposals (California, Massachusetts, New Jersey, and Wisconsin) were initiated by Democrats and, for the most part, opposed by Republicans. If enacted, all four bills would have represented unpaid leave and applied to both public and private sectors. There was greater variation, however, in the length of leave, ranging from twelve weeks (New Jersey) to twenty-four weeks (Wisconsin), as well as in the size of firms to which it should apply— from six employees (Massachusetts) to twenty-five (California and New Jersey). Only one state (Massachusetts) addressed the issue of wage replacement, and only one state (Wisconsin) managed to get some endorsements, though limited, from the business community.

Two states (New Jersey and Wisconsin) supported family leave while California and Massachusetts advocated parental leave. Only one state (California) came close to enacting a bill, having seen it pass both houses before being vetoed by the governor. New Jersey and Wisconsin both witnessed Senate approval only, and Massachusetts' proposal remained locked in the committee system. By 1990, however, New Jersey and Wisconsin passed family leave laws, as did at least eight other states.

Although unsuccessful in their efforts, the initiatives put forth by these states are important for two reasons. First, all four states are generally regarded as among the more progressive and innovative in social policy. The results of legislative efforts in these states can serve as important sentinels for the future prospects of parental and family leave elsewhere. Second, it can also be argued that these unsuccessful proposals contain specific provisions that will help broaden the debate as this issue is addressed more frequently on a national scale.

With respect to other important family-oriented policy initiatives, the following points can be made. In 1987 the California State Assembly passed a resolution that requires the Office of Legislative Research to develop a family impact statement methodology. The purpose of such a statement parallels that of the environmental impact statement. Before legislation is enacted or policies are implemented, a process would be completed to measure the impact such initiatives might have on the family. The California Assembly also has established a Joint Commission on the Changing Family. Composed of bipartisan members, the commission meets monthly and is exploring long-range needs of California's families.

In 1983 Illinois enacted the Family Impact Statement Act (P.A. 83–96), which requires certain state agencies to indicate to what extent their actions have impacted on family stability. Annual reports must be submitted to the governor, and a thirty-five-member family policy task force is responsible for monitoring implementation of the 1983 law by human service agencies.

Also, in 1987 the state of Nebraska enacted the Family Policy Act (L.B. 637), which is directed at family-centered home-based services for chronically dependent family members of all ages. It also establishes standards for communities and agencies in the executive, legislative, and judicial branches of the government. Other states, such as Delaware, Florida, and New Mexico, have taken similar steps but experienced little or no success to date. But, according to works by T. Ooms and S. Preister (1988), Wisensale (1990), as well as S. L. Zimmerman (1988), more states are directing their attention toward families each year.

THE FUTURE OF STATE FAMILY POLICY INITIATIVES

It has been argued here that particularly since the 1980 White House Conference on Families, there has been increasing interest in the overall health and well-being of the American family. This is reflected in the almost constant flow of research literature that not only outlines major demographic changes in the family but also recommends particular policies designed to address specific needs of families. It is also reflected in the emergence of family-oriented policies at both the federal and state levels.

Connecticut declared 1987 the Year of the Family in the state legislature and then proceeded to pass a family policy package consisting of sixteen bills that ranged from family leave to job training for displaced homemakers. California, Massachusetts, Nebraska, Rhode Island, and other states established special family policy task forces, and numerous states enacted laws that were family-oriented in structure. These included parental leave bills, daycare policies, family protection and preservation legislation, and acts targeted at child abuse and neglect.

At the federal level the Reagan administration issued a special policy paper (*The Family: Preserving America's Future*) and handed down an executive order mandating the implementation of a family impact statement. Congress, meanwhile, was also active in the area of family-oriented issues. Although unsuccessful in raising the minimum wage and in passing either daycare legislation or the parental leave bill, it did pass the Family Support Act, which represents the first successful attempt at welfare reform in fifty-three years. It is expected that family-oriented policies will continue to be addressed and debated in future congressional sessions, but expectations are never tantamount to certainties.

In attempting to predict the future course of family policy, it is essential that one be clear about its past. In doing so, at least two important points should be kept in mind. First, it was the Carter administration's White House Conference on Families that drew national attention and raised expectations for a federally based family policy initiative. But second, and perhaps most important, just as the Conference on Families was taking down its tent in 1980, the Reagan administration was moving into the White House. It was Reagan's philosophy of New Federalism that shifted more policymaking from the federal government to the states. This in turn produced two significant outcomes: (1) it became clear that the federal government would not act on a major scale with respect to a national family policy; and (2) it also became clear that the states would have to take the initiative in this area. Thus, it was the latter of these two outcomes that became the focus of this chapter.

Whether or not we will witness a continuation of family policy legislation at the state level ultimately depends on two key factors: (1) the tone and general direction of the Bush administration; and (2) the extent to which individual states have the same four important ingredients that enabled Connecticut to push through its family policy package in 1987. These include political power and whether or not a clear electoral mandate has been established, the role of party leadership, the level of economic resources, and the comprehensiveness of legislative proposals.

With respect to the first factor, it is likely that the Bush administration will differ little from its predecessor. That is, the popular themes of the Reagan years such as deregulation, privatization, and New Federalism will not find themselves among the huddled homeless in Washington. More specifically, and based on Bush's positions during his presidential campaign, he will most likely continue to oppose the minimum wage, limit daycare to voluntary tax credits, oppose mandatory parental leave and national health insurance, and continue to view the voluntary sector (including the family) as a major component of the social safety net. In short, it appears clear that the burden will continue to fall on the states to design family policy and/or initiate family-oriented legislation as they see fit.

With respect to the second factor, whether or not states will be successful in initiating family policy may well depend on four important ingredients that contributed to Connecticut's success in this area. First, although family issues tend to be bipartisan, states in which legislatures are dominated by the same party as the governor's are in a strong position to enact family-oriented legislation—particularly if the power base was produced recently (within two years) by a major election.

Second, support from the leadership of the party in power is crucial to the enactment of family policy initiatives. It is essential that key legislators on important committees be supportive of such legislative efforts. Part of Connecticut's success can certainly be attributed to the party leadership's creation of a special Family and Workplace Committee that was designed to escort the family policy package through the legislature. Other states may find a similar strategy beneficial.

Third, states with solid economic resources such as a low unemployment rate, a solid tax base, and a budget surplus are obviously in a much better position to enact social legislation such as daycare, parental leave, and universal health insurance. A low unemployment rate may also spur on corporations to adopt various family support programs such as parental leave and daycare as a means of recruiting and retaining employees. Clearly, states less well-off economically are unlikely to be aggressive in enacting family-oriented legislation.

Finally, the comprehensiveness of legislation introduced may well determine its outcome. Policy proposals must appeal to legislators from all parts of a given state, be it the inner city, rural areas, or the suburbs. It should also be comprehensive enough to appeal to numerous interest groups so that important coalitions are maintained and opposition to key initiatives is held to a minimum. However, legislators in particular should be wary of specific interest groups that might seek to employ a state family policy agenda as a vehicle to achieve their particular goals. Connecticut, for example, successfully sidestepped both a major labor union and a welfare rights organization that attempted to utilize such a strategy. Other states should be aware of such pitfalls.

In summary, an administration under George Bush will most likely result in a pattern of policymaking not unlike that of Ronald Reagan's. That is, family-oriented initiatives will be expected to originate in the states, not in Washington, D.C. A case in point concerns President Bush's veto of the 1990 Family Leave Act. Despite passing both houses by comfortable margins, President Bush issued his veto on the grounds that such a policy should be made mandatory for private corporations. States that may have placed their family leave legislation on hold, pending the outcome of the debate in Washington, will now most likely move forward on their own initiative as several states did in 1987. For better or for worse, such action will produce a patchwork of family policies throughout the country. The strongest states politically and economically will create and act upon broad-based family policy agendas. On the other hand, those states that lack solid political support and are economically weak will most likely move incrementally, if at all.

6
Latchkey Children and After-School Care: A Feminist Dilemma?

Clifton P. Flynn and Hyman Rodman

Public funding for programs that benefit women and children has traditionally been difficult to obtain. Political and legislative insensitivity serves as a challenge to feminists and others to provide convincing evidence of the need for such programs. In some instances, however, apparently strong evidence in support of a policy or program may be flawed or suspect. Advocates then face difficult judgments about whether to use suspect data in pursuit of a laudable goal. In other instances, the evidence and the argument it engenders may, on further analysis, reveal the risk of unintended consequences that are detrimental to women and children.

The ethical problem posed by suspect data and the strategic problem posed by the risk of unintended consequences can arise in a variety of areas. L. J. Weitzman (1985) has demonstrated the unexpected negative consequences for women and children stemming from the apparently desirable goals of the movement toward no-fault divorce and equitable sharing of property. The "revolution" in divorce laws failed to bring about the desired equality for women because it ignored the economic inequalities that are created in marriage. Supporters did not envision the serious financial hardships most divorcing women would face under no-fault divorce. We may now be in the early stages of a similar development regarding latchkey children and after-school care. On the one hand there is a clear need for policies and programs to provide improved child care generally and care for school-age children in particular. On the other hand, we face a dilemma posed by suspect data and potentially unintended consequences.

Many scholars, policy makers, and child care advocates are convinced that latchkey children face serious physical and psychological risks. The alleged negative effects of self-care receive extensive coverage in the media. In fact, however, existing knowledge about the consequences of self-care for children's development is quite limited. The available evidence certainly does not permit any strong conclusion that latchkey children face serious developmental risks. As will become clear in our later discussion, the limited evidence suggests that there are few or no differences in the social and cognitive development of self-care children when compared to children in adult care. Nonetheless, arguments about the dangers of self-care persist, maintained largely by conclusions drawn from research that is methodologically flawed, by vested professional interests that are served by the creation of a "latchkey problem," and by media hype.

As part of their funding strategy, child care advocates are relying on the latchkey problem to convince legislators to support after-school care programs. This approach, however, may result in unintended, negative consequences for women, particularly for working mothers. Stressing the risks of self-care may increase the opposition to working mothers and may cause some working mothers who feel guilty to quit their jobs. Thus, feminists must decide if questionable findings about the dangers of self-care should be part of the strategy to obtain funding for after-school care. That is the feminist dilemma, and it is also the dilemma faced by others concerned with bringing about improvements in child care policies and programs.

This chapter reviews the research on latchkey children and traces how, in spite of the findings, the problem of self-care has been created by flawed research, by the media, and by child care professionals who have a vested interest in perceiving a latchkey problem. Excerpts from federal hearings on after-school care are presented to illustrate the use of suspect data to achieve a desirable goal—funding for school-age child care. Finally, we question the wisdom of such a strategy by pointing to the potential negative impact it may have on women, and we suggest that a better approach would emphasize the major logistical problems that parents experience in finding child care.

WHAT IS SELF-CARE?

Before beginning this analysis, it is important to be clear about the definition of self-care children and self-care arrangements. C. Cole and H. Rodman define a self-care child as "one between the ages of approximately 6 and 13 who spends time at home alone or with a younger sibling on a periodic basis" (1987, p. 93). Children who fall below this age range require full-time adult supervision; those above the range generally do not. Most would agree, for example, that a 4-year-old child should not be left at home alone for an hour or two each day. Such an arrangement clearly falls under the heading of neglect and does not qualify as a self-care arrangement. By and large, children within the stated age range are capable of spending at least some time alone, but require adult care most of the time.

Reasonable individuals may disagree on when a child is ready for self-care. The age of the child, the child's level of maturity, the amount of time alone, the accessibility of an adult in the event of an emergency—all are important factors to consider. Some children are ready for self-care sooner than others, while some are never ready. It would be a mistake, however, to assume that no child is capable of spending time alone or to decide that all children who do are victims of neglect or are at serious risk (Cole and Rodman, 1987; Rodman and Cole, 1987).

RESEARCH ON LATCHKEY CHILDREN

The impact of mothers' employment and other-than-mother care on children has received considerable attention since the 1970s (Bronfenbrenner and Crouter, 1982; Etaugh, 1980; Scarr, 1984). Scholarly and public interest has focused mainly on formal daycare arrangements for preschool children, ignoring similar arrangements for school-age children. Even less attention has been given to children who regularly care for themselves before and after school. This oversight has occurred despite the fact that children in self-care, commonly referred to as latchkey children, far outnumber children in daycare settings (Rodman, Pratto, and Nelson, 1985).

Researchers in the 1980s, recognizing this oversight, took the first steps in empirically investigating school-age children in self-care arrangements. Five studies have examined self-care by comparing latchkey children with children in adult care. In these studies, researchers were particularly interested in determining whether self-care arrangements have negative consequences for children's social and psychological development.

T. J. Long and L. Long (1982) interviewed fifty-three latchkey children and thirty-two children in adult care from an all-black parochial school in Washington, D.C. The Longs reported that latchkey children have higher levels of fear than children under adult supervision. They also suggested that limited opportunities for social play may have negative developmental consequences for latchkey children.

N. L. Galambos and J. Garbarino (1983) compared self-care and adult-care children, using fifth and seventh graders in a rural community. Latchkey children did not differ from children supervised by adults in school adjustment, in academic achievement, or in levels of fear.

Rodman et al. (1985) compared forty-eight self-care children with forty-eight matched children in adult care on several areas of social and psychological functioning. Twenty-six pairs of fourth graders and twenty-two pairs of seventh graders were matched on age, race, family composition, and social status. No significant differences were found in measures of self-esteem, locus of control, or teachers' ratings of social adjustment and interpersonal relationships.

L. Steinberg (1986) examined peer susceptibility and after-school care status among 768 fifth, sixth, eighth, and ninth graders. He found no differences in peer susceptibility between adolescents who were at home with a parent and those who were in self-care. This finding held for boys and girls. Steinberg did report that, for both boys and girls, those who were unsupervised at a friend's house or said they were just "hanging out" were more susceptible to peer pressure than adolescents in self-care.

Finally, D. L. Vandell and M. A. Corasaniti (1988) compared 150 white, predominantly middle-class third graders from a suburban Dallas school district, who were in a variety of after-school care arrangements (mother care, daycare, sitter care, and self-care). The researchers reported no differences between children in mother care and those in self-care on an array of developmental measures, including school performance, standardized test scores, conduct grades, and children's ratings of self-competence. Additionally, no differences between the two groups emerged in teachers' and parents' ratings of children's emotional well-being, relationships with peers and adults, and work/study skills.

The results of these few studies are mixed. Some negative consequences of self-care have been reported, but the best evidence seems to indicate that the social and psychological functioning of latchkey children is not significantly different from that of children under adult supervision.

THE "PROBLEM" OF SELF-CARE

The popular assumption, however, is that self-care is a problem and that self-care children are at risk. Professional concerns about self-care, supported and reinforced by the media, go far beyond the available evidence (e.g., Turkington, 1983). Newspaper and magazine articles, focusing on the fear and loneliness experienced by latchkey children, make exaggerated claims about the physical and psychological risks of self-care, usually deemphasizing or ignoring evidence to the contrary (such as Rodman, 1984). Many commentators refer to the Longs' (1983; 1982) research to substantiate their claims. The Longs themselves, though acknowledging both positive and negative consequences of self-care, clearly stress the negative in their own writings.

There are methodological problems in the Longs' studies that severely limit the validity of their findings. First, the comparisons of fear level made between latchkey and adult-care children were not based on standardized questions. Second, other variables that may account for observed differences in level of fear, such as the age of the child or the safety of the neighborhood, were not controlled. Third, the semistructured interview schedule employed in the study is open to lack of precision and interviewer bias, weaknesses acknowledged by the authors (Long and Long, 1982). Thus, conclusions about the negative consequences of self-care are premature and are typically based on suspect data.

Steinberg's (1986) study raises certain questions as well. He expands the definition of self-care to include (a) children who are over age 13 and (b) children who are unsupervised but not at home. While knowledge concerning the psychosocial development of both groups is important, such a broad definition confuses, rather than clarifies, the issue.

By extending the definitional boundaries of latchkey children and reporting greater susceptibility to antisocial peer pressure, Steinberg's report will become grist for the mill of those who are already all too prone to see risks in the latchkey situation. The specific details of Steinberg's careful study are in danger of being lost in the overgeneralization that latchkey children are at risk (Rodman et al., 1988, p. 293).

(For an excellent debate on the definition of self-care, see Rodman et al., 1988, and Steinberg, 1988.) Clearly, reports of and beliefs in the dangers of self-care persist. These reports have recently been used in the political arena. Efforts at the state and federal levels for legislation to fund after-school child care programs have been based largely on alleviating the "latchkey problem."

AFTER-SCHOOL CARE LEGISLATION

School-age child care has received little legislative support from the states or from the federal government. Consequently, most after-school care programs have been established locally in communities throughout the country. A few states, including California, New York, and Pennsylvania, have funded school-age child care (Seligson, 1986).

At the federal level, the Dependent Care Grants program was authorized in October 1984 by Congress for $20 million in 1984 and in 1985. Under this legislation, states could apply for block grants for activities related to dependent care resource and referral systems and school-age child care in public or private school facilities. However, no funds were appropriated in 1985 and only $5 million in 1986, with 60 percent of the total allocated for school-age child care ("States applying," 1986). Congress reauthorized the Dependent Care Grant program for 1987–1990 at $20 million per year. As in the previous year, only $5 million was appropriated for 1987 ("Congress reauthorizes," 1986).

The first national legislation on school-age child care was introduced in Congress in the summer of 1983. The School Facilities Child Care Act would have provided funds to use public school facilities to operate child care programs, both before and after school, for school-age children. An amended version of the original bill passed the House but was never brought to a vote in the Senate. A major part of the strategy employed by proponents was to emphasize the dangers of self-care.

The language of the bill refers to the negative effects of self-care. Phrases such as "unsupervised children run physical and psychological risks, including accidents and feelings of loneliness and fear" and "research studies have indicated increased likelihood of alcohol and drug abuse and delinquent behavior among unsupervised 'latchkey' children" are stated as if they are facts.

In the congressional hearings that followed, it was evident that the bill's supporters relied heavily on the notion that the lives of latchkey children are in jeopardy. Witnesses presented vivid, emotional, yet scientifically questionable accounts of the fate of latchkey children. In a prepared statement before a House subcommittee, Ellen Gannett delivered the following testimony:

> Although there exists relatively little research in the area of self-care, the few studies that do exist support the idea that self-care for the most vulnerable children (low income, minority, urban) has negative effects on adjustment, school achievement, and self-image. In addition, studies by Long and Long in Washington, D.C., ACYF in the states of Virginia and Minnesota, indicate that among others [sic], many children experience loneliness, boredom, fear, and some appear to be at risk for accidents and abuse by other children and adults. At best, many of these latchkey children experience severely constrained play and social experiences during the time they are out of school (House Committee on Education and Labor, 1984, p. 33).

Similar testimony was offered by Helen Blank, director of Child Care and Family Support Services at the Children's Defense Fund:

> Psychologists are deeply concerned about the damaging effects of the premature granting of responsibility to very young children caring for themselves or for even younger siblings. Children are also developing a sense of alienation, loneliness, and fear. One-third of the school children in New York City state that they are afraid to go outside their apartment.
> Thomas S. Long at Catholic University has been conducting research on latchkey children since 1979 interviewing hundreds of current and former children who were left alone in the early morning and/or after-school hours. He and

others have found that children who cared for themselves expressed more feelings of fear, loneliness and boredom than did children in adult care (House Committee on Education and Labor, 1984, p. 41).

The hearing before the Senate Subcommittee on Education, Arts, and Humanities was no different. Rita Clark, Human Services Program Analyst for the Florida Department of Health and Rehabilitative Services testified that "the emotional strain on these children can be devastating. Fears and anxieties that develop lead to serious and costly mental health problems in children" (Senate Committee on Labor and Human Resources, 1984, p. 28). Judge Hugh Glickstein, representing the American Bar Association, presented this testimony:

We can only postulate how many injuries, abductions, sexual assaults, and even deaths from fire, drownings, et cetera result from young children having to fend for themselves. . . .

It does not take an expert to reach the additional conclusion that there is an adverse effect on these children, even if they escape physical harm, to be left alone and face the fear of entering an empty house, or wander in the streets, or fill the void by watching endless hours of television (Senate Committee on Labor and Human Resources, 1984, p. 35).

Clearly, proponents of the bill believe that self-care is a problem.

Political realities make it easy to understand why the supporters of after-school care legislation are inclined to define the self-care arrangement as a problem. Budget deficits, pressures to reduce government spending, and a revival of conservatism present formidable obstacles for all child care proposals. In addition, there is an historical reluctance on the part of government to support activities, such as child care, that may be viewed as an invasion of the family's right to privacy (Adams and Winston, 1980; Steiner, 1981). Policy makers must be convinced that a problem exists before spending money on a solution. Consequently, some social scientists, child care professionals, and other well-intentioned individuals have, consciously or unconsciously, constructed a questionable social problem—latchkey children—to solve a real social problem—inadequate child care for school-age children. Stories depicting the horrors of the latchkey experience, based on information derived from limited research and suspect data, paint a dramatic picture of children in jeopardy. That picture may influence legislators to loosen the public purse strings and fund after-school care.

Let us make our position clear. Along with many others, we recognize the great need for child care in this country. We wholeheartedly support efforts seeking to increase the availability of quality child care services for parents in general and especially for working mothers. But we question whether the best way to achieve that goal is to emphasize the presumed negative effects of self-care. Such a strategy ultimately may prove to be counterproductive, particularly from a feminist perspective, as its implementation holds unforeseen consequences for women.

THE FEMINIST DILEMMA

Feminists are by no means a cohesive group, and there are some sharp differences among those who identify as feminists. Certain core beliefs are nevertheless shared by most feminists. They ardently support a woman's right to work. Further, they believe that women should not be prevented from working because they have children, that child care is not the sole responsibility of the mother, and that regular nonmaternal care is not harmful to children's development.

The issue of child care is especially salient for women (Kamerman, 1985). Feminists realize the importance of quality child care services to working mothers. They strongly favor government-sponsored programs for school-age children but know from experience that it is difficult to obtain public funds for such programs.

Feminists are also aware that, because most mothers in this country are employed, many children spend time at home alone or spend time in other types of nonmaternal care.

Feminists have argued that this is not, in itself, undesirable; children of any age do not require the full-time attendance by a mother to develop into happy, healthy adults. They cite the many advantages of jobs and careers for women and suggest that other societal institutions and new family arrangements can provide for the care of our nation's children (Feinstein, 1984, p. 298).

Most people, whether feminist or not, recognize that latchkey children, particularly those from single-parent families, may have special needs that should be addressed. Yet, unlike many others, most feminists do not automatically characterize self-care arrangements as negative or undesirable. Self-care makes it possible for many women to work outside the home who would otherwise be unable to do so. Just as employment provides fulfillment for women, self-care may engender responsibility and self-reliance in children. Thus feminists are faced with a dilemma: Should they use suspect data on the negative consequences of self-care as part of their strategy to obtain funding for after-school programs?

This dilemma, of course, confronts many who do not consider themselves as feminists, but it is particularly salient for feminists. Though some feminists may have considered the problems for women that could arise from a funding strategy emphasizing the dangers of self-care, this chapter is the first instance in which this concern is formally and directly articulated as a feminist dilemma.

What are the possible outcomes of adopting such a strategy? One possibility is success in getting funds for after-school programs. But unintended consequences may also occur. Three possible consequences point out why such a strategy is problematic from a feminist perspective.

Fewer Women Working

One unintended consequence could be a reduction of women in the work force. Although there are no empirical data to substantiate this possibility, and although large numbers of women are unlikely to be affected, there are certainly some women who already are reacting in this way. Unfounded fears about self-care may cause some mothers who are currently using a self-care arrangement to quit work and stay home with their children. Other women may delay entering or reentering the labor force in order to be absolutely certain that their child is old enough to handle self-care. Some mothers may continue to work but with unnecessarily high levels of anxiety and guilt.

Prematurely condemning self-care may eliminate a child care option for working mothers. Each mother must be free to evaluate her child care needs based on her unique situation. As C. Safilios-Rothschild stated, "it is preferable that a number of alternatives for handling child care be available, so that each parent can choose the one most appropriate to her . . . needs and preferences" (1974, p. 19).

Some children are embarrassed by having a baby sitter thrust upon them. Many children possess the maturity and responsibility to be successful latchkey children. Mothers of these children should be able to choose self-care without being made to feel like unfit mothers. Self-care may be the only alternative for women who are poor, who are single parents, or who live where quality child care is not available. Some of these families would undoubtedly benefit from after-school programs, but for many a self-care arrangement may be entirely appropriate.

Heightened Opposition to Working Mothers

Proclaiming negative consequences for latchkey children could lead to serious problems for women and for the feminist movement. Such a strategy may provide conservative political and religious groups with ammunition to revitalize their opposition to working mothers.

The New Right opposes all forms of government-sponsored child care. For the New Right, state-supported child care is another example of how "the welfare state is responsible for undermining the traditional patriarchal family by taking over different family functions. The health, welfare, and education of individuals, it believes, should be the purview of the family" (Eisenstein, 1982, p. 77).

The working mother receives the brunt of the New Right's attack. At the heart of that attack is the claim that maternal employment is detrimental to children. If latchkey children are said to be at serious physical and psychological risk, and if latchkey arrangements exist because mothers work, then it follows, according to the logic of the New Right, that mothers should not work. Conservatives will not miss this new opportunity to stereotype and stigmatize "selfish" women who go to work each day and "neglect" their children.

A similar argument has been made before by the conservative right. During the 1960s, opposition to maternal employment took the form of unsubstantiated claims of the horrors of daycare. In the future, we may confront a parallel argument against working mothers with equally unsubstantiated claims of the horrors of self care.

Most research reports have vindicated working mothers and formal daycare arrangements (Bronfenbrenner and Crouter, 1982; Etaugh, 1980; Scarr, 1984). For many children, daycare has been a positive influence on their social and psychological development. It is conceivable that subsequent research on the effects of self-care may arrive at similar conclusions.

The goals of the New Right are simple and straightforward: "it desires to establish the model of the traditional white patriarchal family by dismantling the welfare state and by removing wage-earning married women from the labor force and returning them to the home" (Eisenstein, 1982, p. 78). Calling for increased funding for after-school care based on the negative consequences of self-care may play right into the conservatives' hands.

Weakened Argument for Funding

Finally, what will happen if further research reveals that latchkey children are not at risk, that they are not developmentally disadvantaged, perhaps even that the arrangement contributes to independence and responsibility? Arguments to obtain funding for after-school care would be weakened considerably, and the credibility of those making the argument would suffer. Valid reasons for publicly supported after-school care would also be tarnished. The challenge of obtaining funding for child care is difficult enough without the addition of this self-imposed handicap. Ultimately, funding for after-school care may be threatened or rejected because of the questionable strategy currently being used by its supporters.

SOCIAL CONSTRUCTION OF THE LATCHKEY PROBLEM

The social construction of the "latchkey problem," although not a central focus of this chapter, is a phenomenon worthy of separate investigation. This would involve investigating the processes by which a set of conditions is defined as a problem (Gusfield, 1984; Spector and Kitsuse, 1977). From a constructionist perspective, social problems are defined as claims-making activities about perceived conditions, not the conditions themselves. "Thus, the significance of objective conditions . . . is the *assertions made about them*, not the validity of those assertions as judged from some independent standpoint, as for example, that of a scientist" (Spector and Kitsuse, 1977, p. 76).

We have alluded to the partisan use of research and to the role of the media in the claims-making activities regarding the danger that self-care poses for children. Another example concerns claims about the number of children in self-care arrangements (for a complete discussion of this topic, see Hobbs and Rodman, 1987). According to the U.S. Bureau of the Census, in 1974 approximately 1.8 million children between the ages of 7 and 13 cared for themselves during out-of-school hours (U.S. Bureau of the Census, 1976). For those defining self-care as a problem, however, it is advantageous to be able to refer to much larger numbers. This attracts greater attention from the media and from policy makers. After reviewing estimates made by others, Long and Long suggest that "the number of latchkey children age thirteen and under can range from a low of less than 2.5 million to a high of nearly 15 million. Even conservative estimates put the figure between 5 and 10 million" (1983, p. 24). Most media reports ignored the 1.8 million figure and used much higher estimates, often in the 5 to 10 million range. Some justified these higher estimates by suggesting that the number of latchkey children had grown dramatically since 1974. But in 1987, based on a survey done in 1984, the U.S. Bureau of the Census estimated that there were approximately 2.4 million latchkey children between the ages of 5 and 13 (Cain and Hofferth, 1989; Rich, 1987; U.S. Bureau of the Census, 1987a).

We have provided only a brief outline of the claims-making activities concerning the "latchkey problem" and of their validity. Rodman (1990) presents a more detailed analysis of these claims-making activities, including the role of researchers, the media, child care professionals and advocates, and policy makers. Beyond that, he carefully scrutinizes the claims, concluding that they often fail to reflect accurately current knowledge about latchkey children and self-care arrangements.

Rodman argues that three ingredients are required for the successful construction of the latchkey problem. First, latchkey children must be shown to be at risk. Second, large and growing numbers of latchkey children must be demonstrated. Third, the media must be used to spread the word about the great numbers of latchkey children and the grave dangers they face. "It remains to be seen whether the latchkey issue has the necessary ingredients to be accepted as a social problem requiring policy and program solutions. The process of the social construction of the latchkey problem is underway, however, although the outcome is still in doubt" (Rodman, 1990, p. 172).

CONCLUSIONS

Should suspect findings reporting negative consequences of self-care be used in an attempt to obtain funding for after-school care? It is tempting to use them because the strategy may succeed, at least in the short term. But the strategy poses a feminist dilemma—it may backfire and lead to several undesirable consequences.

First, women who believe the worst about self-care may leave or delay returning to the work force. Second, drawing attention to the risks of self-care could lead to a conservative backlash, with increased opposition to working mothers. Third, if research shows that latchkey children are not at risk, then those who base their funding arguments on the negative consequences of self-care will lose their credibility.

What is the solution to this feminist dilemma? The solution lies in stressing several compelling reasons that argue for the funding of after-school programs: (1) Most mothers of school-age children work; (2) many more who want to work are at home because quality after-school care is not available, not accessible, or not affordable; (3) the number of single-parent families (typically headed by females) has increased dramatically; and (4) economic disadvantages experienced by women household heads limit their child care options. These reasons form a convincing and powerful argument that is not dependent on using suspect data to construct a latchkey problem.

Efforts to understand self-care and its effects on children have only just begun. Knowledge about self-care has implications for children and families and for policies that address their needs. Researchers need to approach self-care objectively, with an open mind as to whether the experience is harmful or beneficial to children's development. Researchers also need to be keenly aware of other factors that influence children's development. There is, of course, no guarantee that objective research will lead to improvements in social policy. As this analysis has demonstrated, the path from research to public policy is complicated and is influenced not only by the research but also by professional self-interest, by committed policy advocates, and by partisan interpretations of research findings.

Future studies may reveal that latchkey children really are at risk or that they benefit from the self-care experience. More likely, future research will reveal the circumstances under which the self-care arrangement may be harmful or beneficial. Cole and Rodman (1987) suggest that characteristics of the child, the family, and the community are important factors in determining how a child is affected by self care. "For example, a family going through a divorce and living in a high-risk urban neighborhood without friendly neighbors may find that their children are adversely affected by self-care while their cousins of the same age who live in a stable family in a small town do well with the same arrangement" (p. 95).

Many questions about self-care remain unanswered. For the present, however, skepticism would seem to be an appropriate response to those who claim that we are experiencing a serious "latchkey problem."

NOTE

We thank the William T. Grant Foundation and the Ford Foundation for their support of Hyman Rodman's research on self-care children. We also thank Barrie Thorne for her helpful comments on an earlier draft of this paper.

7
Translating the Problems of the Elderly into Effective Policies: Filial Responsibility

Doris E. Dinkins Ford

The public policy debate of the 1980s and for the next twenty-five years will be dominated by the issues of cost containment in the delivery of health care and social services to the elderly. Recent federal policies have emphasized a reduction in federal expenditures for Medicare and Medicaid, resulting in a shifting of the cost of care to other levels of government and to elderly individuals and their families (Estes, Newcomer, and Associates, 1983). This cost containment policy may ironically push elderly persons into physical dependency situations, such as multigenerational living, because many elderly may delay needed health and social services (Gilliland, 1986). In fact, recent evidence has shown a national trend in the reduction of Medicaid recipients (Harrington et al., 1985). This shifting of the cost of care to the elderly and their families has also generated a renewed interest in the policy of mandating family responsibility (Gilliland, 1986; Byrd, 1988; Bulcroft et al., 1989; Indest, 1988).

This chapter evaluates the political implications of public opinion regarding multigenerational living—a behavioral expression of filial responsibility. In the process, particular attention is focused on the efficacy of current aging and social policies to achieve a balance between the needs of the elderly and their family members. More important, at the heart of this analysis are political issues concerning:

1. the potential danger of the growing care gap and the supply of informal caregivers and the impact of such phenomena on the decisionmaking and policy implementation process; and

2. the impact of the current cost containment thrust of long-term care policies on intergenerational relationships and subsequent policies.

THE POLITICAL ECONOMY OF AGING

The well-being of elderly persons has been enhanced through social policies and their resulting benefits. However, policy makers and the general public have begun to examine the link between elderly people and social policy. A. Walker and C. Phillipson argue that the primary thrust behind current economic and social policies is an ideological construct based on "the public burden" model, which characterizes expenditures on public social services as a burden to the economy (1986, p. 10). Implicit in these considerations is the presumption of the supremacy of economic policy over social policy. The result has been the acceptance of narrowly defined "economic objectives" (i.e., profit maximization, economic growth, and cost efficiency) as legitimate policy objectives. Social objectives (e.g., good health and community care), therefore, "must secure their legitimacy in the policy for their achievement" (p. 11). For example, the growth in the number of persons over age 65 has been used to justify the current federal expenditures and curtailment of entitlement (Myles, 1984).

J. Hendricks and T. Calasanti, pursuing this argument further, note that "contemporary debates are often concluded in terms of an 'intergenerational struggle,' in which younger members of society are said to resent the increasing burden that support for the elderly entails" (1986, p. 251). They contend that age-dependency data do not support the increased burden thesis. Rather, dependency is a socially constructed status—that is, a product of the division of labor and structure inequality and not a product of the aging process itself (Walker, 1981).

Thus, there is a need for social analysis of the environmental dynamics of aging—a critical factor in policy decision making. However, the current push for cost-cutting measures in long-term care policy implementation appears to be based on an inadequate analysis of the social and political dynamics of the elderly persons' environment. Medicare most aptly illustrates this point, for physician and selected outpatient services (part "B") was not based on an analysis of the health care needs or financing and access issues of elderly persons, but it was a last minute initiative by Republican party members of Congress to claim part of the credit for its existence (Hudson, 1987). R. Hudson notes that limiting Medicare to a "financing vehicle" is a "clear recognition of the limits of what American Liberalism and well-placed groups are prepared to allow" (1987, p. 527).

Similar arguments have also been presented as the root causes of current decisionmaking efforts that underpin recent cost-cutting measures for federally supported programs serving the elderly. C. Offe's (1972) work offers a useful framework for understanding current policy shifts—that is, the struggle between commodification (buying and selling of goods in the marketplace) and decommodification (the removal of goods from the marketplace, such as through welfare). Hendricks and Calasanti point to the relevance of these arguments in current long-term care policy implementation. They contend that much of the current controversy in aging policy decision making and implementation is due to the constant "tension to re-commodify those things which have been taken out of the marketplace" (1986, p. 260), such as health care for the elderly.

Researchers have also documented trends toward recommodification of welfare and social services for elderly persons like the profit-making nature of the nursing home industry, recent amendments in social and welfare policies that favor the for-profit sector, and so on (Gilbert, 1983; Olson, 1982). The ultimate question, however, will be: Does recommodification or profit making in the social welfare arena improve and enhance the well-being of elderly persons?

In this regard, current policy changes that favor the private sector (e.g., shifts of the cost of care to other levels of government and to elderly individuals and their families) are problematic in that they leave most of the decision making concerning elder care to the provider, which reduces the input of the client and in many cases the quality of care. It can be further argued that the "decentralization drive" of current long-term care policy creates a highly politicized environment where local interests are more powerful (Estes, Newcomer, and Associates, 1983). These current policy changes also raise questions concerning the public and private roles in long-term care cost containment policy development.

LONG-TERM CARE COST CONTAINMENT

The growth and expansion of inhome care services has provided an additional impetus to the push of elderly persons into multigenerational living arrangements. For example, the number of Medicare-certified home health service agencies increased 27 percent from 1966 to 1984 (Phillips et al., 1987). Because in-home health care depends on the existing social networks within the community for the promotion of independence and well-being through an array of health and social support services, it will become increasingly difficult to tailor support services to the specific needs of the patient without increasing the caregiving demands on adult children and family members of the elderly. Thus, the cost-containment value of inhome care coupled with the potential possibility of shared living arrangements present special social policy concerns as well as the concerns of overtaxing family caregivers.

Given the direction of long-term care policies, several areas of inter-generational conflicts along with increased expectations of filial respon-sibilities have been created. Although the family is the major source of emotional and tangible support, it has been suggested that multigener-ational living is not a preferred type of living arrangement. Yet, it is a given fact that multigenerational living may be an outcome of current long-term cost containment policies. The reality, therefore, is that most home care agencies are limited in the types of services provided because they are based on the medical model of care that is largely determined by their Medicare and Medicaid reimbursement mechanisms. In other words, basic essential resources and avenues for securing needed social and nonmedical services are excluded even though these services are needed by families who provide care to the elderly.

Consequently, the expansion of home care services raises further con-cerns regarding overtaxing the family caregivers because current policies appear to make it more difficult for elderly persons to receive acute and long-term care services. The current growth of inhome health care ser-vices is a direct response to the Tax Equity and Fiscal Responsibility Act (e.g., prospective cost reimbursement and reduced length-of-stay re-quirements), which is perceived by many as a cost containment measure. Hence, home health care services fill the gaps created by current policies by providing a mechanism to deal with the high cost of caring for fragile and poor elderly that are precipitately discharged from the hospital into the community. Home health care, therefore, has become a substitute for hospital care and a supplement for institutional care.

Several demographic, social, and economic factors also greatly influ-ence the structure and nature of home care services. The increasing incidence of disability in the older cohorts of the aging elderly will place additional strain on existing and predicated nursing home and long-term care institutions. In fact, it is estimated that 20 percent of the elderly population until the year 2004 will require intermediate and extended care for some type of functional impairment (LaVor, 1979). This high incidence in functional dependency will require lifetime medical sur-veillance and some form of long-term care (Sommers, 1985).

A painful reality most families face is that there will not be enough long-term care facilities to accommodate the anticipated growth of func-tionally dependent elderly. Daniels (1988) notes that long-term care ser-vices will have to increase their current daily units from 6.9 million daily units of services to 19.8 million by the year 2040. The current policy emphasis of cost containment will most likely restrict the development of nursing home beds since institutional care is not perceived as cost effective or efficient. Consequently, more elderly will be pushed into the community to be cared for at home and by significant others.

The privatization of publicly supported aging services and programs and the politicalization of filial responsibility have given rise to the medieval ethos that "community is not responsible until children have made their maximum effort" (Schorr, 1960, p. 2)—that is, in regards to the well-being of their parents. This ethos also suggests that adult children ought to support parents without economic benefits or laws mandating such responsibility. Filial responsibility "emphasizes duty rather than satisfaction," especially "the duties required by law, by custom or by personal attitude" to assist in the protection, care, or financial support of a family member (p. 1). Thus, filial responsibility is intimately intermixed with family, kinship responsibilities, law, and sociocultural values, like parental and marital obligations. This new direction in aging policy implementation—that is, a disestablishment of organized care systems for the aged (Sussman, 1985)—will increase expectations for filial responsibility and discontinuities in intergenerational relationships.

In general, family responsibility laws require more of the cost of social and health care services to be shifted to the elderly and their families. Supporters argue that policies of this kind strengthen family bonds. Research data, however, do not provide evidence to support this contention. On the contrary, the delicate balance of filial responsibility and reciprocity will most likely be seriously threatened. As noted by N. Gilliland, "the impact of family responsibility laws will be greatest on adult children who, although not denying their filial responsibility, must impoverish themselves and their children to make a financial contribution to their parents' care" (1986, p. 33). Such expectations of filial responsibility (i.e., through legislated financial support) will increase generational conflicts although filial responsibility is considered to be an internalized norm (Sussman, 1985). More than forty states require, but do not enforce, financial support of needy elderly patients. Generally, the most common behavioral examples of filial responsibility have been expressed as emotional support and help in times of illness and disability (Hagestad, 1987, p. 248).

Ironically, as the population ages the family shrinks—more working women, later marriages, more divorces, fewer children, and so on (Sommers, 1985). These trends seriously threaten the supply of family care, which is an essential factor in the informal network of services actuated through inhome care policies. Of major political and social significance is the growing care gap; the changing status of women will have a significant impact on the availability of "kinkeepers." The mass entrance of women into the work force, changing attitudes concerning "gender-appropriate roles," and rising inflation which necessitates the two-income family have also reduced the availability of "kinkeepers" (Hamon, 1986).

Improvements in life expectancy coupled with increasing disability and decreasing fertility rates among younger generations mean that there will be fewer children to care for elderly kin, restricted access to elderly kin because of the mobility of the American society, and simultaneous demands placed upon adult children by their elderly parents and by their own children. Divorce, separations, widowhood, or remarriage may create a sense of less filial obligation and limitations, thereby making filial responsibility a hardship (Hamon, 1986; Cicirelli, 1983).

In fact, the critical reality is that extended families are not and have never been the norm in the United States (Daniels, 1988; Hagestad, 1987). Additionally, "intimacy at a distance" is preferred by older generations (Rosenmayer, 1984). In light of these considerations, serious questions are raised about the inadequacy of current social policy analysis. Concerns about the discontinuities in values and attitudes between younger and older age cohorts have also resurfaced the issues of "generation gap" and "intergenerational conflict." More important, and of importance to political science, is the question: Is society willing to accept the family structure of kin network as an alternative for publicly organized systems of care for the aged?

The paradox, however, is that the bulk of care currently received by elderly persons is given by families. According to the National Center for Health Statistics (1972), 62 percent of the personal and medically related care given to persons over age 65 was provided in the home by family members and not through the public sector. Currently, 80 percent of all long-term care is provided by families, especially the partially disabled (Daniels, 1988).

Recent cost-cutting policies, however, appear to be chopping away at this established community support system. Deep cuts in programs supported by the Older Americans Act pose a serious threat to the well-being of elderly persons and their families, especially in their quest to maintain residences outside of institutions. The National Nutrition Program for the elderly has been severely cut and relegated to serving meals rather than creating multiservice environments as initially planned (e.g., primary health care, recreation, socializing, and outreach) (Austin, 1987). Food stamps and housing subsidies have increased their eligibility requirements, and, by doing so, a large percentage of elderly persons or their families will be eliminated from receiving these benefits. Community-oriented programs, therefore, are considered by many elderly persons to be symbolic referents of the federal government's understanding of their health and social needs, which cannot be neatly separated. They are also illustrative of the fact that the needs of the elderly span beyond economic issues and health concerns (Phillipson and Walker, 1986; Lammers, 1987).

Adult children have become important in the provision of assistance and services to elderly kin. The current thrust in long-term care policy

may greatly influence the willingness or ability of adult children to assume filial duties. Recent policy changes will ultimately have an extraordinary impact on intergenerational relationships and expectations in
assuming filial responsibility.

PUBLIC OPINION: POLICY IMPLICATIONS
AND TRENDS

Public opinion can be important in the support of public policy (Page
et al., 1987). It has "substantial proximate" effects upon public policy
in the United States and determines "what governments do" (p. 23).
Public opinion, therefore, can be an important element of political support for aging policies, especially subsequent to the cost-cutting movement by the federal government to privatize aging services. Thus public
opinion concerning the expectations of increased filial responsibility is
one way to judge the extent of readiness within society for such major
policy changes. "Policies are judged in terms of expected costs and
benefits to the individual and for his or her family, friends, favored
groups and the nation or world as a whole" (Page et al., 1987, p. 23).
Public sentiment, therefore, can be critical to understanding the alacrity
of families to accept a more critical role in the care of their aging parents
or kin.

INTERGENERATIONAL CONFLICT AND
POLITICAL IMPLICATIONS

Current long-term policy thrusts—that is, the shifting of care and cost
for caring of the elderly to the individual and the family—appear to be
predicated on a "mythic past" where aging individuals enjoyed the
"fortunes and company of kin" and participated in multigenerational
living arrangements (Treas, 1975; Daniels, 1988). Multigenerational
households have never been the standard (Daniels, 1988; Treas, 1975;
Laslett and Wall, 1972). Earlier studies by Treas (1975) noted that less
than 3 percent of elderly persons living in multigenerational households
were either heading their own households or living as guests in the
homes of their children. In fact, all data tend to suggest that in the past
very few people survived to old age (Laslett and Wall, 1972; Daniels,
1988). Most elderly persons (approximately 84 percent) lived in two
household families, that is, with an aged spouse (Shanas, 1977). Additionally, as noted by Treas (1975) and Daniels (1988), little evidence
has been produced that proves older persons today would be substantially meliorated by their fusing into extended households. Data have
consistently found that even in widowhood the preference is independent living arrangements; for example, only about a third of elderly

persons whose spouses have died live with their kin (Treas, 1975). However, current rough estimates tend to suggest that about one out of thirty-six households is generationally inverse with adult children providing daily care for dependent parents (Steinmetz, 1988).

Intergenerational Conflict

As can be seen from Figure 7.1, the older cohort (ages 70 to 79) is less predisposed to the idea of multigenerational living. Data in this study clearly indicate that more than 50 percent of the selected age cohorts are less likely to support multigenerational living arrangements. The attitudes expressed by the cohorts bolster data and findings of potential conflicts in multigenerational living arrangements. In this regard, data concerning widows point to lifestyle dissimilarities, struggles over authority or household division of tasks, and the irritating tumultuousness of grandchildren as potential areas for intergenerational friction (Treas, 1975).

Recent studies have also raised questions concerning role strain, value and role conflict, filial responsibility and expectations, composition of the informal caregiving network, increased family complexity, and the capacity of the informal care system to provide the mass volume of long-term care (Krach, 1990; Finch and Mason, 1990; Scharlach, 1987; Stone et al., 1987; Hamon and Blieszner, 1990; Hagestad, 1987). These data tend to indicate that older cohorts acknowledge filial responsibility but are for the most part unwilling to assume the expressions of filial responsibility by sharing households with adult children.

The Growing Care Gap

The growing care gap, the progressive reduction in caregivers, raises concerns about the capacity of the family or the kin network to provide long-term care for elderly relatives. Concerns have been raised concerning the growing numbers of middle-aged women who are actively pursuing careers, job opportunities, and family responsibilities. These activities may gravely affect the type and quality of care provided to elderly parents. Future concerns are also raised concerning the low rate of fertility among the "baby boomers," in that the boomers will have fewer kin to care for them in their old age.

The Political Context of Filial Responsibility

Social legislation emulates the values of the society it typifies. Therefore, "public policy is a reflection of what the time or better yet the market will bear" (Kerschner and Hirschfield, 1975, pp. 355–356). Legis-

Figure 7.1
**Percent Response by Age Cohorts Who Think Elderly Parents Should Live
with Their Adult Children, Selected Years**

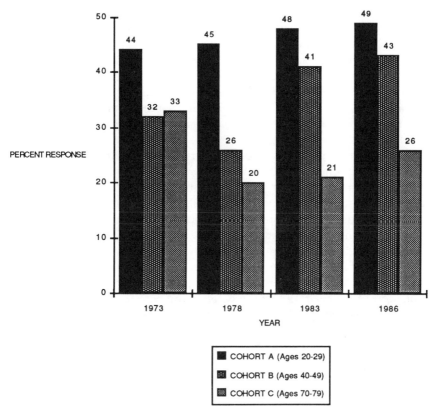

The data for this study are derived from national surveys conducted by the National Opinion Research Center (NORC) at the University of Chicago. Attitudes concerning multigenerational living arrangements are measured by responses respondents gave when asked the question: "As you know, many older people share a home with their children. Do you think this is generally a good idea or a bad idea?" (Davis and Smith, 1986). The 1973, 1978, 1983, and 1986 respondents participating in the NORC survey are included for analysis.

Three age cohorts were selected for analysis. Cohort A consists of age group 20–29. This cohort represents the young end of the aging cycle. Cohort B consists of age group 40–49, representing the middle of the aging cycle. It is also representative of persons who are at the point of reaching *filial maturity*, that is, persons with changing perspectives toward parents and ones who are better able to see their parents as real people (Blenkner, 1965; Troll, Miller and Atchley, 1979). Cohort C consists of age group 70–79, which represents persons that are at the older end of the aging cycle.

lation, therefore, is rarely based on future needs and is often predicated upon predominant social norms and existing conditions. In this regard, public policy becomes reactive and is seldom initiatory (Kerschner and Hirschfield, 1975). This poor conceptual framework for long-term care (e.g., policies that are implemented based on the crisis approach) has long dictated the major programs serving the elderly. For instance, the Social Security Act was a direct result of the Depression, and Medicare and Medicaid were the result of the health care crisis of the 1960s (Kerschner and Hirschfield, 1975; Ford, 1989). It appears that the current thrust to redistribute the burden of cost for the elderly to the private sector, namely the individual or the family, may be the result of the morass created by the inefficiency of the current system. Such efforts lack a clear philosophy for which to design public policy (Kerschner and Hirschfield, 1975).

The current long-term care policy arena has been dominated by the New Right opponents of state welfare who are eager to shift the onus of costs and responsibility of care for the elderly back to the private sector (Goodin, 1986). Family responsibility, therefore, has become the underpinning of current long-term care policy implementation and formulation. Although the family plays a significant role in deferring and halting institutionalization among elderly residents, a contradiction between social values and norms has been created, that is, the moral obligation of adult children to care for their elderly parents and the obligation of the welfare state to care for the elderly.

It can be noted here that the current thrust to make families and individuals more responsible for the care of the elderly is the result of the "crisis reaction" of the 1980s (i.e., the high costs of care for the elderly and inflation). The ideological constructs of the New Right also exert a tremendous influence on current policy development, thus they gain the opportunity to fashion their ideologies into public policy. In short, the overall social results may not be salubrious, especially for the frail and dependent elderly. In this regard, Gilliland (1986) notes that the policy of mandating family responsibility has been revived in order for supporters of federal budget reductions to shift more of the cost burden of long-term care to the elderly and their families. She further notes that mandated responsibility can save money for a public agency (namely, the state) through the collection of revenues and through deterrence to nursing home utilization.

J. L. Lopes (1975) and A. L. Schorr (1980) both conclude that family responsibility laws have not produced substantial revenues for states. Family responsibility laws, therefore, have harmful effects on families and are time consuming to manage and difficult to enforce (Bulcroft et al., 1989; Gilliland, 1986). Others have found that high administrative and judicial costs associated with the enforcement of family responsibility laws have not proven to be cost effective or beneficial (Bulcroft et al., 1989; Baldus, 1973; Garrett, 1979–1980). One can, therefore, conclude that family responsibility laws are contradictory and value laden.

The policy of deterrence may inadvertently push elderly persons into multigenerational living. This fact is even more of a reality given the current social, political, and economic conditions that have produced a shortage in affordable and safe housing for the elderly, the high costs of institutionalization, the reduction of community support systems, and the poorly constructed income maintenance system. The policy of deterrence also implies that elderly persons may delay or refuse to seek needed services because of the desire to retain control over their independence, self-respect, and authority in the family exchange (Gilliland, 1986). Additionally, researchers have noted that caregivers for the elderly are also adversely affected (Cantor, 1983). Forced filial responsibility has contributed to new social and political concerns. For example, "elder abuse" is more common where families are forced into the burden of elderly care, especially multigenerational living, because the cost of care such as nursing home care may be prohibitive (Gilliland, 1986).

Inhome Care: A Complex Environment

Research studies have shown that home health costs have been cheaper for patients "primarily living with others, those less likely to be married, those whose families were willing to have them at home, those with higher anticipated functional scores, and those taking more medications while in the hospital" (Vogel and Palmer, 1985, p. 351). Naturally, these facts raise questions concerning client characteristics and needs for service, family-service agency cooperation, and mobilization of family and volunteer supports. These facts raise further concerns about public support of the role of the family in the provision of in-home care.

Home care is discussed in this section because of its importance to defining the role of the family in the care of the elderly kin and the degree of filial responsibility assumed. Home care changes and expansions also shed light on the issues of access to long-term care services, social as well as health, which are integral to the support of aging kin by adult family members.

Home health care has now become one of the most competitive areas in the health care industry (Kane, 1989; Burke and Koren, 1984). In 1977, 46.8 percent of the home health agencies were government-sponsored delivery structures; however, by 1984 only 27.6 percent of the agencies were sponsored by the government (see Figure 7.2). Of the 6,000 home health agencies in the United States in 1984, 78 percent were certified

Linking Ideology to Action

Figure 7.2
Growth in Home Health Agencies by Percent of Total Medicare-Certified
Agencies, 1977 and 1986

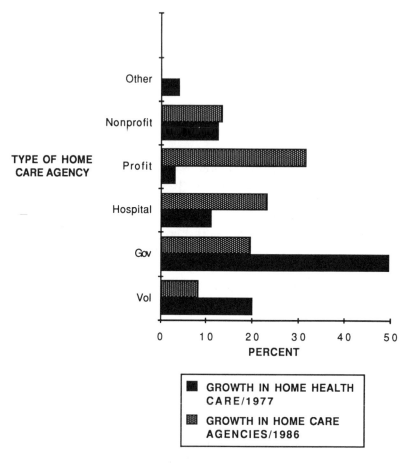

Source: Health Care Financing Administration, Program Studies, 1987.

for participation in Medicare, which reflects a 53 percent increase in home health agencies certified for participation in Medicare between 1977 and 1984.

Additionally, between 1967 and 1983 there was a 27.4 percent increase in amount reimbursed by the federal government for elderly persons enrolled in Medicare's hospital insurance coverage (see Table 7.1). The per person reimbursement covered under Medicare's hospital insurance plans also increased 10.6 percent between 1967 and 1983 (Health Care Financing Administration, 1987).

In spite of the tremendous growth and competitive nature of home

Table 7.1
**Home Health Care Medicare Utilization, Amount of Reimbursement, and
Percent Change by Type of Coverage and Selected Years, 1967–1983**

Coverage	1967	YEAR 1982	1983	PERCENTAGE CHANGE 1967-83	1982-83
		Reimbursement in Millions			
Hospital Insurance	26	992	1,258	27.4	26.8
Supplementary Insurance	17	19	22	1.6	15.8
		Reimbursement Per Person			
Hospital Insurance	204	923	1,025	10.6	11.1
Supplementary Insurance	145	1,091	1,098	13.5	1.0

Source: Health Care Financing Administration, Bureau of Data Management Strategy, June 1987.

health care services, the home care delivery system still lacks uniformity and reliable methods for the collection of data concerning costs and impact of services. The structure and dynamics of home health care is comparatively immature and poorly articulated as a system for the delivery of long-term health care services in the United States. Methodological problems, for example, impede effective cost-effectiveness analysis in that home care data and institutional data are not comparable.

Institutional data concerning costs are expressed in *per diem* terms, while home care data is expressed in per visit or per service unit terms. Additionally, home care data and cost factors reflect primarily health or health-related services and not housekeeping or personal care (Vogel and Palmer, 1985). The merits of the system—that is, the provision of long-term health care in appropriate settings based on a diverse set of patient needs—may never be realized because of the system's poor design and rapid expansion efforts that may initially increase cost outlays by the government.

Home health care is comprised of two systems: "one designed for acute, short-term patients; the other to provide in-home services for more chronically ill, long-term patients" (Burke and Koren, 1984, p. 10). The growth in Medicare-certified home care agencies tends to suggest that both public and private health insurance plans are more likely to focus on the short-term acute nature of the homebound patient. In many cases, most of the insurance plans (especially private plans) are restrictive, limiting services to skilled care following an acute hospitalization. On the public side, Medicare is one of the largest payers for short-term home health care. For example, in 1985 Medicare spent $1.7 billion on home health benefits (Kane, 1989).

The chronic home care system poses the greatest amount of concern because of its complex structure and poorly defined payment system. The short-term home care service system has been lauded as one that is most cost effective, if one accepts the notion that home care services have saved costs related to institutionalized stays (e.g., reduced the number and length of acute hospital or nursing home stays). Thus, short-term home care services appear to have an advantage over chronic care home care services in that costs and expenditures can be directly linked with therapeutic intervention and outcomes.

Chronic care patients present the most significant concerns in terms of payment and reimbursement. Adequate payment systems have not been developed to defray the costs of supportive and personal care services (e.g., chore services, home-health aid, or meals-on-wheels services). In many cases, chronic care persons who may require personal support services often "spend down" to Medicaid eligibility or select more costly institutionalized settings in order to secure services that are reimbursable. This group is also heavily dependent on the availability of family or other personal supports. The employment of primary caregivers outside the home also suggests the need for additional services such as daycare and respite care services to augment the role of the primary caregiver (Burke and Koren, 1984).

The current trend and expansion (i.e., the growth of proprietary and nongovernment Medicare-certified home health agencies), however, appears to be solely based on the perceived cost efficiency nature of home care. This emphasis on acute care is firmly rooted in the medical model where costs can be more easily justified and guaranteed through public reimbursement. Naturally, this line of thinking implies that it may become increasingly difficult to justify personal home care delivery mechanisms, which are less clearly defined types of service concepts.

The heterogenous nature of home care suggests the provision of a variety of levels of care that have been debated since the federal government's initial involvement. The Kerr-Mills legislation allowed for the payment of home health aides to perform light housekeeping in the patient's room. This law was initially linked to Old Age Assistance and, in effect, divided housekeeping and health care for reimbursement purposes, thereby creating a false distinction in the provision of long-term care services (Trager, 1973; Vogel and Palmer, 1985).

In a broad sense, home care is still a rather undefined area of provision of services to the nation's elderly. Home care is primarily financed by Medicare, which focuses on the provision of acute care services to the elderly, thereby making home care a byproduct of an acute illness rather than a result of a long-term or chronic condition, which requires multiple levels of services (Davis and Rowland, 1986). In this respect, "services can be furnished only to a beneficiary who is homebound and needs either skilled nursing or speech or physical therapy occasionally" (Davis and Rowland, 1986, p. 66).

Thus, the classification of home health care as a part-time or intermittent nursing service requiring professional supervision and authorization by a physician implies a more costly approach to the provision of services and a limited definition of home health care. Naturally, most definitions refer to home health care as "an array of health and social support services provided to sustain individuals in the home or community" (Quinn, 1987, p. 324). Implied here are broader and far-reaching purposes such as maintaining and restoring health, maximizing limitations, and minimizing disabilities (Lundberg, 1984; Quinn, 1987). Also implied here are commitments from the informal network (e.g., family, spouse, or significant others) for support and execution of in-home services.

The growing number of proprietary Medicare-certified home health agencies also raise serious concerns about adequate protection of the "most vulnerable of all consumer groups—those receiving care in their homes, away from public and professional scrutiny" (Roybal, 1987, p. 11). Objective data concerning quality of home care is sparse and often nonexistent. Data are lacking on the providers of services, the number of persons being served, and the amount of public and private funding going into home care (Roybal, 1987).

Quality assurance standards and monitoring systems for personal care services are nonexistent at the federal level; however, they do exist in thirty-four states and the District of Columbia. Additionally, acute care standards at the federal level primarily focus on "problems of reimbursement, fraud and abuse," and not on care standards, consumer protection and enforcement, training, data collection, and monitoring (Roybal, 1987, p. 12). There is a need for the government to take a much more active and concerted role in the development of effective and equitable long-term care systems, especially the home care system.

However, the current support of inhome services at the federal level (i.e., as a means of controlling health costs), coupled with decreased funding for services at the community level, has been interpreted as a move in the direction of promoting the single service concept (Wood and Estes, 1985). The single service concept, however, presents serious concerns about access to services, especially since there is a movement away from community-based multiple-entry service points of access. This change in funding has also been seen as a means of shifting more of the paying clients to the private sector, including increased support from adult kin. Such changes raise questions about the viability of the public home care system (Phillips et al., 1987) and the role of family or kin (filial responsibility) in the payment for services.

Additionally, the expenditures by Medicare for inhome services in 1985, which totaled more than $8 billion, plus the increase in the number of Medicare-certified home health care agencies (e.g., from 1,275 in 1966 to more than 4,703 in 1984) tend to suggest a growth in "third party" government, the indirect provision of services through private agencies. D. J. Palumbo and J. Maupin contend that "the complex nature of public-private partnerships are susceptible to connivance and 'back-scratching' rather than the arms-length, objective service delivery system that they presumably are supposed to have" (1987, p. 11).

Although privatization is supposed to introduce competition to stimulate quality improvements, innovation, and efficiency, it may not be the direction needed for home health care because of the focus on the acute aspect of home care. As J. L. Sundquist (1984) notes, privatization may not cut the financial outlays made by the federal government, especially in regards to services to the poor, but it may draw the government's attention away from the need to make social programs work as they should. In this same light, it can be argued that the impact on the competence of government programs to achieve a sense of social equity, to assure quality care, and to provide an effective and systematic mechanism for the delivery of home health care services will be weakened. Cost effectiveness of home care is still largely an unanswered question (Kane, 1989; Vogel and Palmer, 1985); any savings in actual costs may be illusory.

Therefore, from the political arena, privatization questions concerning competition for resources and clients (i.e., quality of care), the role of the government as decision maker and financier of private enterprise (i.e., stability of financial resources of the public inhome care agencies), and the role of family, spouse, and the informal network as providers of support services must be answered. Answers must be sought and obtained before filial responsibility for elderly kin is a realistic consideration in the provision of long-term care services, especially inhome care services.

A cost effective and comprehensive system is needed to address the diverse aspects of home health care. The role of the family must be clearly defined since the bulk of caregiving, especially for the chronic homebound elderly person, is dependent upon the family unit and the nature of living arrangements within the unit.

AN ECOLOGICAL FRAMEWORK FOR PRACTICE
AND RESEARCH

As the elderly continue to grow in numbers, the political debate concerning the delivery of coordinated long-term care services has become more intense and critical because of shrinking federal budgetary resources. The various long-term care reforms proposed and implemented over the last decade have generally agreed on the array of services and the types of services necessary that would enable the frail elderly and disabled to function independently within the community (Davis and Rowland, 1986). Nevertheless, they all fail to define adequately the relationship between need for a service and the subsequent demand, utilization, and availability of resources (formal and informal) at the community level.

What is still missing is an understanding of long-term care needs from an ecological perspective—the functional relationship of elderly persons to their social, physical, and biological environments. This view assumes that the adaptation of elderly persons to their environment causes a modification of the disease process or the conditions that contribute to institutionalization. Such a perspective requires an understanding of the role of the social environment and its impact on the conditions that produce conflicts within the milieu.

In short, the social environment is an important feature of the human ecology of aging individuals because it is the component of the ecosystem that relates to the interaction and the association of elderly persons with other individuals within their milieu. This is an important concept for policy makers and decision makers to understand—older individuals are more dependent on their social networks because of the impact of aging (e.g., illness, retirement, limited income, death of spouse, etc.) upon the dynamic and changing nature of the sociocultural environment (Hayslip et al., 1980). Therefore, the informal network is a primary source of support for dependent elderly (Hayslip et al., 1980).

The social ecological perspective also suggests that systematic intervention, through environmental manipulation (e.g., the development and implementation of effective social policy and intervention efforts), can moderate many of the variables affecting the environment of elderly persons and enhance their ability to respond to changes, thereby aiding in their successful adaptation to environmental constraints.

In this regard, P. G. Windley notes that "age-related deficits in environmental abilities are likely to be more a function of society's failure to provide and maintain supportive environmental situations than of any organismic factor" (1982, p. 67). E. E. Hassinger (1982) provides evidence to support this contention through his comments concerning the environment of rural elderly persons. He notes that the organizational characteristics of rural society—that is, informal group networks and extralocal organizational relationships—affect the delivery of health services in rural areas. To understand interrelationships within a given environment, especially in the social milieu, an epidemiological perspective is required. Such a perspective requires an understanding of all of the surroundings in which elderly persons find themselves: biological, physical, and social.

It should be increasingly evident to policy and decision makers that the health and functional well-being of elderly persons is not only dependent upon their ability to adapt to physical and biological constraints within their environment but also to their social, cultural, and political influences. The social environment, therefore, is an indicator of past and future events in the life of elderly persons and is worthy of more consideration from policy and decision makers in the design and implementation of social policy. Thus, policies and planning strategies addressing the general living environment of the aged must deliberately depart from the traditional medical conceptual framework and move to a more holistic framework.

It is recommended that research efforts be directed toward an examination of social and psychological issues that are a part of the social context of families of elderly persons. The relationship of family caretaking to resource availability and functional well-being has not been fully examined. Specifically, studies should be undertaken to examine and specify the conditions under which family caretakers or informal caretakers can provide beneficial support to elderly persons.

The growth and privatization of home health care have not been fully examined or evaluated as to their impact on the quality and comparability of care and, more importantly, upon the family or informal support systems of the elderly. Research studies should be developed that would maintain and improve systems of home care. Such studies should examine the social and political implications of these recent events. Studies should be pursued to examine the environmental and organizational responses to the private sector expansion and growth in the home service industry. Research studies should also examine the role and the viability of public systems of home health care, as well as issues of access to services and the development and maintenance of nonmedical support services, such as chore services, homemaker services, adult day care, and so on.

National and local policy makers and planners should engage in environmental engineering in the provision of long-term care services and the development or implementation of effective and efficient long-term care policies. *Environmental engineering* can be defined as the development of appropriate policies or services based on factual evidence of need, which afford the creative blend or allocation of resources for human service systems that meet the long-term care needs of elderly persons and subsequently afford adaptation to various environmental constraints.

CONCLUSION

This chapter sheds light on public sentiment regarding the behavioral expression of filial responsibility—multigenerational living. Attitudes expressed in this research study (i.e., among the older cohorts) indicate that multigenerational living is not in accord with current societal norms. O. H. Mindel (1979) aptly notes that such living arrangements are the last resort prior to institutionalization. In addition, given the lack of support and enforcement of current and past family responsibility laws, it appears that the public is unwilling to shoulder the burden of elderly care that requires extended commitments and behavioral expression of filial responsibility, such as multigenerational living. The findings of this study and others strongly suggest that it may not be realistic for families to assume the total responsibility for care of aging parents or family members (Gilliland, 1986).

Social legislation for the elderly needs to be framed on clear data and facts that are consistent with societal norms and realities (Kerschner and Hirschfield, 1975). The lack of a clear philosophy upon which to build long-term care policy has continued to lead to the development of poorly constructed policies for the elderly. Ill-planned policies for the elderly will continue to increase the costs of long-term care because the implementation of such policies are in many cases in direct contradiction with societal norms.

NOTE

An earlier version of this chapter was prepared for delivery at the Annual Meeting of the American Political Science Association, Chicago, Illinois, 3–6 September 1987.

8

Abortion and Family Policy: A Mental Health Perspective

Gregory H. Wilmoth, Danielle Bussell, and
Brian L. Wilcox

This chapter focuses on abortion as a public health issue as it relates to family policy. Other researchers have used similar approaches when discussing abortion. G. Steiner asserts that "if the pursuit of family policy turns from generalities to specifics, abortion is a subject from which there is no escape" (1981, p. 51). Brigitte and Peter Berger, who generally favor a national family policy and who personally oppose abortion, maintain the opposite view that "it does not seem to us that abortion properly belongs to the topic of family policy; it raises fundamental questions of human and civil rights that touch on every political issue and not just on 'the problem of the family' " (1984, p. 73).

In this chapter we examine the research on the mental health sequelae of abortion and suggest the family policy implications of these research findings. More important, we set out an agenda for the discussion of abortion and mental health as related to family policy. This agenda covers the following areas: (1) abortion as a potential public health issue in family policy; (2) abortion as one option among others concerning pregnancy resolution; (3) abortion as a policy construct to be evaluated; (4) cautions about the adequacy of postabortion sequelae research methodology; (5) research findings on the psychological sequelae of abortion; and (6) public health policies warranted by these research findings. We attempt to address the major concerns and policy options presented by profamily, antiabortion proponents.

THE PUBLIC HEALTH POLICY CONTEXT

On 30 July 1987 President Reagan attempted to refocus the abortion debate away from legal and moral issues to health issues (Victor, 1987).

President Reagan, speaking to a prolife assembly, noted that abortion was inconsistent with his family policy. He directed Surgeon General C. Everett Koop to compile a report on the physical and psychological sequelae of abortion. The rationale for the president's directive was the documentation and dissemination of the risks associated with abortion in order to begin a campaign similar to the surgeon general's antismoking campaign.

President Reagan is not the only person to have expressed public health concerns about abortion. The prolife group Women Exploited by Abortion claims that abortion causes, in addition to numerous physical complications, severe psychological problems for the majority of women who have abortions (S. Smith, 1988). There is also an effort to have an as yet unsubstantiated complication, postabortion syndrome (PAS), recognized as a major psychiatric disorder (Speckhard, 1987a). Some prolife groups hoped the surgeon general's report would validate these claims and sequelae.

The surgeon general refused, however, to issue a report, stating instead that the scientific data prevented reaching any scientific conclusions (Koop, 1989a). The U.S. House of Representatives' Committee on Government Operations, Subcommittee on Human Resources and Intergovernmental Relations held a hearing on 16 March 1989, which resulted in the public release of Koop's report (1989b)[1] in the Congressional Record. Koop's report concluded that "[v]alid scientific studies have documented that . . . there is not a significant risk of physical complications" (Koop, 1989b, p. E908). The report does, however, emphasize the "[i]nconclusiveness regarding the psychological outcomes of abortion" (p. E908). The Surgeon General's conclusions did not provide the public health foundation for an attack on abortion for which the prolife advocates hoped. Instead, it rejected the prolife group's claim of significant physical risks, and it failed to substantiate the psychological sequelae claims of either the prolife or prochoice groups.

HEALTH DIMENSIONS OF ABORTION

Among the numerous grounds used as a basis for family policy, public health is one that should have wide appeal and be less controversial than others. Clear, uncontaminated statistics of widespread, severe complications (either physical and/or psychological) could be compelling in public policy debate.

The incidence of abortion and demographics of those having abortions indicate the reason for public health concerns. Over a million women have abortions each year, and an estimated 21 percent of women of reproductive age have had an abortion (Forrest, 1987). Of all women having abortions, 80 percent are under 30 years old and are thus in their prime reproductive years (Henshaw and Silverman, 1988). Over half (52 percent) of women having abortions have never had children, and 80 percent are unmarried at the time of the abortion (Henshaw and Silverman, 1988). These statistics demonstrate that if abortion has negative health sequelae for women, then abortion would affect a large percentage of women and thus their current and/or future families. It seems prudent, therefore, to investigate the health sequelae of abortion as one aspect of national family policy.

Public health arguments have been raised over the years around the sequelae of abortion. The Centers for Disease Control (CDC) collect data on mortality and physical morbidity associated with abortion, but the CDC does not gather similar data on psychological morbidity associated with abortion. Although some prolife groups challenge the CDC's statistics on abortion mortality and physical morbidity, the surgeon general's report (Koop, 1989b) confirms the CDC's statistics. What is primarily at issue then is what effect abortion has on the psychological health of women.

The current debate about the psychological sequelae of abortion is not new. We are, in fact, revisiting a previous debate with new data and new sequelae. Prior to 1960, the prevailing belief that inevitable, harmful psychological sequelae followed abortion was supported by several case studies. Proponents of legal abortion successfully argued in the 1960s that abortion could be therapeutic in preventing suicide and other serious emotional problems. In 1967 and 1968, five states (California, Colorado, Georgia, Maryland, and North Carolina) revised their abortion laws on medical grounds to permit therapeutic abortions if the continuance of the pregnancy would threaten the emotional health of the woman. These laws expanded the legal definition of health to include mental as well as physical health.

Although the Supreme Court's 1973 ruling in *Roe v. Wade* "settled" the legal issue of abortions during the first trimester of pregnancy, its opinion specifically emphasized the state's compelling concern for public health related to pregnancy and abortion. Koop's report (1989b) did not, however, provide a public health concern to sanction state and federally legislated, and/or court-mandated, restrictions on abortions.

Lewis and Carr (1986) provide details about abortion policy in the 1980s and how it changed over three decades. As is the case for most public policy, a change in policy in one area impacts other areas. In the case of abortion policy, changes would probably impact the rate of births to unwed mothers, welfare and Medicaid costs, and so on.

ABORTION AS A CONSTRUCT

Any attempt to assess the health impacts of abortion must confront the important and changing dimensions of abortion. First, there are two major types of abortion: elective and therapeutic. Therapeutic abortions need to be further differentiated into those performed because (1) of suspected defects in the fetus, (2) the pregnancy is due to rape or incest, and (3) the woman's life is endangered by continuation of the pregnancy. An elective abortion is one that is not a therapeutic abortion. Over 90 percent of all abortions are elective abortions (Torres and Forrest, 1988).

The major debate about the health consequences of abortion centers on elective abortion. If there are indeed health benefits for therapeutic abortion, then we must include research conducted on women receiving therapeutic abortions. Given the four major circumstances of abortion (therapeutic–congenital, therapeutic–rape/incest, therapeutic–life saving, and elective), it is likely that there would be variations in the type and degree of psychological sequelae.

The procedures used to perform abortions have changed over time, and there are different abortion procedures used in first trimester abortions versus late second trimester abortions. In the early 1970s the majority of abortions were either dilation-curettage procedures (D&C) or saline injection procedures. Today most first trimester abortions are performed by vacuum aspiration. Late second trimester abortions are dilation-evacuation procedures and saline injection. First trimester procedures used today involve less anesthesia, less time, and are less painful than those used in the early 1970s or in current procedures used in late second trimester abortions. Approximately 10 percent of all abortions are performed in the second trimester (Henshaw, Forrest, and Van Vort, 1987). A tenable hypothesis would be that the mental health consequences of abortion vary as a function of the amount of time, pain, and intrusiveness of the procedure used. Thus studies from the early 1970s and studies on second trimester abortion patients should show more severe postabortion sequelae compared to more recent studies on first trimester abortion patients. Although the overall incidence of sequelae was low, women aborting in the second trimester were five times as likely to feel guilt and six times as likely to report feelings of depression as women aborting in the first trimester (Osofsky, Osofsky, and Rajan, 1973). Women who experienced greater pain during an abortion reported significantly more negative psychological reactions after the abortion (Bracken, 1978).

ABORTION IN THE CONTEXT OF PREGNANCY RESOLUTION

Impact assessments, whether of health impacts or economic impacts, rely upon a standard for comparison. A program or policy is better or worse than something; so it must also be when assessing the psychological sequelae of abortion. Abortion is one of the legal options that a woman has to manage a pregnancy. Her other options are to give birth and raise the child or to give birth and surrender the child for adoption. Of those who decide to give birth, between 8 and 13 percent experience a miscarriage (spontaneous abortion).

The choice among these options is influenced by several factors; for example, marital status is a major consideration. In one study, 50 percent of abortion clients stated that they aborted because they wanted to avoid single parenthood or because their relationship with the father was poor (Torres and Forrest, 1988). An additional 18 percent of abortion patients were either separated, divorced, or widowed (Henshaw and Silverman, 1988). The consequences for a woman having and raising a child are significantly different if she is single than if she is married.

METHODOLOGICAL LIMITATIONS OF
ABORTION RESEARCH

When family policy involves public health goals and/or concerns, then it too should be based on empirical knowledge. Although the literature concerning the psychological consequences of abortion is extensive, conclusions based on this body of research are tenuous due to the inadequate methodology generally characterizing these studies (Lyons et al., 1988).

The primary limitation is the lack of consensus on what dependent variables to study when investigating the psychological sequelae of abortion. Many diverse operational definitions have been chosen to indicate "psychiatric sequelae" to abortion, including anxiety, guilt, depression, anger, shame, hostility, sense of loss, disappointment in self, embarrassment, doubt, fear of disapproval, regret, satisfaction with the decision to abort, neurosis, and psychosis, as well as behavioral manifestations of stress such as suicide attempts or sexual dysfunction. However, many of the above indications of distress (e.g., regret or guilt) are not necessarily indicative of psychiatric disorders (Illsley and Hall, 1976).

In many studies, it is unclear what criteria (i.e., operational definition) for diagnostic judgment were used and whether or not the judgment was validated by independent observers. For example, J. Osofsky and H. Osofsky (1972) operationalized "sadness" as "much crying" and "happiness" as "much smiling." Other researchers use their summary judgment of an interview or the subject's response on a particular question as the dependent variable. These judgments may be subject to bias as well as unreliability and uncertain validity.

Case studies on the mental health of women who underwent abortions have limited scientific applicability because they are not objective and inferences cannot be separated from the predilections and biases of the clinical researcher. Women described in these case studies may have differed along a number of dimensions prior to the abortion and represent only a small proportion of women who come to therapeutic attention. As a result, case studies on abortion cannot support inferences about its effect.

A large number of researchers have used nonstandardized questionnaires and/or interviews to examine the mental health of abortion patients. Thus, there is no way to demonstrate their accuracy, their consistency over time, whether they can predict future responses, or whether they truly sample the information they intend to measure. Additionally, interviews are subject to interviewer bias and other contaminants.

Some studies have utilized psychometric scales or tests, such as the Minnesota Multiphasic Personality Inventory (MMPI), to supplement information gained in interviews and/or questionnaires. Considerable disagreement exists among investigators as to which cutoff scores are appropriate for designating a psychiatric disorder. Moreover, there may be a statistically significant difference in scale scores between women who have abortions and women who carry to term, but the average scores for both groups may be in the subclinical range (i.e., normal).

Another difficulty is the widespread variability in the timing of followup tests. Postabortion tests have been conducted from immediately after the procedure while the patient is in the recovery room to followup tests anywhere from less than three months (the majority of studies) to several years after abortion. Antiabortion groups claim that severe emotional problems caused by an abortion frequently do not appear for five to ten years postabortion. It is important, therefore, to have long-term studies, but large scale studies do not exist. Researchers do not agree on when negative sequelae become manifest and how enduring they are. Further, not all investigators collect data before the abortion. It is difficult to interpret tests conducted after abortion when performed in the absence of pretest data, especially when a woman has a history of psychiatric illness.

Little consensus exists as to what comparison group would be most appropriate for studies of abortion patients. Possible comparison groups include: (1) women carrying unwanted pregnancies to term; (2) women refused abortions; (3) pregnant women; (4) the general population of women; (5) women who have never had an abortion; and (6) women who have had spontaneous abortions. This chapter examines evidence for most of these groups.

The representativeness of samples is another methodological issue in abortion research. Sample characteristics are very important in studies of the psychological sequelae of abortion because research has noted that differential responses to abortion are related to women's intrapersonal and interpersonal contexts. It is possible that subjects with certain distinguishing characteristics are more likely to "self-select" themselves into an abortion sample, especially if the study relies on volunteers at a particular clinic. In particular, studies of psychiatric indication on samples of women receiving therapeutic abortions are biased to include only the most psychologically disturbed women.

Unfortunately, most abortion studies have been forced to use small samples of subjects due to lack of volunteers. The problem of sample size is often exacerbated by attrition from the original sample before the study is completed, which varies between 13 and 86 percent (Adler, 1976). Noncompleters appear to differ from completers in variables found to be risk factors for abortion sequelae (Adler, 1976; Freeman, 1977). Cumulatively, these differences between completers and noncompleters suggests a high probability that many samples in abortion research are nonrepresentative of the total population of women receiving abortions.

The majority of studies have obtained samples from particular clinics or counseling agencies. Findings drawn from a single clinic are likely to reflect the rules and procedures of that specific clinic and thus not be generalizable.

Relatedly, all studies do not examine the same event when they investigate abortion. Research conducted in the 1940s, 1950s, and 1960s examined illegal or therapeutic abortion. J. Handy concludes that "from a research perspective, the influence of sociological factors on psychological aspects of abortion means that past literature, even when relatively recent, may not be applicable to current problems if the attitudes of women, their families and doctors have changed, and/or if legal, economic or welfare provisions regarding pregnancy have changed" (1982, p. 29).

PSYCHOLOGICAL SEQUELAE OF ABORTION

Postabortion psychological sequelae are those emotional and mental experiences that occur in the time period following an abortion. We are not assuming or prejudging that all or certain psychological experiences following an abortion are caused by or are a result of having an abortion. The question of what causes experiences or disorders that follow some event are scientific questions that must be answered by carefully controlled and designed research rather than being assumed *a priori*.

The issue of the psychological sequelae of abortion is not a single, simple question. From a public health perspective, we need to know: (1) the prevalence and severity of both positive and negative psychological sequelae; (2) the onset(s) (immediate and/or delayed) of sequelae; (3) the duration of sequelae (acute or chronic); (4) the risk factors associated with sequelae; and (5) the causal links between abortion and

psychological sequelae, if any. Which emotional and mental disturbances that occur some time after an abortion are the result of the abortion rather than some other life event either preceeding or following the
abortion? Information answering these questions is fragmentary and of
questionable reliability. Research has investigated questions of prevalence and severity of sequelae and risk factors associated with sequelae
more than onset, duration, and the causal factors of sequelae.

The methodological weaknesses of the research, described previously,
prohibit any conclusions about whether abortion causes psychological
sequelae. Despite the conclusion of the surgeon general's report (Koop,
1989b) that the psychological evidence is inconclusive, the research repeatedly documents both positive and negative abortion sequelae as
well as possible risk factors.

Expressions of guilt and regret are frequent following an abortion
(Adler, 1975; Blumberg and Golbus, 1975; Friedman, Greenspan, and
Mittleman, 1974; and Speckhard, 1987b); but these responses are usually
mild and short-term. Abortion is a difficult decision (Cohen and Roth,
1984), and it is not surprising to find such reports. Guilt and regret are
feelings that most individuals experience several times in their lives,
sometimes intensely. They are common to the grieving process following
a variety of forms of loss. Self-report measures of emotions such as guilt
and regret by abortion patients were, however, unrelated to clinical
scores on the MMPI (Robbins, 1979). These emotions by themselves are
not signs of emotional or mental disturbances and must be distinguished
from psychiatric disorders.

From the point of view of public health policy, limited resources require that public health efforts be directed at physical or mental disturbances severe enough to warrant treatment. Normal guilt and regret
experienced as part of the grieving process rarely require professional
treatment (see "Adjustment Disorder" in American Psychiatric Association, 1987). In mental health, when emotional or mental states become
dysfunctional they are classified as *psychiatric disorders*.

Few studies measured emotional disorders classifiable as psychiatric
disorders. In Denmark (David, 1985), only separated, divorced, or widowed women having abortions had significantly higher rates of admissions to psychiatric hospitals than women giving birth. The actual rates
of admissions were, however, very low for both term-birth women (.1
percent) and women having abortions (.2 percent). Further, even fewer
studies used standardized instruments to measure these disorders.
Depression was the major disturbance that could be considered a psychiatric disorder and was measured with standardized scales. For these
reasons and others to be explained, we concentrate on postabortion
depression.

Depression and Abortion

Depression has been widely studied in various populations of women (Kierman and Weissman, 1980; Nolen-Hoeksema, 1987). This allows comparisons of postabortion depression rates with depression rates related to other life events experienced by women. Such comparisons permit approximations of the relative severity of abortion as a precursor of depression. Another advantage is that depression research has identified numerous risk factors that might be relevant to postabortion depression.

Baseline Depression Rates for Women. One way of estimating the relative psychological harmfulness of abortion is to compare postabortion depression rates to depression rates for the general population of childbearing age women and for women during pregnancy. Rates of depression on the Beck Depression Inventory (BDI) (Beck et al., 1961) for women in general range from 17 percent to 29 percent (Atkeson et al., 1982; Tanaka-Matsumi and Kameoka, 1986). B. Major (1987) reported a postabortion BDI depression rate of 15 percent, which is within these ranges of depression for nonpregnant women. One-year postabortion BDI depression scores as well as guilt, state anxiety, and trait anxiety scores were not significantly different for abortion patients compared to those of students and health professionals (Baluk and O'Neill, 1980).

Depression Rates for Pregnancy. The depression rate for women during pregnancy is about 16 percent (Nolen-Hoeksema, 1987) compared to the postabortion rate of 15 percent. Bradley (1984) found no differences of anxiety or self-esteem during pregnancy carried to term between women who had prior abortions and women with no prior abortions. During the third trimester, however, women with prior abortions did report higher levels of depressive affect. There were no differences in gestation and delivery for these two groups of women or in birthweight and Apgar scores for their infants (Bradley, 1984).

Postpartum Depression Rates. A comparison of postpartum depression rates and postabortion depression rates provides some indication of whether abortion is followed by more or less depression than the choice of giving birth and raising the child. Postpartum depression rates varied from 10 percent (those who sought treatment) to 21 percent on the BDI (Hopkins et al., 1984; Nolen-Hoeksema, 1987). Abortion appears to have a depression rate (15 percent) similar to that associated with parturition.

Studies comparing postpartum depression in women with previous abortions compared to those with no previous abortions provide a more direct assessment. There were no differences twelve to sixteen months postpartum in anxiety (Bradley, 1984); MMPI scores on defensiveness, hypochondriasis, hysteria, psychopathy, introversion, mania, or schizophrenia; or alienation (Athanasiou et al., 1973). R. Athanasiou et al. (1973) found no difference in self-esteem or MMPI depression scores, whereas Bradley (1984) found that women with previous abortions had significantly higher depression levels and lower self-esteem postpartum. Bradley also noted that the women with higher depression scores were not dysfunctional (psychiatrically depressed).

Depression Rates Following Surgery. Current methods of abortion are intrusive, surgical procedures. When women experience anxiety and stress prior to, during, and after an abortion (Cohen and Roth, 1984; Rosen, 1988), it might be because they are undergoing a medical procedure *per se* rather than or in addition to the termination of a pregnancy. Hysterectomy is intrusive surgery on the reproductive system, which furnishes a comparison for assessing the depression sequelae of surgery *per se.* A total of 32 percent of women receiving hysterectomies for noncancerous reasons experienced depression (measured on the Zung SDS; Zung, 1965) after their surgery (Moore and Tolley, 1976) while other studies have found rates between 4 percent and 24 percent (Lalinec-Michaud and Engelsmann, 1984). The rate of postabortion depression (15 percent) (Major, 1987) is within the midrange of these rates for hysterectomy.

Risk Factors for Depression. Given that only a small percentage of women experience postabortion depression, do the risk factors for postpartum depression and posthysterectomy depression resemble those for postabortion depression? The major risk factors for depression are similar: (1) previous emotional problems; (2) history of mental illness in family; (3) deficits in social skills; (4) marital or relationship problems and dissatisfaction; and (5) lack of social support (Moseley et al., 1981; Robbins and DeLamater, 1985). Ambivalent feelings about the pregnancy are highly predictive for both postpartum and postabortion depression (Hopkins et al., 1984). Women's cognitive coping styles also predict their postabortion reactions (Cohen and Roth, 1984; Major et al., 1985; Mueller and Major, 1989).

Positive Psychological Sequelae

The emphasis of abortion foes on negative sequelae is misleading. It distracts from clearly documented, positive psychological sequelae of abortion (Zabin et al., 1989). Between 70 percent and 85 percent of women report feelings of relief and/or happiness after abortion (Adler, 1975). Pre-post studies generally find a decrease in negative emotions, anxiety, and depression following abortion (Peck and Marcus, 1966; Moseley et al., 1981). This evidence further supports the proposition that abortion is a coping adjustment in response to the distress of an unwanted pregnancy.

Abortion, Subsequent Pregnancy, and Child Abuse

Most women (70 percent) having abortions report an intention of having another child (Henshaw and Silverman, 1988). Does a subsequent pregnancy carried to term reactivate unresolved emotional reactions to a prior abortion or result in less nurturance for the child? Bradley (1984) compared women with and without prior abortions during their first pregnancy carried to term. The women with prior abortions showed no evidence of inadequate maternal functioning. They did not differ from nonaborting mothers with respect to: (1) level of preparation for the mothering role; (2) confidence in caregiving; (3) their feelings, attitudes, and behavior toward their infants; (4) their perception of their infant's temperament; (5) the number of problems their infants had; and (6) their infant's scores on the Bayley Scales of Infant Development. These findings are important because they indicate that abortion does not adversely affect the nurturance that subsequent children receive. This refutes the belief by some that women who abort lack maternal caring and parenting abilities.

P. Nye (1979) has argued that abortion increases child abuse. Studies of child abuse have not examined prior abortions as a variable, however, thus providing no substantiation for Nye's claim. Conversely, the surgeon general's report concluded that "well-conducted studies document that children born as a result of an unwanted pregnancy are more likely to experience detrimental psychosocial development, emotional adjustment problems, and a poorer quality of life than are children born to women who desired or otherwise accepted their pregnancies" (Koop, 1989b, p. E908).

Postabortion Syndrome

Antiabortion researchers (Speckhard, 1987a) argue for a new clinical disease: postabortion syndrome (PAS). PAS is defined as a type of post-traumatic stress disorder (PTSD). PAS is in the formative stages of conceptualization and operationalization and is not found in the recent DSM-III-R (American Psychiatric Association, 1987). No standardized diagnostic criteria or instruments for PAS exist. Abortion foes claim that the prevalence of PAS is epidemic among women who have had abortions. Prolife groups assert that women who have had abortions, and who do not show symptoms of PAS, are in resistance and denial thus masking the illness.

There are conceptual problems with PAS as a type of PTSD. All of the events described in the DSM-III-R as precursors of PTSD are non-volitional: The person is a victim of a disaster that is outside the range of usual human experience. Abortion is not mentioned in the DSM-III-R as an example of the type of event that is associated with PTSD. A more accurate diagnosis of women who experience emotional problems following an abortion may be adjustment disorder (DSM-III-R). In addition, PTSD is a diagnosis for severe emotional distress caused by any source; creating a special subclassification based on the source of the stress seems like a purely political diagnosis rather than a medical or psychological diagnosis.

Further, no research on abortion uses any of the standardized PTSD assessment scales or research interview schedules. Researchers should be using these diagnostic instruments in their research instead of the nonstandardized mood questionnaires they have previously used (Speckhard, 1987b). Until PAS is a recognized diagnostic category with standardized diagnostic criteria, it seems ill-advised to base public policy on it.

Beliefs about Postabortion Psychological Sequelae

The psychological sequelae of abortion are either similar to those of normal subjects not experiencing traumatic events or similar to those of women experiencing childbirth or surgery. Some evidence suggests, however, that the public's beliefs about the psychological sequelae of abortion are drastically more extreme than the actual sequelae (Baluk and O'Neill, 1980; Fingerer, 1973). M. Fingerer (1973) also found that preabortion patients significantly overestimated the severity of post-abortion depression and anxiety that they actually experienced after the procedure. It is not surprising that prolife advocates who believe abortion is murder (Smith, 1988) also believe that women having abortions must experience severe guilt, regret, and depression.

Adoption and Psychological Sequelae

Adoption is often proposed by prolife groups as the option of choice for women with unwanted pregnancies. For that reason, it is reasonable to compare the psychological sequelae of abortion with the psychological sequelae of adoption.

The amount of research on the psychological sequelae of relinquishing a child for adoption is minuscule and of a lower scientific quality than the research on abortion. Although recognizing the limitations of the research on adoption, it is worthwhile to examine it for the types of sequelae reported. The picture that emerges is one in which very similar types of sequelae are reported for both abortion and adoption.

Women report both relief (23 percent) and improved outlook on life (55 percent) as well as guilt (15 percent), regret (18 percent), increased anxiety (38 percent), and worsened outlook on life (24 percent) after surrendering a child for adoption (Burnell and Norfleet, 1979). As many as 40 percent expressed frequent and/or severe depression, 20 percent received therapy for emotional problems, and 3 percent were hospitalized for emotional problems (Burnell and Norfleet, 1979). Women reported recurring dreams about the loss of the baby during the first two years postadoption (Rynearson, 1982), and 43 percent stated their subsequent marriage was negatively affected by their decision to surrender their child for adoption (Deykin, Campbell, and Patti, 1984). These findings are of further concern because unwed mothers who relinquish their children for adoption are less maladjusted than those who keep their infants (Horn and Turner, 1976).

Adoption and abortion are both difficult choices for women. Both have similar types of negative sequelae. Research tentatively suggests that abortion and adoption have equally serious sequelae. In addition, Surgeon General Koop noted that "[n]ot all children unwanted by the mother will be placed for adoption, nor will all children placed for adoption be adopted" (Koop, 1989b, E908).

POLICY IMPLICATIONS

Current evidence does not support claims by abortion opponents that abortion causes high rates of mental disorders (Adler et al., 1990). Neither can abortion be said to be a psychologically benign procedure. A small percentage of women do experience depression following abortion, and a much smaller percentage (less than 1 percent; David, 1985) are admitted to a psychiatric hospital. In many cases, if not most, abortion appears to either trigger preexisting mental conditions and/or be compounded by preexisting weaknesses in the woman's coping abilities and social support network.

The available evidence on the psychological sequelae of abortion does not warrant policy decisions about the desirability of legal abortion or on restrictions to legal abortion. The evidence does have implications for: (1) research policy; (2) educational policy; (3) prevention policy; and (4) service delivery policy.

Research Policy

Research on Sequelae. Although the available research supports the conclusion that there are few and mild psychological sequelae after abortion, there is a serious need for additional systematic research. The research is characterized by small-scale, piecemeal, nontheoretical, short-term studies. We have emphasized the methodological weaknesses of the research. We have suggested some areas in which research does not exist.

It is easy for proponents or opponents of abortion to discount the research evidence or to misuse the research evidence for their own needs. One result is that the public and policy makers do not know who or what to believe. There is a real policy need for research that is methodologically sound, programmatic, and as objective as possible. Considering the numbers of abortions, adoptions, out-of-wedlock parenting, and in-wedlock parenting by adolescents, it seems a prudent policy to fund increased research on each of these options. We believe that the federal research agencies should fund a series of studies that: (1) are methodologically sound; (2) assess both short-term and long-term sequelae; (3) collect comparable data on abortion, adoption, single parenthood, and dual parenthood; (4) incorporate relevant risk factors; and (5) investigate the symptoms asserted for postabortion syndrome as compared to posttraumatic stress disorder and adjustment disorder. The surgeon general's report (1989b) on the physical and psychological sequelae of abortion recommended such research. Research should also be expanded to include the psychological, economic, and social sequelae for children born out of wedlock and to women denied abortions because that is the policy alternative to outlawing abortion (David and Matejcek, 1981).

Research on Safer Procedures. Research that leads to the development of procedures that are less invasive, less surgical, and less painful holds the potential for reducing both physical and psychological sequelae. Congress has either forbidden or not funded research on improving abortion procedures. Medical science and technology are moving in directions that will lead to earlier and less invasive procedures. France has approved use of an abortifacient pill (RU 486). Pregnancy testing technology now makes home pregnancy testing possible as early as nine days past the last missed menstrual period. Advances in this technology will likely decrease this waiting period.

Early medical administration of an abortifacient pill might reduce physical and psychological sequelae. From the perspectives of public health, research on an abortifacient pill seems prudent. There is a serious need for government funding of clinical trials of RU 486 or equivalents.

Educational Policy

Objective Information. Opponents of abortion have sought to require women with unwanted pregnancies be provided information on the negative physical and psychological sequelae of abortion (Pennsylvania Abortion Control Act of 1988). The justification given for this requirement is phrased as a public health one: Women have a right to be informed of the risks of medical procedures. Unfortunately, the political agenda has distorted this requirement in two ways. First, it draws attention to the risks while ignoring possible benefits. The woman is given only half the information. Second, the information is distorted because the risks are given without their respective rates. Many women will incorrectly assume that the risk is greater than statistically indicated. Imagine being given a list of the risks, without rates, of receiving the live polio vaccine. You would be confronted with a list of dire consequences with no information on the extreme rarity of these risks or of the benefit of receiving the vaccine.

Public health policy would be best served if all legislation and regulations requiring information on the risks of abortion also required inclusion of the incidence rates for each risk, the benefits with their incidence rates, and identical information for term birth for women of the appropriate age group. Impediments such as waiting periods and mandatory information designed to complicate the decisionmaking process serve to potentially increase negative psychological sequelae.

Prevention Policy

Surgeon General Koop (1989b) emphasizes that the best prevention for the possible negative effects of abortion is the prevention of unintended pregnancy. When contraception falls, he recommends a profamily policy of support programs including government-funded prenatal, delivery, daycare, educational, and job benefits to enable the woman to give birth and then either surrender the infant for adoption or raise the child herself. Koop's report does not address whether these benefits would be means tested or universal. Although such benefits would respond to the needs of those women who have abortions because they feel unable economically to care for a child, it does not address the needs of those women who abort for other reasons.

Research has identified several risk factors that predispose women to postabortion disorders. Such women can be helped if they are identified. For example, a short questionnaire or interview might be used to select women who might then be encouraged to receive additional counseling before receiving an abortion. Vulnerability to postabortion distress, however, should not be grounds for restricting a woman's access to abortion. Ideally, preabortion counseling should be expanded to include components that address some of these risk factors and increase the woman's coping ability. Previous research has shown the effectiveness of such a counseling session (only seven minutes long) (Mueller and Major, 1989).

Most abortion clinics schedule a postabortion examination. This would be a good time to administer a postabortion screening for psychological coping. Any woman who shows signs of coping difficulty through this screening should be offered short-term, sliding scale therapy by the clinic and/or offered a support group (Lemkau, 1988; Zakus and Wilday, 1987).

Women should also be given the names and addresses of mental health professionals.

Service Delivery Policy (Access Issues)

Funding Issues. Congress and the states have imposed a number of impediments to abortion access. Most of these impediments affect poor women, adolescents, and those covered by government-paid insurance. Currently, only abortions to protect the woman's life are funded by Medicaid, government-paid insurance, or performed by the military and Public Health Service. We believe that there are important public health reasons for a policy in which all government entitlement programs, government-paid insurance plans, and military and Public Health Service clinics and hospitals should cover or perform abortions on request. There is considerable evidence that abortion improves the mental health of women distressed by an unwanted pregnancy. Current federal policy denies poor women easy access to a potentially therapeutic procedure. The prospect for such a policy change, however, is very unlikely.

Liability Issues. Another attempt to limit access to abortions has taken the form of legislation designed to exclude abortifacients and contraceptives from federal liability legislation. This would statutorily define abortifacients and contraceptives as inherently dangerous products, thereby completely sidestepping the existing FDA scientific approval process. While the amendment to so exclude abortifacients and contraceptives passed at the committee level, it died along with the overall legislation at the end of the 100th Congress. Again, there is no public health justification for excluding abortifacients and contraceptives from liability coverage. To do so would increase the public's fears and thus likely increase the negative psychological sequelae of abortion. Equally important, this policy if adopted would discourage pharmaceutical companies from developing and marketing abortifacients.

Abortion Counseling and Referrals. Family planning clinics are a primary source for pregnancy testing for poor women and adolescents. The Reagan administration, in response to prolife groups, promulgated regulations (*Federal Register*, 1988) forbidding federally funded family planning clinics from providing information about abortion as an option in unwanted pregnancies or providing referrals when requested to abortion providers. These regulations were challenged in, and blocked by, federal courts. They are now before the U.S. Supreme Court under *Rust v. Sullivan*, and the decision will not be released before this book goes to press (May 1991). In terms of public health, it is counterproductive to force separation of pregnancy testing from provision of information on options to unwanted pregnancy. An overriding public health principle has been the idea of one-stop, integrated health services. Fragmentation of services is less effective and more expensive in meeting health needs. This is yet one more example of how antiabortion policies are not consistent with public health policy.

Parental Consent for Minors. Several states have tried to require that minors seeking an abortion either show proof of having notified their parents of their plans or proof of actual parental or judicial consent. This impediment to abortion has been rejected in the majority of federal court cases reviewing it. The courts, however, have generally argued that the right to privacy in abortion decisions is limited to minors who are capable of mature decision making. Minors fearing their parents' reaction or merely protective of their privacy must be granted judicial review as an option to parental notification or consent. Either parental or judicial involvement increases the likelihood of emotional stress and embarrassment as well as delay in having the abortion. We believe that such requirements increase the vulnerability of the adolescent to postabortion distress and thus are not justified on public health grounds.

SUMMARY

Abortion is a public health issue with relevance to family policy. It is only one among the many issues that provide a basis for forming family policy. Based on the research investigating the mental health consequences of abortion, there are good public health reasons for legalized abortion without various statutory, judicial, or financial restrictions.

NOTE

1. Although referred to as the "Surgeon General's Report" in congressional hearings (Koop, 1989b), this draft report was written at Dr. Koop's direction by his special assistant, George Walter. Dr. Koop testified on 16 March 1989 before the Human Resources and Intergovernmental Relations Subcommittee of the House of Representatives that he never released the report, not because it was an incorrect report, but because he had already delivered his letter of 9 January 1989 to President Reagan and closed the abortion study prior to receiving the draft report on 17 January 1989.

9
Women Under the Collective: The Exigencies of Family Policies in China

Jean Robinson

During the late 1960s, Chinese women were encouraged to participate fully in mass action and public life. Issues of domestic labor and family life were considered personal and bourgeois. Just a decade later, the leadership of the People's Republic of China (PRC) launched major efforts to downplay mass action and political involvement while reforming relations within the family and encouraging women's work in both the public sector and the household. Most recently a return to more traditional family life has been indirectly encouraged as part of the "Get Rich" policy in Chinese economic reforms. This variability in state policy is indicative of changes in economic development strategy in China, a subject of perennial interest among China watchers. However, equally significant and much less noticed, the policies are testimony to the way ideology and economic development plans jointly shape the lives of women and families under socialism.

The chapter presents the argument that policies directed at family change are determined by a complex interaction among social, economic, and political factors. One part of this complex puzzle is shrouded by regime references to the *collective interest*—a term which provides ideological justification for both regime goals and short-term policy programs but which is premised on certain presumptions about the relations among families, economy, and society. In socialist countries and indeed in liberal Western societies, the collective interest serves to legitimate strategies, priorities, and policies while mystifying actual social relations.

In this chapter, I examine recent trends in Chinese family policies, focusing specifically on marriage and divorce reform and family planning in the 1980s (see Robinson [1985] for other family-related issues). These

issues continue to concern the Chinese leadership because of their presumed positive and direct impact on economic growth. Analyzing the
state's intent and implementation in these areas, I show not only the
connection between economic policies and family change but also, more
importantly, in what ways the collective interest as defined by the political elite legitimizes ignoring the needs of women as a distinct group
and obfuscates the relation between production and reproduction.

WOMEN AND THE COLLECTIVE INTEREST

The collective interest is often used by regimes as the rationalization
for the pursuit, or lack thereof, of particular public policies. The term
suggests that the collective interest is the aggregated needs of an entire
population but in fact it ignores the interests of significant segments of
the population, particularly of women. Indeed while the membership
and treatment of dominated groups varies cross-nationally, it appears
that women and homosexuals share similar fates—that is, their interests
are disaggregated from the collective in all societies.

When used with reference to public policy, the collective interest is a
difficult concept to limit. Some issues, such as national defense, may be
above particular group interests, but many domestic policies tend to
reflect the particular interests of the dominant group in society, usually
represented by the ruling elite. This confounding of the particular with
the general can occur whether the elite is an elected legislature, a central
committee, or a group of economic managers. Decisions may be made
in the name of the collective, but they are based on the self-interest of
the ruling group, on an exclusionary definition of the members of the
collective, and on, at best, a paternalistic view of what the collective
needs. When the leadership asserts that pursing a particular issue or
policy is not in the collective interest, it withholds legitimacy from that
issue or policy. Simultaneously, this denies the validity of the needs or
interests of the affected group.

In one sense the collective interest merely serves then as a cover for
the actions of a self-interested elite. Yet it also has two far-reaching
ideological functions, both of which serve as legitimating mechanisms
for the regime. On the one hand, the collective interest represents the
founding principles for the existence of the regime, say, for instance
the pursuit of equality, socialism, and prosperity. On the other hand,
the collective interest is the formula for rationalizing and legitimating
specific policies, even if such policies contradict founding principles.
Thus, in China, the regime uses Marxism-Leninism with its references
to the collective's social equality to assert regime legitimacy while simultaneously using the collective interest to legitimate public policies
that undermine social equality.

The two levels of operation of the collective interest often result in dissonance and indeed contradiction. In terms of public policies, the PRC despite its broad commitment to equality has allowed family policies to be determined by narrowly defined material and production interests. In those instances where family change has been attempted or where certain aspects of women's domination are addressed, policy success has been incomplete. It is unfinished because to pursue further change would require a redefinition of the collective interest, and this means a fundamental reordering of society. The collective interest is the tool of discourse that sets the parameters of justified action; when the definition of the collective is fundamentally flawed, the policy options for leaders are narrowed. The problem derives from assuming that the collective is synonymous with the producers and that production is exclusively materialist. Given the propensity to see both men and women as productive workers, socialist political leaders have blithely pursued policies under the tacit assumption that the collective interest represents both men's and women's needs impartially or indeed that once women engage in productive labor, they are for most intents "men" (Stolcke, 1981). It has not been acknowledged that women's and men's interests may differ due to the fact that their lives are experienced differentially because of the way *reproduction* structures the family and society.

Male needs are taken as the norm for policymaking partially because of the socialist (mis)understanding of reproduction. Contemporary socialist leaders have by and large accepted Marx's and Engels' wisdom that production produces value but reproduction only produces babies. While social reproduction was given a nod, women's role in reproduction was merely instinctual activity through which the species continued. But, of course, reproduction is more than gestation and birth, although this too has labor value. Reproduction also creates people out of babies, people who become consumers, producers, even citizens. Furthermore, reproduction produces society: the nurturing of children and adults, provision of emotional and psychic care, education and socialization— all of which reconstruct society anew in every generation. In most societies, in most centuries, this reproductive labor has been primarily performed by women. While this labor has not been ignored by socialist policy makers, neither has it been seen as something requiring change or valuation.

So what? we may ask. Aside from the attempt to secure equality, which is fundamental to the goals of socialist regimes, the issue of reproduction is significant because the formulation of family policy is pursued within the parameters, at both levels, of the collective interest. Only issues that have been determined as having *direct* relevance to production or to reducing pressure on the market or labor force are pursued by socialist regimes. Problems related to social reproduction or to the gendered division of labor are not addressed. Yet these also affect the family, the economy, and society. And all of these decisions have been made in the name of the collective interest. It becomes clear that what may be good for the economy or the collective is not necessarily good for women.

In less developed societies such as China, economic growth has a dominating impact on policy choices. Nevertheless, economic development must be seen as much more than a mechanistic process involving "objective" choices aimed at increasing the gross national product (GNP). Instead in all societies it is a set of political acts that involve value choices based upon given sets of circumstances (Anderson, 1975, pp. 225–227). These choices include ideological perceptions of the goals of development and of the state's ability and right to intervene effectively in personal lives. This is especially true in the PRC where not only development but the aim of the Chinese revolution itself has been equated with *both* economic growth and social equality.

The Chinese leadership has interpreted the tension between economic growth and equality to mean that addressing the domination of women or the transformation of the family as goals separate from economic aims is impermissible. Family reform remains subject to the opposing exigencies of economic development. Thus, although the state intermittently advocates the socialization of domestic labor, the provision of nurseries and child care facilities, the redefinition of marital relations, family planning, and the like, it has also tacitly approved the maintenance of a division of labor in which women, by virtue of their reproductive functions, remain outside the collective.

Traditional Chinese culture as well as current norms hold that families rather than individuals are the legitimate social and economic base of Chinese society. The vast majority of Chinese men and women marry. Never married adults are considered abnormal and pitiable and confront difficulties in obtaining housing or even job promotions. In the case of women, it is expected by both sexes that women will marry *and* have children (for the "experience of being a woman," Sheridan, 1976, p. 64). Public discussions inevitably link women's rights, their status, and future with the nurturing of the next generation. Thus, women and family are confounded in the context of policymaking in China such that policies with regard to one cannot be understood without reference to the other.

Furthermore, China's myriad problems, stemming from a huge population, a relative lack of capital for investment, a large unwieldy bureaucracy, and a tradition of popular conservative attitudes, have led to the national or collective interest as having the highest priority. Li Chang of the Chinese Academy of Sciences has argued that China's "socialist spiritual civilization" promotes "moral concepts [which] imply identification of individual interests with the interests of the people and, when the two fall into contradiction, subordination of personal interests to the overall interests of the people" (Li, 1981, pp. 16–17). Women in China have been urged to adopt Central Communist Party (CCP) defined goals as their own and to put aside other, more "personal" demands until the "interests of the people" are met. Yet because of the special character of women as a group, they are especially disadvantaged when it comes to divergences between their interests and the collective's.

MODERNIZATION, THE FAMILY, AND WOMEN

Since 1978, the leaders of the PRC have emphasized the modernization of the economic system through the application of modern science and technology, through a decentralization of economic planning combined with the use of market forces in industrial and agricultural development, and through greater acknowledgment of the effects of education and birth rates on economic progress.

The internationally publicized efforts to win Chinese women's co-operation in the birth planning campaign have been accompanied by attempts to restructure family relationships and to provide some services to support working parents of only children. Complementing the distribution policy characterized by the maxim "from each according to his ability, to each according to his work," both men and women are expected to engage in socialist construction and to arrange their family life around their work. Since 1982, Chinese peasant families have been encouraged to "get rich" by signing production contracts with the state and using their knowledge and labor as investments to build both national and family wealth. More recently, these "market" reforms have been extended to industrial production and the service sector, with individuals and families urged to use their own resources to modernize their lives. For its part, the Chinese government has reversed its policies that guaranteed jobs to school graduates, life-long tenure to employees, and wage equality to peasants and workers. The "iron rice bowl" has been smashed, the headlines read, and in its place, individual effort will be rewarded. The effect of these new policies has been to rebuild the family as the basic economic unit of society, reinforcing the patriarchal structures that socialism had vowed to eradicate.

Marriage and Divorce

The reform of marriage has played an important role in Chinese politics since the early days of the revolution when Mao Zedong, as a young radical, called for freedom of marriage in response to the suicides of women faced with arranged marriages (Mao, 1970, pp. 334–337). By 1950 the CCP had promulgated a new marriage law that not only outlawed arranged marriages and bride price but also provided for divorce and for equal rights in the ownership, management, and inheritance of family property. The new marriage law was contemporaneous with a program to distribute land to all peasants. The association of the marriage law with the land reform program was crucial for the economic liberation of women (and their resultant support of the CCP), but that same association led to discontent among older people and many males who saw freedom of marriage and female ownership of land as a frightening betrayal of their traditional world. The marriage law campaign was not a complete success in any case; it was opposed by state and party cadres as well as by more traditional husbands and mothers-in-law (Parish and Whyte, 1978, p. 159).

Over the next twenty years, marriage customs changed slowly with pressure for closer compliance with the 1950 marriage law occurring during periods of political activism and economic experimentation, for example during the Great Leap Forward (1957–1958) and the anti–Lin Biao anti-Confucius campaign (1973–1975) of the Cultural Revolution. Yet despite these episodic efforts to change marital relations, reports in China suggest that bride price, arranged marriages, and other "feudal" customs continue to be practiced (*Renmin Ribao*, 28 November 1980; *Anhui Ribao*, 20 February 1980; Honig and Hershatter, 1988). With the regime's recent encouragement of entrepreneurship and material gain, both parents and children have perceived marriage as an overt material relationship. Notably, arranged marriages; expensive wedding ceremonies and feasts; the physical abuse of wives, children, and elderly people; and inequality between husbands and wives have been seen by the Chinese state not as a result of recent policy initiatives but rather as an inheritance of China's prerevolutionary superstitions and practices and of the anarchy and economic disorder associated with the Cultural Revolution (*Xinhua*, 8 January 1981).

The current emphasis on "revolutionary, democratic and harmonious new families" establishes new norms for partners in marriage, including being considerate, helpful, thrifty, industrious, respectful of the aged, and supportive of women's equality with men. Political correctness, valued during the Cultural Revolution, is now a minor consideration except for marriages of Party cadres (Chinese women discuss life and work, 8 March 1979). Rather, the Party presumes that marriages based on love, understanding, and mutual respect will result in loyalty, labor, and dedication to the nation. The decision to formulate a new marriage law to strengthen families was founded on the belief of the Chinese leadership that familial harmony will enhance economic growth and social progress (*Renmin Ribao*, 16 September 1980). This view of the relationship between the family and society is reminiscent of Confucian tradition that held that only the harmonious family could produce children who would act for the best interests of the state. More recently, the Communist Party set a precedent in 1950 with the first CCP marriage law, that was designed to ensure that potential producers would lend their support to consequent economic reforms. Similarly, the 1980 marriage law was a foundation upon which the regime could inaugurate a new set of economic policies.

The 1980 law attempted to strengthen the nuclear family by reminding people of their rights and responsibilities in marriage. The law led initially to a spate of divorces, but it also led to renewed efforts to stabilize family life through wide-ranging media discussions. Simultaneously, the legislation served as a didactive device to promote the intensive effort to control population growth. This was especially significant given the political controversy over proposed legislation concerning mandatory population control. The marriage law became effective 1 January 1981 and was preceded by three months of public preparation in the media and through women's federations around the country. The law, which covers issues ranging from freedom of marriage and parental responsibilities to inheritance and the naming of children, concentrates on achieving three goals: the provision of legal supports for state control of population growth; the enhancement of the rights of women and children in families; and the control of monetary exchange for and in marriage (see *Tianjin Ribao*, 26 October 1984; Hao and Liu, 1984; *Xinhua*, 15 March 1985; and Marriage Law, 1980).

The law stipulates that "family planning is practiced" in marriage and that both husband and wife share the responsibility for contraception. Couples are told that from the practice of planned and late parenthood, happy homes and economic and social progress will develop. A minimum legal marriage age was set at 22 years for men and 20 years for women, with exceptions made for the national minority groups where the age limit is lower and family planning is not enforced (*Renmin Ribao*, 16 September 1980; *FBIS*, 15 December 1980; *Xinhua*, 4 September 1980; *Xinhua*, 10 February 1981). Success in achieving both later marriages and later births is critical in light of the fact that 65 percent of China's population is under age 30. The propaganda accompanying the new law was unusual in asserting that "marriage and birth can be separated and marriage does not necessarily include birth" (*Xinhua*, 10 February 1981). But more to the point is the lack of adequate housing, the disproportion of women to men, and inflation and unemployment, all of which act to delay urban marriages and thus births until the late 20s for both men and women.

In rural areas, the situation is different. With the promotion of family enterprises in agriculture through the "responsibility system," both marriage and childbirth are encouraged. The "responsibility system" (*baogan daohu* is the most common form) is a contract arrangement whereby families agree to sell a certain amount of produce to the state at set prices, with all remaining produce to be sold at the families' discretion. This economic reform encourages large families since the more workers in a family, the more wealth can be accumulated. With the return to family contracting, the head of the household has been reinforced in his control over other family members since it is he who signs the contract. This gives parents greater resources to control children's behavior in marriage, divorce, and births. Thus, marriages get entangled in the web of traditional custom, including "parents meddling with the freedom of marriage of their children" (*Renmin Ribao*, 28 November 1980).

The marriage law, which disputes the right of parents to determine their children's spouses, also advocates the individual rights of women. The All-China Women's Federation (ACWF) has acclaimed several statutes of the new law, hailing them as extensions of women's rights under socialism. These articles include:

Article 9: Husband and wife enjoy equal status in the home.

Article 10: Husband and wife each has the right to use his or her family name.

Article 11: Husband and wife have the freedom to engage in production, to work, to study, and to participate in social activities; neither party is allowed to restrain or interfere with the other.

Article 16: Children may adopt either their father's or their mother's family name (Marriage Law, 1980).

Despite the fact that Articles 10 and 16 are the only new additions and that no enforcing legislation has been written, the intended effect of the articles is to ensure that equal rights are practiced within the household. Articles 10 and 16 are connected specifically with the birth control campaign and aim especially at parental efforts to ensure they will have heirs to carry on the family name. The significance of naming is tied to patriarchal notions of the continuity of the kinship line, a continuity that traditionally demanded sons. If daughters and wives can retain their natal names, then the family may continue, even without sons. Of course the family's patriarchal character has then been changed significantly. Fundamentally an unacknowledged mother right has been legislated here (see Engels, 1972; Sacks, 1974). Thus the CCP has insisted that

when female babies grow up, they are as good a source of labor as males and may work even better at certain jobs. They can do better housework and can let their husbands live with the bride's family. The people of new China, particularly the younger generation, must overcome the old idea of looking down on female babies and insure that, if an only child is a girl, the parents take just as good care of her. . . . [I]t is necessary to conscientiously implement the policy of equal pay for equal work for men and women. . . . Party members and cadres must take the lead in overcoming the feudal idea and erroneous concept that only a male child can carry forward the family name (*Xinhua*, 25 September 1980).

Money is the link between the family name and equality. Only if women have the same access to employment and income as men will peasants agree to the one-child stipulation. It is in the interests of the economic reform that patrilocality and overt patrilineal and patriarchal practices be stemmed. Suggestions in the Chinese press that women see no value in working strenuously for the economic development program are explained by reference to sexual discrimination in employment and inequality in the home (Executive committee, 12 December 1980). Only with a direct attack by the state on patriarchal customs can the regime make effective arguments that will help to overcome gender inequality and population increase (see *Xinhua*, 8 December 1984; Luo Qiong, 1985; *Xinhua*, 10 December 1985).

Since 1985, public policy efforts in China have attempted to find integrative solutions for women's involvement in the economic reforms and their situation within the traditional patriarchal order of the family. There have been "newlywed courses" that seek to convince husbands and wives to share housework (*Renmin Ribao*, 9 March 1986), press reports that laud the intelligence and labor capacities of women (Luo Qiong, 1985; *Xinhua*, 6 October 1986), and seminars that discuss the ways in which women can balance their "feminine" duties with their responsibility for productive labor (*Xinhua*, 23 March 1985). Controversy has raged in particular over the cultural assumption that women are wives and mothers first (Luo Qiong, 1985; Wei Shu, 1985; *Xinhua*, 6 October 1986). While numerous professional women have pleaded for the importance of their contributions outside the home, women are being urged by the ACWF—the conduit for communicating state interest and policy—to be "virtuous wives and good mothers" (*xianqi liangmu*) (Tao, 1987). This is only part of women's task, but nevertheless it imposes a heavy burden. "Because of their physiology, psychology and temperament, women excel in childcare. On the basis of this fact alone, women are made to take on more duties than husbands" (Xian, 1987). The state recognizes that women need assistance in completing their "rear-area work" (*Renmin Ribao*, 9 March 1986) but attributes the problem to the "underdeveloped state of China's present economy" (Luo Qiong, 1985).

What becomes very clear is that Chinese equality assumes innate differences and roles for women and men, and that the valuation of these roles is also differentiated. *Hongqi*, the official theoretical journal of the CCP, has stated that while social reproductive work is necessary, it is not as valuable as productive labor (Luo Qiong, 1985). But women are also encouraged to wear makeup (*Zhongguo Funu*, 6 June 1985), cook well for their husbands, bear children, and be centrally engaged in child-hood socialization and education (Honig and Hershatter, 1988). Marital policies have contributed to the burden of women's work in the 1980s, such that both customary patriarchal demands as well as legislated so-cialist demands are legitimized by the state.

Divorce has also been connected in state propaganda to the question of equality and economic progress, with nods to both traditional values and collective needs. The marriage law sanctions more easily obtainable divorce, "in light of women's growing economic independence and more equal position in the family" (*Xinhua*, 5 October 1980). Divorce is to be granted when both husband and wife desire; when only one party re-quests dissolution, reconciliation is attempted under the auspices of the people's court system. Child custody decisions tend to favor the mother, and the disposal of joint property, while subject to agreement between husband and wife, can be decided by a people's court after "taking into consideration the actual state of the family property and the rights and interests of the wife and the child" (Marriage Law, 1980; *Women of China*, 1987). Both the 1950 Marriage Law and the 1980 law were intended to protect women's rights; in the past, however, court practice favored the male side, so the 1980 law has attempted to reinforce the legal protection of women in divorce. In general, the emphasis remains on reconciliation except in cases of wife abuse or forced marriage (*Renmin Ribao*, 4 January 1980; *Renmin Ribao*, 16 September 1980; *Beijing Xinhua*, 5 February 1980; *Beijing Review*, 4 May 1981).

Because 70 percent of all divorce cases since 1980 have been initiated by women, policy makers have focused on women in the recent effort to stabilize marriages. Women are encouraged to find ways to solve marital conflicts by compromising, helping their husbands, and sharing their enthusiasm for work (*Women of China*, October 1985). The ACWF has advised against divorce because "marriage is a safeguard of women's interests" (Wei Shu, 1985, pp. 30–31). Thus, although the existence of legal divorce is necessary to ensure that women have an escape from male hostility, extramarital affairs (see *Xinhua*, 15 March 1985), and so on, organizations representing collectivist values persist in situating women in a context that embeds them in their social reproduction role.

Only early focus of the propaganda on marriage and divorce reform has been the "practice of using marriage to extort money and goods from suitors" (*Xinhua*, 5 September 1980). While noting that the persis-tence of arranged marriages is a sign of feudal practices that are not only illegal but contravene personal rights, it is the exchange of money for marriage and the expenditure of large sums of money on ceremonies which seems to draw the most ire from the state. The leadership has blamed the Cultural Revolution (and its leaders) for giving rise to prac-tices that are now seen as extravagant and wasteful. While large feasts, gift exchanges, and monetary presents have had a long association with weddings in China (as elsewhere) the regime since 1957 has attempted to convince couples to disdain these customs as relics of the past. Yet the practices continue and indeed have increased in number in the 1980s. Women in urban areas want future husbands to provide them with televisions, sofas, and tape decks before they will agree to marry (Schwarz, 1981; Woman leader on new marriage law, 1981; Robinson, 1982); parents in the rural areas insist on large feasts, sumptuous presents, and traditional ceremonies. In Beijing the problem became so severe as to warrant the issuing of a municipal circular that condemned ostentation, extravagance, and "displaying one's wealth in marriage ceremonies" (*Xinhua*, 7 February 1980; Kong, 1981).

State criticism of these practices links them with the growth of corruption and the decline in industrial production. A series of letters in *Gongren Ribao* (*Worker's Daily*) have told of factory department heads using factory-owned vehicles and fuel to transport guests to their children's weddings; of factory workshops ceasing operations because the workers took the day off to attend ceremonies and celebrations; and of people selling factory-issued clothing in order to purchase wedding presents (see *China Daily*, 4 August 1981; Extravagant weddings criticized, 1981). The Communist Youth League, trade unions, and women's federations have called upon parents and engaged couples to be more economical in wedding ceremonies, to guard against the waste of state property, and to deemphasize ritual. In the early 1980s, moral exemplars were made of such phenomena as group weddings in which fifty or more couples married *en masse*, no gifts were exchanged, and only the lunch hour was used to celebrate the event. By middecade, group weddings gave way to traditional one-couple affairs, but the message from the state was the same. Money spent on rituals is wasted. Nevertheless, there appears to be approval of honeymoons and the purchase of consumer durables for the new home (see, for example, *Women in China*, November 1985). What is of interest here is that as economic productivity has increased, "bourgeois" weddings have become more acceptable.

The state clearly does not want to hinder marriages. Indeed given the "correct" ages and the promise to use contraceptive measures faithfully, the PRC avidly supports marriage as a way to satisfy the emotional, productive, and reproductive needs of individuals in society. What the government wants to prevent is the waste of people's income and/or savings on what it considers "nonproductive purposes." Marriage and divorce policies attempt to ensure that all available family resources be used to enhance economic growth through savings, education, training, and family sideline production (Contributions of rural women, 1980; Executive committee, 1980; Sixth Gansu provincial women's federation, 1980; *Zhongguo Xiao Feizhe Bao*, 1987). The stipulations on marriage and divorce established since 1980 are designed to counteract traditional attitudes that inhibit women's participation in labor outside the home but to merge with customary attitudes that assume women will naturally (and without recompense) engage in social reproduction. Thus the current emphasis is on building a stable and harmonious foundation in the family, which reproduces both patriarchal and socialist values.

Family Planning

Family planning in China has always been influenced by ideological perceptions concerning overpopulation and by whether development strategies rely on labor-intensive or capital-intensive plans. Until 1956, the CCP considered family planning to be unnecessary. For many Chinese socialists, the Malthusian explanation of overpopulation merely justified capitalists' use of induced unemployment to exploit workers. It followed that overpopulation could not exist in a socialist society that had no desire to exploit labor. Yet by the mid–1950s and again in the early 1960s, family planning was encouraged not only to safeguard the health of women and children but to contribute to the growth of national prosperity. With the start of the Cultural Revolution, family planning as a national program disappeared. Contraceptives and free abortion (legalized in 1958) were available, but little effort was made to convince men and women to practice contraception. In 1969, however, population control was held to be a crucial link in the task of modernization and development that lay ahead for China. Contraceptive techniques were widely publicized and disseminated, and by 1972 there was even public discussion of possible restrictions on food and clothing rations for "excess" children. Families were urged to have no more than two children each.

A revised population policy was initiated in 1978. For the first time, Chinese officials noted that reproduction is a form of production and that "the production of people must be connected to the production of materials" (Nationwide demographic science discussion, 1979). To achieve a satisfactory balance between economic growth and population increase, the thrust of the population policy called on couples to marry later and to have only one child (*wanxishao*).

By mid-1979, both rural and urban couples were encouraged to take pledges to have no more than one child. Before the agricultural reforms of 1982, a benefit system was enacted for couples who promised to limit their family size. The systems varied from province to province but shared certain characteristics. They all provided different guidelines for urban and rural areas with incentives that included monetary benefits and larger housing and food allocations for one-child families (*Renmin Ribao*, 11 August 1979). These state-encouraged incentives substituted material benefits for that which additional children traditionally provided parents. As the new market economy swept through rural China, these incentives lost effectiveness. If families with more workers (otherwise known as children) could gain more wealth, they could afford to lose population control incentives and still be better off then before. By 1984, adherence to the population program began to backslide.

The program has been dogged with problems from the start. Culturally and economically induced preferences for sons, fear of losing old-age security, concern about maintaining the good health of only children, and fears about loss of femininity/masculinity all contributed to opposition to the population control measures. Both childbearing women and birth control officials have borne the brunt of the failure to accede to the one-child policy (*Guizhou Ribao*, 27 June 1980; Butterfield, 1979; Gui, 1980; Robinson, 1985). Throughout the 1980s there have been reports of violent disagreement with the one-child policy, especially on the part of rural men. Although the level of hostility is unclear, provincial newspapers have frequently commented on incidents where husbands divorced their wives who chose abortion against their wishes and where family planning cadres were physically attacked by male peasants. Daughters-in-law have been urged to get abortions when it was determined their fetus was female; other women have been beaten by their husbands upon giving birth to girls (Robinson, 1982; Honig and Hershatter, 1988). Thus antagonism appears to be directed not only at government cadres but also at childbearing women themselves. There is scant evidence of how women feel about this policy (but see Honig and Hershatter [1988] for some tantalizing clues). Peasant women say they would prefer to have a son since this ensures domestic tranquility and economic security. (See Wolf [1972] and Wolf [1985] for further discussion of the importance of the Chinese "uterine family.") Educated urban women oppose wife beatings and forced abortions as well as preferences for sons. In general, however, they have been convinced of the importance of the one-child policy but appalled by the actions taken against wives and mothers. Disagreement with the one-child policy and its consequences is both an elite-mass conflict and a gender conflict.

With the implementation of the economic reform measures between 1982 and 1985, conflict eased as coercion lost its effectiveness. By 1985, China's birth rate began to rise. The one-child policy had pushed the average number of births for a Chinese woman from 2.66 in 1979 to 1.94 in 1984 (Greenhalgh and Bongaarts, 1987), but in light of peasant opposition, local officials began to ease up on the stringency with which they enforced the birth policy. By 1985, the fertility rate had risen to 2.2, and in 1986 Chinese women were bearing an average 2.4 children (Kristof, 1987).

The reactions of the public and officials responsible for implementing the population control programs have led the Chinese leadership to argue that population control is necessary for the collective interest. A law of family planning has yet to be approved by the legislative bodies in China, but there has been considerable effort to redraw the policy in line with popular complaints. Before official changes were made in the policy, local officials began to show some flexibility, but in the end the legitimacy upon which they acted was based on reassessments by the top leadership. In April 1984, the CCP Central Committee issued Document 7, enumerating and expanding the conditions under which a couple could have two children (e.g., the first child being a girl). The Party also urged more ideological work to ensure voluntary cooperation. The following year, the CCP revised its population target for the year 2000 from 1.2 billion to "around 1.2 billion." This apparent flexibility was, however, overshadowed in 1986 when the Central Committee, in Document 13, called for stronger measures to enforce the one-child policy. The policy leadership is clearly frustrated by the demographic situation, but as Shen Yimin, a population official at the PRC State Statistical Bureau, admitted, "we cannot rely on punishment anymore. People don't mind paying for a second child" (Kristof, 1987). As of fall 1988, the PRC initiated an experimental program in several provinces that would allow families with a single, female child to try again for a son. This policy modification appeases the peasants' desire for sons, albeit at the cost of devaluing daughters. It is likely to lead to conflicts between one-son and two-children families, as well as to greater sexual equality problems.

Despite the lack of a formal law, the PRC leadership, advised by a Family Planning Commission, has created mechanisms for influencing the decision to have children. Recent measures taken by the state have included expulsion of any university, college, or technical student who parents a child. Rewards for having only one child and penalties for more than one child have both increased. A one-child mother is often given extended postnatal leaves and full payment of pregnancy expenses for first pregnancies. Free schooling and medical care are provided for the only child in addition to extra housing, food, and, in some instances, preferential placement in elementary, secondary, and university schooling. Couples may be given pay increases up to 40 percent. In some cities, if a couple has more than one child, the mother may forfeit not only pregnancy and postnatal paid leaves but in certain cases must pay all medical charges for prenatal and delivery services. The family can be charged an "excess child fee" up to 10 to 15 percent of their income until the extra child reaches the age of 14. Both spouses may lose their jobs and in urban areas face heavy barrages of peer criticism. Notably most of these disincentives focus on urban dwellers; in the countryside now, people are apt to be self-employed, women have no maternity leave anyway, and income is dependent on agricultural production.

It should be noted here that while both husbands and wives can be punished for excess children, women seem to be punished more severely. In the early 1980s, the Chinese press covered a number of cases in which couples did not conform. In one case, where both husband and wife were CCP members and yet had a fourth child (because they had three daughters and wanted a son), the husband was denied work bonuses for one year; the wife was denied bonuses for three years. In another case, the wife, upon birth of a third child, lost her job and thus economic independence; her husband was forced to have a vasectomy. Both parents were criticized for the preference for a male child (Guizhou couple punished, 1980; Beijing couple suffers, 1980). More recently, there has been less coverage of these punishments but notification to the public that, in the face of the 1986 growth spurt, "unplanned second and more births will be strictly forbidden" (Population policy key, 1987).

Despite the recent vacillations of the Communist Party on the issue since 1985, there has been consistent emphasis on the relation between the economy and birth control policy. Contraception is viewed as a responsibility of all citizens since it is in the "collective interest." Population control has been connected to equality of opportunity for women by the state, but the greatest emphasis of the state's argument is that family planning is necessary for economic progress. Because of this direct impact, state budgetary commissions have allotted scarce resources for solving the social problems that are connected to getting popular support for planned births. For instance, expenditures for social welfare have increased despite general cuts in the budget, and some peasants have been provided with retirement pensions to offset the cost to rural families of the one-child policy (Zhao, 1981; Retirement in the countryside, 1981). The state has begun devising ways to provide other social security measures for elderly people with only one child. In addition, more money has been budgeted for health services for mothers and children to reduce health risks and hence to assuage fears that an only child may die and leave parents childless. The Party has even begun to inform young people about contraception and conception in newly instituted sex education classes. Family planning has clearly become part of the collective interest—at both the level of ideology and the level of policy. Yet even as women's reproductive capacities have become more controlled by the state, women's inclusion within the collective remains questionable. At best, one can say that women's reproductive functions have become a factor in public policy.

CONCLUSION

The persistence of bride price, expensive marriage feasts, patrilocality, traditional sex roles within the household, and preferences for male children exemplify the difficulty the Chinese regime has had in reforming the family. So, too, the Chinese leadership has had problems in liberating women. Part of the explanation for these failures is not so much the economic backwardness of Chinese society, as the leadership claims, but rather the manipulation of women's issues, which fails to deal with women's lives as distinct from men's except as they are shaped by women's reproductive role.

Furthermore, family policies in China serve as indispensable underpinnings of the sexual division of labor in the family. Clearly there are times when state control and intervention in family life has coincided with the interests of women. The general support of population control and the ideological campaigns to institutionalize equality may be beneficial to women. On the other hand, coerced abortions, the devaluation of women, and the assumption that women have the main responsibility for social reproduction may serve economic goals but do not necessarily represent the best interests of women.

Women are objects of political control. The arguments for family planning and marriage law reform suggest that economic growth, at least currently, is synonymous with the collective interest. In a very real sense, the state is promoting the idea that women are primarily wives and mothers and thus defined by their reproductive capacities. Lacking political control and control over their reproduction, sexuality, and lives, women have remained dependent and their interests remain external to the collective interest.

The paucity of female representation in the Communist Party and government elite as well as the observed inequities between men and women suggest that women are an especially disadvantaged group. The failure of the leadership to change the basic sexual division of labor in the family contributes to this disadvantaged status. Furthermore, the likelihood of women as a group becoming less disadvantaged in this respect in the near future seems slight: the potential cost to the state in terms of allocating resources to the resolution of women's double duty, to disestablishing preferences for sons, and to correcting the contradictions between the market reforms and the one-child policy is great. Given the dominance of economic growth as a defining factor in the collective interest, such expenditures may seem irrational. It appears that little consideration is given to the notion that resolving women's problems may indeed generate greater economic growth for the system by freeing women to be more productive.

The importance of political power to the expression of interests becomes obvious in this context. If women's interests are to be included in national policies, they must be articulated and presented by members of the elite itself. This means that more forceful representation for women is necessary. Successful family policies, in terms of providing personal nurturing and emotional space as well as liberating women, appear to be dependent on the ability of women to mobilize themselves for protection of their own interests. But female representation is not enough. Until social reproduction is perceived by the leadership and by members of society as affecting productive relations and forces in the same way that traditional values do, women's interests will continue to be either ignored or manipulated to serve the collective interest.

NOTE

I would like to thank the East Asian Exchange Committee and the Women's Studies Program, Indiana University for providing funding for this research. I also want to express my thanks to Jack Bielasiak, Margery Wolf, and Irene Diamond for comments on earlier versions of this chapter.

III

Exploring Impacts

10

Post-Mortem on the Deterioration of the Welfare Grant

Theresa Funiciello and Sanford F. Schram

The politics of welfare in recent years has taken an ominous turn. The idea that welfare benefits have gotten too high has acquired a virtually unquestioned status. It has become part of what many liberals and conservatives alike are calling the New Consensus on welfare reform.[1] In the final weeks of the 1988 session of the 100th Congress, both houses agreed on welfare reform legislation reflecting the New Consensus and revising the main welfare program—Aid to Families with Dependent Children (AFDC). The reforms, however, did not include any mechanisms for increasing welfare benefit levels and in fact were based on the assumption that they were too generous and that the government needed to institute more serious work requirements (Mead, 1990; Ellwood, 1988; Kosterlitz, 1989; Stevens, 1988; Rich, 1988).

This was all part of an emerging outlook that suggests that the poverty we were so concerned about in the 1960s was no longer the critical problem. Instead, by the 1980s, "welfare dependency" had become the pressing issue (Murray, 1984). Conservatives such as Charles Murray (1986) and James Q. Wilson (1985) were quick to remind us that traditionally the true test of public policies was whether or not they promote private virtue—in other words, whether or not they make us better people. For them, welfare worked to undermine private virtue, and high welfare benefits discouraged individual responsibility among the poor. Welfare failed the test conservatives set for public policy because it discouraged us from being responsible for ourselves, our families, and our communities. High welfare benefits were corrupting the poor working class and eating away at the moral fiber of the nation.

In the face of all this rhetoric regarding welfare and the poor, the deterioration of the purchasing power of the welfare grant in recent years is often overlooked (Ellwood and Summers, 1986; Peterson and Rom, 1989). If one can say there is a crisis in welfare, it stems from the fact that we have allowed the grant to decline in real terms while failing to appreciate the constraints operating on it. In spite of protestations to the contrary, the grant simply now is generally lower in real dollars than it was in the past. In addition, the grant often comes in a form which welfare recipients are unable to use as effectively as the sums for which they may be eligible imply. And even in those states with relatively higher grants, recipients often get less than the maximum possible. The following analysis examines these limitations in an effort to put the discussion about the welfare grant into a more informed perspective.

First, we review the recent reforms. Next, we examine national trends with respect to the real value of the welfare grant, and then we look at New York State as one of those states which has witnessed the sharpest decline. This analysis highlights how the welfare grant is structured in at least one state so that recipients end up with even less buying power than the declining gross sums in the real value of benefits indicate.

THE NEW CONSENSUS, THE REFORMS, AND THE GRANT

The 1988 Family Support Act has been heralded as a major piece of welfare legislation (Mead, 1990). Some observers have called it the most significant welfare reform in decades (Stevens, 1988). While there is good reason to dispute this, the claim is in itself significant because it tells us much about how the focus of welfare policy dialogue has changed (Handler, 1988). This legislation represents the culmination of several years of effort in Congress to forge a compromise between liberals and conservatives under the New Consensus on welfare reform. Only from the perspective of reducing "dependency" can the new legislation be seen as an advance in welfare policy. Yet, even from that perspective, the new legislation is of questionable value as it emphasizes work and training programs that were tried and failed repeatedly over the 1970s and 1980s (Jencks and Edin, 1990). From a perspective that concentrates on poverty as the main problem confronting the poor, the new legislation can be seen at best as insignificant and at worst as further eroding the already limited ability of AFDC to help poor families cope (Handler, 1988).

The 1988 reforms follow legislation in 1981, 1982, 1984, and 1987 that in all years included provisions for tightening and standardizing eligibility (U.S. House of Representatives, Committee on Ways and Means, 1988). The 1981 reforms made numerous changes in determining eligibility, including reducing and eliminating several income deductions while taking into account various previously uncounted sources of income, such as from stepparents. The 1984 reforms, among other things, standardized the definition of the filing unit. These and other changes produced over $650 million in reduced expenditures annually in AFDC since 1981, largely due to benefit reductions and, to a lesser extent, through the denial of aid. The 1981 reforms also gave states the option of expanding work requirements for "employable" AFDC parents. By the mid-1980s, most states had adopted a number of these work programs (U.S. General Accounting Office, 1987; Gueron, 1988; Block and Noakes, 1988).

The 1988 reforms continued this trend. By October 1, 1990, all states were required to start to phase-in programs as part of what is euphemistically called the JOBS (Jobs Opportunity and Basic Skills) program. JOBS requires most AFDC mothers with children over age 3, as well as other employable adults receiving such aid, to complete high school, get training, or work. As of 1991, 7 percent of the eligible caseload was required to participate, rising incrementally to 20 percent in 1995. Participants must average twenty hours a week in JOBS-related activities before they can be counted as participating in the program. States must spend at least 55 percent of their JOBS funds on individuals who have been targeted by the legislation as likely to become long-term welfare recipients. These are heads of AFDC families who are either: (1) parents who are under 24 and have not completed high school; (2) parents who have had little or no work experience from the previous year; (3) parents who have been on public assistance for more than thirty-six of the previous sixty months; or (4) those whose youngest child is within two years of no longer being eligible for assistance. In addition, two-parent families receiving AFDC must have at least one parent enrolled in the JOBS program or complete sixteen hours a week of community service work. Also, the law provides for limited extensions of child care and Medicaid benefits up to one year after a family leaves AFDC for paid employment. The 1988 legislation also requires that states extend aid up to six months each year to a two-parent family where the principal wage earner is unemployed (AFDC-UP). Last, the law requires states to establish automatic payroll deductions of child support payments from absent parents of AFDC children (Kosterlitz, 1989; Rich, 1988). Whether or not these reforms will reduce welfare dependency remains uncertain. What is certain is that they do little if anything to increase cash benefits many poor people need.

The 1988 reforms also require each state to examine the standard of need they use to determine eligibility. Yet the act does not require states to upgrade their need standards (Welsh and Franklin, 1988). Also, there is nothing in the 1988 reforms that does anything to increase the real value of welfare benefits for families currently receiving full assistance. On the contrary, the 1988 reforms are very much dedicated to

Table 10.1

Maximum Monthly AFDC Benefits for a Four-Person Family for the Continental United States[1] (in 1988 dollars)[2]

State Group	1960	1968	1980	1988	PERCENT CHANGE 1960-1988
Low States[3]	375.83	438.28	319.87	289.50	-22.97
Middle States	631.95	696.71	544.69	455.88	-27.86
High States	836.85	856.29	620.15	502.35	-39.97
All States	609.99	659.16	497.46	417.67	-31.53
Weighted Average[4]	624.83	719.55	505.82	471.05	-24.61

1. Data for 1960 and 1968 are from U.S. House of Representatives (1987, pp. 660–62). Data for 1980 and 1988 are from U.S. Department of Health and Human Services (1980, pp. 59–60; 1989, p. 375).

2. Benefits are adjusted according to the annual consumer price index as it is reported in U.S. Department of Commerce (1981 and 1986, p. s–5).

3. High, moderate, and low benefit states are the upper, middle, and lower thirds of the state welfare grant distribution for 1960.

4. The Weighted Average is the maximum monthly benefit for a four-person family for the average recipient family. The Weighted Average is calculated by multiplying the total number of recipient families in each state by the maximum benefit, taking the sum, and dividing by the total number of recipient families for the Nation. The Weighted Average enables us to specify the average maximum benefit in a way which takes into account that states vary in the number of families receiving assistance. The number of AFDC recipients are for December of each year. For 1960 and 1980, the number of recipient families is taken from U.S. Bureau of the Census (1961, p. 286; 1981, p. 344); for 1968 the numbers are from U.S. Social Security Administration (April 1969, p. 64); and for 1988 the number of AFDC families is from U.S. Department of Health and Human Services (1989).

reducing "welfare dependency" even at the price of ignoring the deterioration in the real value of welfare benefits.

THE DETERIORATION OF THE GRANT: 1960–1988

Table 10.1 shows the change in the real value of benefits in AFDC. In constant 1988 dollars, the average state's AFDC monthly guarantee (or maximum benefit) for a four-person family with no income increased from $609.99 in 1960 to $659.16 in 1968—an increase of 8.1 percent—only to decline to $417.67 in 1988—a decline of 37 percent.

AFDC is, however, only part of the benefit package. Food stamps is the other major component, replacing the earlier food commodity program on a national basis in 1972 with full implementation coming by 1974 and 1975 (U.S. House of Representatives, Committee on Ways and Means, 1988. pp. 795–796). Food stamps already existed in some counties, but elsewhere the national stamp program represented a major improvement in benefits.[2] Yet, the food stamp program itself continues to be plagued by underutilization. More important, the interaction of AFDC and food stamps has since then created a perhaps inadvertently negative effect on the overall system.

AFDC is a program in which states administer their own programs within national guidelines. Costs are shared between the state and the national government with no state paying more than 50 percent of the cost. States set their own AFDC benefit levels. Food stamps is a national program run according to national standards and fully financed by the federal government. Most AFDC families are eligible for food stamps. (Until 1979 all were.) Food stamps benefit levels are based on recipient income from any and all sources including AFDC. Food stamps also is usually adjusted automatically for inflation whereas AFDC benefits are not.

With the advent of the food stamp program, the federal logic implicit in the combination of AFDC and food stamps took hold. States became intent on optimizing the flow of federal funds. They closely scrutinized how changes in AFDC affected the flow of food stamp dollars into their jurisdictions. Food stamps would be reduced about thirty cents for each dollar increase in AFDC. This then would replace some food stamps, which were entirely federally funded, with AFDC, which could be as much as half financed by the state. States accordingly became reluctant to increase AFDC benefits. AFDC benefits were often left unadjusted for inflation, and, as a result, food stamps came to assume a greater proportion of the total benefit package.

The consequences of this insidious federal logic are visible in Table 10.2. Combined AFDC–food stamp benefits for a four-person family without countable income on average dropped from $805.04 (1988 dollars) in July 1974 when food stamps operated under uniform national rules to $659.52 in July 1988. This drop amounted to 18.1 percent and was almost wholly due to shrinkage in AFDC purchasing power. Food stamp maximum benefits were virtually unchanged since they were adjusted for food price inflation in almost all years. It was largely state declines in AFDC that ate into the real value of the post–1972 benefit package.

Virtually all states practiced this sort of budgetary brinkmanship with their AFDC grants in the food stamp era to the point that the real value of their combined benefits declined from 1974 on. For the lowest third of states receiving benefits in 1960, the average real value of their combined AFDC–food stamp benefits declined from $645.83 in 1974 to $564.63 in 1988. Table 10.2 indicates that low state benefits in 1988 were still above their average of $375.83 for AFDC benefits in 1960 and $438.28 in 1968. There may be some solace in these last figures; however, we must keep in mind that by the mid-1960s some recipient families in

Table 10.2
Maximum Monthly Combined AFDC–Food Stamp Benefits for a Four-Person
Family for the Continental United States[1] (in 1988 dollars)[2]

	AFDC Only[2]		AFDC-Food Stamps			Percent Change	
State Group	1960	1968	1974	1980	1988	60-88	74-88
Low States[3]	375.83	438.28	645.83	593.16	564.63	+50.24	-12.57
Middle States	631.95	696.71	862.22	753.53	688.91	+ 9.01	-20.10
High States	836.85	856.29	901.07	806.35	721.45	-13.79	-19.93
All States	609.99	659.16	805.04	719.49	659.52	+ 8.12	-18.08
Weighted Avg[4]	624.83	719.55	842.40	733.79	696.15	+11.41	-17.36

1. All data are derived from U.S. House of Representatives (1989).

2. The figures for 1960 and 1968 do not include the value of food commodities.

3. High, moderate, and low benefit states are the upper, middle, and lower thirds of the state welfare grant distribution for 1960.

4. See Note 4 in Table 10.1 for explanation.

selected counties could get food commodities or stamps. Therefore, by 1988, the combined package had probably deteriorated back to the vicinity of the combined value in the mid-1960s of AFDC benefits and food commodities. Nonetheless, it is probably the case that the net effect of food stamps in low benefit states was a rise in benefits, and, in spite of subsequent declines, they remained above pre–food stamp levels.

The trendline in Table 10.2 is the same for the middle third of states; however, things were different for high benefit states. In these states, benefits tended on average to decline so much after 1974 that the real value of the total benefit package was less than that of AFDC alone in 1960. For those recipients who got food commodities, the 1988 combined benefit package would be even lower than the benefit levels of the 1960s. The average in benefits for these states went from $836.85 in 1960 to $901.07 in 1974 and then down to $721.45 in 1988.

In fact, not counting food commodities, the overall average state combined maximum benefit saw at best only the most modest increase of 8 percent from 1960 to 1988, such that welfare benefits were not much better in the mid-1980s than they were in the early 1960s. If benefits are weighted to account for the number of recipient families in each state, the average family's benefits were still only marginally better (11 percent) in 1988 compared to 1960. These data are weighted by the number of recipient families in each state in each year. When other methods such as weighting by the state's total population in 1980 are used, the average family's benefits rose only about 6 percent (Moffitt, 1987; U.S. House of

Representatives, Committee on Ways and Means, 1988). Yet, these averages do not figure the value of food commodities in the 1960s. If that could be done, the overall average in the 1980s would in all likelihood be below that for the mid-1960s.

The data unmistakably demonstrate that benefits have declined. Yet, the reasons for the decline continue to be subject to debate. Paul E. Peterson and Mark Rom (1989) suggest that the declines have mainly come from states trying to avoid being more generous than their counterparts, thereby attracting more poor people from out of state. Russell Hanson (1988) suggests that states have been forced to become more competitive in the leaner years of the 1970s and 1980s and have allowed benefits to decline so as to not lose out in the competition for creating a more attractive business climate. Robert Moffitt (1988) gives greater stress to the substitution effect to which we have alluded.

In any case, conservative protestations to the contrary, the deterioration of welfare benefits since the onset of the food stamps program has been real and dramatic such that welfare is worth little if any more today than it was in the 1960s.

THE WELFARE GRANT IN NEW YORK: WHAT YOU SEE IS NOT WHAT YOU GET

The deteriorating value of the welfare grant is only part of the current dilemma. Another often overlooked facet of the problem is the way in which the welfare grant is structured to limit recipients' ability to use it effectively. New York, one of the states that has suffered sharp declines in the value of welfare benefits, offers an excellent example. New York has the second largest welfare population in the United States. It is also a traditionally liberal state and therefore can serve as a litmus test. If New York's grant is deficient in various ways, it is likely that the grants of less liberal states are as well. The New York grant provides a glimpse at the convolutions inherent in one state's current welfare system and its effects on the ability of recipients to realize the full value of their benefits.

Today, New York has a partially consolidated AFDC grant. It is one of ten states that does not provide its AFDC benefits in one allowance (U.S. Department of Health and Human Services, 1989a). This system can be traced to the late 1960s when the state moved to a "flat grant" (commonly referred to as the "basic allowance") for AFDC. At that time, the state established separate grants for "basic" needs and "shelter." (Since 1981, the state has added a third grant—a home energy allowance.) This grant system actually represented a consolidation. Before 1970, welfare recipients in New York State could receive a series of "special needs grants," such as a furniture allowance every two years, in addition to a recurring monthly grant. The flat grant or basic allowance itself was originally initiated to save money. The state moved to a flat grant system in 1970 largely as a way to counter organized efforts by welfare rights groups to leverage these special grants for all their recipient members. A savings was anticipated by consolidating the grant in such a way as to reduce aggregate payments while at the same time eliminating the important organizing tool for welfare rights organizations that the special needs grants had become (Piven and Cloward, 1977; West, 1981). The flat grant also facilitated a shift to a more routine system by automatically providing the same benefit to each household (adjusted for family size). In short, the flat grant offered standardization and cost savings (Simon, 1983).

The state's flat grant is based on a "standard of need." The development of the standard was precipitated by *Rosado v. Wyman* (1970) in which the U.S. Supreme Court ruled that each state must specify an "*actual* standard of need" as the basis of its AFDC payments. The Court, however, made allowances for a state "to accommodate budgetary realities" and pay recipients less than the standard of need. The Court stated that while this system "leaves the states free to effect downward adjustments in the level of benefits paid, it accomplishes within that framework the goal, however modest, of forcing a State to accept the political consequence of such a cutback and brings to light the true extent to which actual assistance falls short of the minimum acceptable" (*Rosado v. Wyman*, 1970). In other words, states were obligated to set a rational standard based on real costs, but they were not obligated to pay it. The difference between what the state paid and what was "needed" constituted the basis for future political discourse. What the Court overlooked is that a state could underestimate need when setting its standard and then pay recipients the "full amount." In this way, a state could shortchange recipients and save money without paying a political price for the hidden shortfall. This is exactly what New York State did.

The basic grant was based on a modified version of the U.S. Bureau of Labor Statistics Lower Living Standard (LLS). The LLS was the lowest of three budgets developed by the federal government for a four-person family. It was the sum of costs of a specified list of goods and services deemed necessary for a "minimum standard of adequacy." New York's modifications consisted of making various downward adjustments to the LLS. Logically, certain categories of goods and services included in the federal LLS budget were eliminated because they were met by other grants or programs, for example, the shelter allowance. Other LLS categories were eliminated because they were determined nonessential or inappropriate items of consumption for families in need of public assistance. Consequently, the welfare grant still contains no allocation for such items as reading materials, recreation, nonpublic transportation, tobacco, alcohol, gifts, and contributions, as well as food away from home. When New York eliminated the LLS allocation for food away from home, it did not compensate by adding to the food-at-home category. Apparently, a welfare family was not only expected not to eat in restaurants but was expected to do without food completely when the LLS family dined out. Other downward modifications also took place, the most dramatic of which was a final 12 percent reduction of the remaining total based on the composition of the average welfare family and its alleged lesser needs (Downtown Welfare Advocate Center, 1979; *RAM v. Blum*, 1980).

The net result of these modifications was a welfare grant that amounted to 42 percent of the total LLS budget and only about two-thirds of the cost of comparable categories of the LLS (in other words, excluding shelter costs, occupational expenses, medical expenses, tax payments, social security and disability payments, gifts, contributions, insurance, as well as the items mentioned earlier).[3] Worse, although the newly devised grant was issued effective 1 July 1970, it was based on May 1969 prices. A family of four received a maximum of $231 month in 1970 in the basic, or nonshelter, portion of the grant; until 1990, the only actual net increase in the basic grant *per se* occurred in 1974 when benefits were brought up to the prices of the same goods and services for January 1972. All items in the basic allowance (other than utilities, to be discussed later) remained from 1974 until 1990 pegged to the cost of living in January 1972. Excluding utilities, in July 1987 (the last time comparable data were available) it cost $589 to purchase the same quantity of goods and services that the welfare grant only provided $243 to cover. As such, welfare recipients in the compassionate "family of New York" received an average of $196 per person per day to cover about half their food (food stamps added a modest amount), some of their medical expenses (Medicaid is often erroneously assumed to cover all health care needs), and all of their clothing, furniture, transportation, baby bottles, soap, school supplies, toothpaste, toilet paper, kitchen utensils, and so on (see Table 10.3). If a welfare mother took one ride on the subway in search of the elusive job and returned home again, she was already dipping into her children's benefits. Or, just consider the cost of one pair of baby shoes for feet that change size every three months.

The inadequate nature of New York's basic grant cannot be made more painfully obvious than when we consider its effects on the food budget of recipients. Even when food stamps are added to the food-at-home allocation, New York's "food package" falls short of need. In fact, the combined total for food is estimated to be less than the food package available in most other states—including Mississippi, the poorest of the fifty states. In 1979, the food stamp allotment for a four-person family

Table 10.3
The Real Value of the Basic Allowance Excluding Utilities for a Four-Person
Family per Month in New York State

Categories of Goods and Services included in the Basic Allowance (Excluding Utilities)[1]	Original Basic Allowance set at May 1969 Prices	Current Allowance set at January 1972 Prices	Actual Cost of of Items, if Allowance reflected July 1987
Food at Home[2]	$121	$137	$357
Household Furnishings	24	26	54
Public Transportation	7	9	35
Clothing	47	50	85
Personal Care	13	14	39
Education and Miscellaneous	6	7	19
Total (Excluding Utilities)	$218	$243	$589

1. Utilities are also included in the basic allowance; but in recent years, grant increases based on energy related inflation have changed the technical construction of the total welfare grant. These increases have resulted in a somewhat truer-to-real-costs allocation for utilities than for other items in the basic allowance. Originally, utilities were budgeted in the basic allowance at $13 per month and then changed to $15 per month in 1974. This $15 per month is still in the basic allowance in addition to the other items in the table. However, it would be misleading to show it as "unchanged" since 1974, because in 1981 and 1985 "home energy allowances" were added to the total monthly benefits— in effect increasing the utility portion of the grant by $68.70 for a family of four. The Home Energy Allowance is now listed as a separate grant category alongside the basic and shelter allowances.

2. Food, furnishings, clothing and personal care are adjusted according to corresponding items in the Bureau of Labor Statistics' Consumer Price Index (CPI). "Education and Miscellaneous" is no longer used as a category in the CPI and is adjusted according to the cost of the CPI's "other goods and services" category, as the closest rational approximation. Transportation is adjusted by the rate of change in the actual cost of public transportation in New York City, as per the original "standard of need."

receiving maximum AFDC benefits in New York State was $83 per month. The state assumed that $137 (29 percent) of the $476 total monthly AFDC grant was to be spent on food. The total food package for these New York families therefore was $220 a month.

In Mississippi for that year, a four-person family receiving maximum AFDC benefits was eligible for $189 a month in food stamps. Mississippi's welfare grant, which in 1979 was a maximum of $120 per month to a family of four, was designed to include 42 percent, or $50, for food. Adding the food portion of the welfare grant ($50) to the food stamp allotment ($189) brought the Mississippi total monthly "food package" to $239 or $19 more than the money available for food in New York State.[4] Using the same methodology for 1987, the gap widens to $28 with Mississippi's total food package at $331 and New York's at $303.[5]

New York recipients had, of course, more money in the rest of their AFDC budget than recipients in Mississippi and could, theoretically at least, shift funds to cover their food costs. Yet, New Yorkers would be doing this at the expense of other basic needs, which have been underbudgeted from the very beginning of the state's need standard and have fallen increasingly short of actual cost. In addition, by 1990, the position of New York's food budget vis-à-vis other states like Mississippi has not improved and, if anything, has gotten worse as changes in New York State shelter benefits have resulted in decreases in the food stamp allotments for the state's AFDC recipients. In spite of automatic cost-of-living increases in food stamps, on two occasions between 1980 and 1988, a significant downward shift in food stamps for New York State residents took place as shelter allowances were increased—an ironic and troubling circumstance explained below.

The fact that the New York grant is compartmentalized into different allowances serves to limit recipients' access to all of the grant and constrain the extent to which they can juggle it. In New York State, as in nine other states, benefits for shelter are determined separately from other benefits and are specifically allocated for housing. This benefit is paid out according to one's actual rent up to a specified maximum. If a recipient's rent is lower than the maximum (or "shelter ceiling"), the recipient's grant is accordingly lower. On the other hand, if the rent is higher than the ceiling, the excess must be taken from some other portion of the total grant—that is, from the part that is technically allocated for some other item of need. Relatively high shelter grants may make the total New York grant seem high, but they often merely pay inflated rents for the inadequate housing the poor normally get. In addition, since shelter benefits are supposed to be used only for housing, the basic grant is left to cover other needs—a job that, as already seen, it does not do well.

The problem, however, is more serious and more ironic. To be sure, some income increases have accrued to New York's welfare budget in forms other than the basic grant. For instance, the shelter allowance has been raised twice during Governor Mario Cuomo's administration for a total average increase of 51 percent. This sounds like a major benefit increase; it is. Yet the actual beneficiaries are *not* the poor, whose food stamps decrease one dollar for every three-dollar increase they receive in rent allotments. The real beneficiaries are landlords who raise their rents in direct response to each shelter allowance increase. In New York City, for instance, median gross monthly rents had risen by only 6.8 percent during the three-year stretch prior to the first shelter allowance raise implemented in 1984. Experts studying the low rent patterns concluded that the ceiling for welfare rents was acting like an informal rent control. They were right: in the very first year subsequent to the shelter grant increase the median gross monthly rent was up 7 percent and by 1986 swelled 19.7 percent (New York City Human Resources Administration, 1987). The second of these shelter grant increases was implemented in January 1988 and produced similar results.

For the most part, recipients are living in the same quality housing (usually dilapidated), paying more for it, and eating less. Since more dollars pass through their hands on the way to landlords, fewer dollars are available for buying food when their food stamps are automatically reduced. For nonwelfare poor families who share approximately the same low rent market, the effects are likely to be even worse. There is, general housing market increases are not met by automatic wage increases on the job.

There is one portion of the welfare grant in which purchasing power has actually increased: energy. In view of severe oil price inflation, the federal government in 1979 exempted energy-related public assistance grant increases from consideration in the calculation of food stamp budets if states could prove the need for such increases based on actual costs. Since New York State had severely underbudgeted utilities in the first place, and given the impact of inflation, the state was able to take advantage of this provision in 1981 and 1985, instituting and increasing a "home energy" allowance. (Several other northern states with cold winters and high heating costs did likewise.)

The first and larger of these was enacted during Governor Hugh Carey's administration following a two-year organizing drive for basic grant increases led by welfare recipients themselves. The second was initiated by Governor Cuomo, largely to offset the reduction in food stamps precipitated by the first of his two shelter grant increases. Together, these home energy supplements have added a monthly total of $68.70 to the income of a four-person family. As such, energy is the only item of need for which welfare in New York bears a resemblance to real costs.

The basic grant, the shelter allowance, and now the home energy allowance constituted New York State's standard for New York City for a three-person family in 1975 as 110.1 percent of the poverty line. By 1987, the percentage had dropped to 62.9 percent of the poverty level (Baillargeon, 1987). Even when food stamps were added in, recipients generally still fell below 75 percent of the poverty line.

Yet, viewed from the perspective of purchasing power, the New York State welfare grant looked even worse then the numbers show. For instance, the shelter allowance increased 51 percent since the ceiling was first established in 1975. Yet, the housing available to poor people in New York City, where two-thirds of the state's welfare recipients live, has never been more scarce nor in worse condition. Housing also costs far more than it ever did. That is, recipients must pay more and get less.

Purchasing power has therefore decreased even in the part of the grant that had seen the biggest increase over time.

The solution to these problems, however, is not to raise the shelter grant because of the way the housing market responds to such increases. Instead, an increase in the basic allowance would generalize to an overall increase in purchasing power because the market for items covered by the basic allowance is not sensitive to welfare benefit increases. The price of public transportation, for instance, is not sensitive to welfare grant levels in any discernible way. Therefore, increasing the allocation for public transportation should not have any effect on its cost. The result would be an increase, then, in the total purchasing power of recipients. A substantial increase is particularly critical for the basic allowance that declined so much in real value due to inflation.

The logic is clear but has yet to be followed in New York or elsewhere to any great extent (Welsh and Franklin, 1988). The net effect is that most states are currently contributing nil to the overall purchasing power of welfare recipients, while continuing declines in the real value of benefits sink people ever deeper into poverty.

In 1990, New York State finally increased the basic allowance but only by 15 percent, hardly enough to compensate for the ongoing deterioration in the real value of the welfare grant. This increase, of course, resulted in another drop in food stamps for New York State welfare recipients, thereby perhaps promoting the Cuomo administration's political popularity among liberals moreso than the interests of poor families. As of August 1987, the Bureau of Labor Statistics changed the methodology for calculating the Lower Living Standard, making extremely difficult further comparisons between changes in the rising cost of the standard and stagnant welfare grants. Even without such comparisons, the trend was clearly still one of a widening gap between what people needed and what the state was willing to provide.

CONCLUSION

We live in a time when the issues of poverty have been supplanted by the issue of "welfare dependency." Welfare is now seen as part of the problem rather than part of the solution. Increased welfare benefits and liberalized policies that started in the 1960s have allegedly been encouraging irresponsibility among the poor. Yet, the foregoing analysis of the welfare grant raises questions about this perspective.

First, the examination of national trends in welfare benefits indicates serious erosion in their real value. Since the implementation of the nationally funded food stamps program in 1974, states have shifted more of the cost for welfare to the national government. In the process, virtually all states have witnessed substantial benefit declines. Low benefit states retain benefits above their pre–food stamps levels; however, the deterioration of the welfare grant in high benefit states has been so substantial that many of them find their benefits below what they were in 1960, before the decision to wage war on poverty. On average, welfare benefits are only marginally higher than they were three decades ago.

Second, when we examine how the welfare grant has operated in one of the states that has undergone a sharp decline—New York—there is even less reason to be sanguine about the limited assistance the welfare grant affords the poor. The New York grant since 1970 has been based on an inadequate standard of need and has therefore never funded benefits at levels sufficient to meet the needs of recipients. Whereas some states only fund part of their standard of need, others like New York have understated need. In addition, New York like nine other states has a compartmentalized grant, and recipients cannot simply receive benefits and use them as they are needed. Shelter grants, for instance, are limited to housing costs. To compound the problem, in recent years, increases in the shelter allowance have resulted in rent increases. In turn, recipients receive more in AFDC shelter payments only to dole out more in rent and to receive less in food stamps. The problems of New York's grant may not be generalizable to other states, but they may be an indication of how the diversity and complexity of the current welfare grant system operates so as to impose serious limitations on the ability of recipients to use effectively what benefits they do receive.

The problems of the welfare grant today stem less from the prospect that it might encourage "dependency" and more from its ineffectiveness in supplying worthwhile assistance to those who need it. While conservatives have been arguing that welfare benefits are too high, the poor have been getting fewer benefits under conditions that further limit these benefits. It just may be that we have more and deeper poverty not because of "welfare dependency," but because we are providing the poor with less than they need. As simple as this is, the banal reality of the relationship of welfare to poverty is not readily recognized in the current political climate.

NOTES

An earlier version of this paper was presented at the 20th Annual Meeting of the Northeastern Political Science Association, Providence, Rhode Island, 12 November 1988. Evelyn Brodkin, Henry Freedman, Russell Hanson, Richard Hula, Maurice McDonald, and Robert Moffitt provided helpful comments. Thanks are extended to Tina Seda and Ryan Schram for assistance in the research, to Pat Turbett for help on the data calculations, to Michael Wiseman for suggestions regarding national trends, and to Tom Sanzillo and Cynthia Mann for considerations on the New York State analysis.

1. The Reagan administration stressed the idea of an emerging New Consen-

sus on welfare (Domestic Policy Council Low Income Opportunity Working Group, 1987). For the views of conservatives on the New Consensus, see Novak et al. (1987) and Mead (1987). For the views of liberals, see Garfinkel (1987). For a critical assessment of the New Consensus, see Handler (1988).

2. The Commodity Distribution Program started in the 1930s, expanded after changes in 1949 and 1954, and by 1963 reached 7,019,000 recipients. Precise figures for the value of food commodities in all states are unavailable. From 1961, food stamps existed in some counties, while others had the food commodity distribution program. By 1967, more AFDC recipients got food stamps than commodities, though participation in both programs was not high (see Hollings, 1970, pp. 198–268; Kotz, 1969, pp. 44–56; McDonald, 1977).

3. These calculations are based on data from U.S. Department of Labor (1972).

4. For figures on AFDC and food stamps benefits in each state, see Kasten and Todd (1980, Tables 7 and 9). For figures on the proportion of the AFDC budget that went for food in each state in 1979, see U.S. Department of Health and Human Services (1980, pp. 51–52).

5. These calculations are based on AFDC figures from U.S. Department of Health and Human Services (1987a, pp. 402–403) and food stamp amounts from the Center for Social Welfare Policy and Law.

11

Reagan's Federalism and Family Planning Services: Implications for Family Policy

Deborah R. McFarlane

The restructuring of federalism was a major priority for the Reagan administration. President Ronald Reagan believed that many domestic responsibilities had been usurped by the federal government, and he wanted to return those responsibilities to the states (Peterson, 1984). Toward that end, the president envisioned a two-stage process. First, the federal grant system required dramatic changes. Reagan proposed consolidation of eighty-four of the three hundred federal categorical grants into six block grants with reduced funding. In the health area alone, he proposed aggregating twenty-five categorical programs into two block grants. Block grants would remove categorical restrictions and turn most of the policy discretion over to the states (Peterson et al., 1986). The second stage would develop gradually. As states became accustomed to making their own policy decisions with more flexible federal dollars (i.e., block grants), they would slowly assume full responsibility for their own needs and services. The president argued that states would be more responsive to their own needs than was the federal government (Rosoff, 1981).

Reagan did not get all that he wanted, but major changes were implemented. Congress consolidated fifty-seven, instead of eighty-four, categorical grants into nine, not three, block grants. Overall, funds were reduced by approximately 9 percent from the 1981 categorical grant levels. The reductions for individual health programs ranged from 17 percent to 45 percent. Even though these changes were much less than what Reagan had proposed, the 1981 block grant consolidations made up the largest grant agglomeration ever enacted by Congress (Peterson et al., 1986).

FAMILY PLANNING POLICY

Public funding for family planning services began in the 1960s. Although both the federal and state governments provided support for these services, the federal government played the preeminent role. During fiscal 1965–1975, the federal government spent approximately $629.9 million for family planning while the states spent an estimated $70.2 million. Four statutes authorized most of the federal funds that supported publicly subsidized family planning services during fiscal 1976–1985: Title V of the Social Security Act, Title X of the Public Health Service Act, Title XIX of the Social Security Act, and Title XX of the Social Security Act. In spite of Reagan's effort to block federal categorical programs, all of these enactments survived the budgetary politics of 1981, albeit with substantial changes. These federal statutes and their amendments as well as state appropriations for family planning are explained in Table 11.1.

Title V

Under this statute, maternal and child health monies were awarded on a formula basis to state health departments. States were required to match federal dollars one to one. In 1967, Title V was amended to stipulate that 6 percent of all Maternal and Child Health (MCH) funds had to be spent for family planning. However, this requirement was national; individually, states did not have to spend 6 percent of their Title V grants for family planning.

In 1981, the 6 percent requirement was removed, becoming effective in fiscal 1982. The match rate was also changed: for every $3 contributed by the federal government, the states had to match with $4. In the same year, eight existing federal programs—including MCH—were consolidated under Title V, with a 17 percent reduction in the fiscal 1981 appropriation. At the state level, the result of these changes meant that family planning services had to compete with more programs for less money than had been the case during the six-year period prior to the Reagan administration.

Title X

The Family Planning and Population Research Act of 1970 enacted Title X of the Public Health Service Act. Title X was the first and remains the only national legislation addressing just family planning and related issues. Prior to fiscal 1985, Title X was the largest single contributor to public funding for family planning. Unlike the other grants, these categorical funds were administered by the regional offices of the Public

Table 11.1
Federal Statutes Authorizing Federal Funding for Family Planning Services, FY 1976–1987

Statute	Grant and Administrative Mechanisms	Specific Family Planning Provisions	Changes Since Reagan
Title V, Social Security Act (Maternal and Child Health)	Formula grants matched by the states administered by state health departments	FY 68-81: Stipulation that 6% of all Title V funds be spent on family planning.	(1) The 6% requirement was removed. (2) More programs were consolidated under Title V. (3) 17% reduction in funds.
Title X, Public Health Service Act (Family Planning)	Project grants administered by the 10 regional offices of the Public Health Service	Categorical legislation	(1) 20% reduction in funds. (2) Reassignment of many grants to state health departments.
Title XIX, Social Security Act (Medicaid)	Reimbursement of providers for individual services. Federal government matches states' expenditures at different rates. Administered by state agencies, either the health or welfare department. No federal ceiling on Title XIX expenditures.	FY 72-85: 90% federal match for family planning services.	No changes for family planning (1) 90% match retained and (2) no federal ceiling.
Title XX, Social Security Act (Social Services Block Grant)	Block grant to state agency, usually welfare department. FY 76-81: Federal government reimbursed states for services rendered at 75% of cost, up to a certain ceiling based on state population.	FY 76-81: 90% federal match for family planning. 1% penalty for failure to provide family planning services to AFDC recipients.	(1) Elimination of 90% match. (2) Reduction in funds.

Health Service (PHS). Grants were awarded on a competitive basis to projects that either delivered or subcontracted for services. Unlike the other three federal grant programs, Title X did not mandate that a state agency had to be a grantee, though state agencies (e.g., state health departments) were certainly not excluded from seeking these funds.

Title X survived Reagan's effort to block categorical programs. Title X was reauthorized for fiscal 1982 although it was cut sharply, a 20 percent reduction from the fiscal 1981 appropriation. In many states, the Title X grants were consolidated, and the state health department became the only grantee.

Title XIX

Title XIX of the Social Security Act required administration by a state agency. In most states, the state welfare department administered the Medicaid program. In some states, however, Medicaid was managed by the state health department or a state umbrella agency (e.g., health and welfare combined). Medicaid programs reimbursed providers for services rendered to eligible persons. The federal government, in turn, reimbursed the states for 90 percent of their Medicaid expenditures for family planning. This 90 percent match was a more favorable rate than the states received for other Medicaid services; the match rate ranged from 50 percent to 83 percent, depending on the health status of the state.

After Reagan became president, the rates of federal reimbursement to the states were reduced (3 percent in fiscal 1982, 4 percent in fiscal 1983, and 5 percent in fiscal 1985); however, the 90 percent match for family planning services remained. Moreover, the administration's attempts to cap or place a ceiling upon total Medicaid expenditures were unsuccessful. The more states spent, the more the federal government had to spend for this program. It is noteworthy that the Medicaid program was the only one of the four sources of federal funding that actually increased its family planning expenditures during the Reagan years.

Title XX

Title XX block grant funds were allocated to states on the basis of population. Title XX required administration by state welfare departments. During the Ford and Carter years, the federal government reimbursed the states at a $3:1 rate. Family planning and daycare services, however, received a 90 percent federal match ($9:1). Unlike the Medicaid program, Title XX always had a national ceiling, that is, a limit or cap on the total amount that could be spent under this program.

Under Reagan, the new social services block grant was also codified as Title XX of the Social Security Act. Like Title V, the revised Title XX was reduced overall ($2.4 billion for fiscal 1982 from what was to have been $3 billion). States were no longer required to match federal funds, thereby eliminating the favorable 90 percent match for family planning services.

State Appropriations

During the six-year period prior to the Reagan administration, state funds accounted for an average of 13 percent of public expenditures for family planning, as shown in Table 11.2. Throughout both periods, state appropriations gradually increased. They represented a greater share (16 percent) of all public expenditures for family planning during the Reagan years, largely because of the cutbacks in federal funds.

ASSESSING THE EFFECTS OF DECENTRALIZATION

In the case of family planning, the implementation of Reagan's decentralization policy was complex. No simple change occurred from only federal categorical support to just block grants and state appropriations. What changed for family planning was the amount and composition of funds that were available.

How did these changes affect program performance? The most direct measure of family planning program performance is the number of patients served through public programs in a year (Bogue, 1970). Unfortunately, these data are not available. The National Reporting System for Family Planning Statistics, which was designed to collect patient statistics, was disbanded by the Reagan administration in 1981. The other major source of family planning data, the Alan Guttmacher Institute, has not developed estimates of patients served since 1981 (AGI, 1983).

Expenditure data by source of funding are available for fiscal 1982–1987[1] as well as for the six-year period prior to the Reagan administration (Gold and Guardado, 1988). Assuming that the costs of serving family planning patients are relatively standardized across the states, expenditures may be considered reasonable proxies for program outputs. For example, given an average cost of $75 per family planning patient in 1981, a state that spent $150,000 for family planning services would have served an estimated 2,000 patients per year. In terms of actual expenditures, the outputs of the national family planning program decreased nearly 12 percent from fiscal 1981 to $327.7 million in fiscal 1982. These reductions cannot be completely attributed to structural modifications. All of the pertinent federal programs had been cut back significantly, so even in the absence of structural changes, decreases in expenditures would have been expected. In the short run, the slight increases in state

Table 11.2
Public Expenditures for Family Planning Services Adjusted for Inflation by Source of Funding, FY 1976–1987 (in 1982 dollars, dollars in millions)

Source of Funding	Before Reagan					*	During Reagan					
	1976	1977	1978	1979	1980	*	1981	*	1982	1983	1985	1987
Title V	$ 36.5	$ 39.8	$ 32.1	$ 28.0	$ 25.7	*	$ 24.4	*	$ 16.6	$ 17.8	$ 18.9	$23.8
Title X	$160.6	$174.7	$195.6	$175.0	$189.2	*	$167.4	*	$118.1	$109.2	$109.7	$100.5
Title XIX	$ 72.4	$ 76.0	$ 54.4	$ 69.4	$ 85.5	*	$ 98.6	*	$ 93.7	$100.3	$112.7	$27.1
Title XX	$ 55.4	$ 65.1	$ 82.4	$ 70.4	$ 70.5	*	$ 59.8	*	$ 46.2	$ 35.4	$ 32.9	$38.4
State Appropriations	$ 40.3	$ 35.7	$ 48.6	$ 66.7	$ 63.3	*	$ 57.8	*	$ 53.1	$ 53.8	$ 52.5	$38.4
Total	$365.0	$391.4	$410.5	$407.6	$434.2	*	$408.1	*	$327.7	$316.5	$326.8	$228.2

Sources of Raw Data: The Alan Guttmacher Institute and the Survey of Current Business (U.S. Department of Commerce, Bureau of Economic Analysis).

appropriations did not even begin to replace the cutbacks in federal funds.

Inflation, of course, affects the capacity of programs to provide services. Table 11.2 shows national family planning expenditures for fiscal 1976–1987, adjusted for inflation using 1982 dollars as a constant.[2] This adjustment shows an even more pronounced decline in the capacity of programs to deliver services after 1981. Adjusted state appropriations dropped slightly in fiscal 1982 and remained at about the same level through fiscal 1985, dropping off again in 1987. Together, block grant expenditures (Titles V and XX) decreased after fiscal 1981 until 1987 when block grant family planning expenditures showed a slight rise.

The effects of the cutbacks and structural modifications on individual states has been uneven. In fourteen states, public expenditures for family planning were actually less in fiscal 1987 than they had been in fiscal 1981. When these outlays were adjusted for inflation, all but ten states showed a decrease in family planning outlays during the same period. Indeed, twenty states reported more than a 25 percent decrease in public spending for family planning services.

How have the cutbacks and structural modifications affected program effectiveness? One of the most widely used measures of family planning effectiveness is "met need," which is the number of patients served per year divided by the target population. The denominator, "women in need," has been the conventional method for estimating target populations for publicly subsidized family planning programs in the United States for nearly twenty years. "Women in need" includes low income, sexually active, fecund women who are not currently pregnant or trying to become pregnant (Dryfoos, 1973; 1975; Torres et al., 1981; AGI, 1988). As discussed earlier, data for the numerator of the met need measure are unavailable. However, expenditures for family planning services can be used as a proxy for the number of patients served.

Table 11.3 shows the annual adjusted expenditures (1982 dollars) per woman in need by source.[3] The average annual cost for a publicly subsidized patient was $87.62 in 1982 dollars (Chamie and Henshaw, 1981). In other words, the government should be spending at least $87.62 times the number of women in the target population in order to be 100 percent effective. If the public sector is spending less than $87.62 per woman in need, then the public sector is almost certainly not funding services for all the women that have been identified as "in need." The last row in Table 11.3 estimates the percentage of family planning need (WIN) that was met in each fiscal year. Nationally, the public sector had the capacity to serve 66.9 percent ($58.64/$87.62) of the target population in fiscal 1976, while that capacity was only 38.1 percent ($34/$87.62) in fiscal 1983. We would say that, at most, the family planning program was 72 percent effective in fiscal 1977 but only 31 percent effective in fiscal 1987.

Table 11.3
Family Planning Expenditures per "Woman in Need,"[1] FY 1976–1987 (in constant 1982 dollars)

Source of Funding	Before Reagan						*	During Reagan				
	1976	1977	1978	1979	1980	1981		1982	*	1983	1985[4]	1987
Title V	$ 5.86	$ 6.39	$ 4.42	$ 3.86	$ 3.35	$ 3.18	*	$ 1.75	*	$ 1.88	$ 1.99	$ 2.47
Title X	$25.80	$28.05	$26.96	$24.12	$24.64	$21.80	*	$12.44	*	$11.50	$11.56	$ 8.76
Title XIX[2]	$11.62	$12.20	$ 7.50	$ 9.56	$11.13	$12.84	*	$ 9.87	*	$10.57	$11.87	$ 9.00
Title XX[3]	$ 8.89	$10.45	$ 1.36	$ 9.56	$ 9.18	$ 7.79	*	$ 4.87	*	$ 3.73	$ 3.46	$ 2.63
State Appropriations	$ 6.47	$ 5.73	$ 6.70	$ 9.19	$ 8.24	$ 7.52	*	$ 5.59	*	$ 5.67	$ 5.53	$ 4.20
Total	$58.64	$62.82	$55.94	$56.29	$56.54	$53.13	*	$34.46	*	$33.33	$34.41	$27.06
% Need Met	66.9%	71.7%	64.6%	64.1%	64.5%	60.6%	*	39.0%	*	38.1%	39.3%	31.0%

1. Due to rounding, the percentages may not add up to 100.
2. Includes expenditures for contraceptive services only.
3. Includes expenditures for medical services only.
4. Expenditure data were not collected for FY84 or FY86.
Source of Raw Data: The Alan Guttmacher Institute.

The fiscal effectiveness of the family planning program varied by state both before and during the Reagan administration. On the whole, states became less effective in meeting their respective family planning needs after 1981. For example, the average public expenditure (in 1982 dollars) for family planning services in 1981 was $53.13 per woman in need. For fiscal 1982, this figure had dropped to $34.52.

The variation among the states in family planning expenditures per woman in need increased during the Reagan administration.[4] The change in the composition of available funds was the major reason for the increased variation. Across both periods, Title X, the categorical grant program, showed considerably less variation in dollars spent per woman in need than did the other enactments. However, Title X's proportionate share of public family planning funds decreased after 1981. More fiscal discretion had been turned back to the states, meaning that a greater proportion of family planning expenditures emanated from less restrictive state-administered funds. Many states simply chose not to spend their discretionary funds for family planning. For example, twenty-three states reported spending no Title XX dollars for family planning in fiscal 1983, while only two states reported no Title XX family planning expenditures in fiscal 1979. Seven states, however, reported sizeable increases in their Title XX family planning expenditures during the same period.

To summarize, as assessment of the effects of a more decentralized family planning policy includes these findings:

1. Spending for family planning decreased, though it is difficult to separate the effects of structural modifications from actual budget cuts.
2. Accountability was diminished at the same time as budgets were cut. Family planning patient statistics were no longer collected at the national level.
3. The estimated number of patients served by public family planning programs decreased due to both lower expenditures and annual inflation rates.
4. The effectiveness of public family planning programs in serving lower income women in need decreased because of budget cuts, inflation, and growing target populations.
5. The variation in family planning program effectiveness among the states increased largely because of the difference in the composition of public funds. State-administered public funds—including Titles V, XIX, and XX and state appropriations—showed much more variation than did Title X throughout fiscal 1976–87.

IMPACT ON WOMEN AND FAMILIES

The above effects have had profound implications for low income women and their families. As a result of the budget cuts, fewer low income women received services from organized family planning programs. Even though many agencies implemented efficient measures such as sliding fee scales and greater utilization of nurse practitioners, these were not nearly enough to offset the decrease in funding (Torres et al., 1981; Orr, 1983). Moreover, inflation continued so that the budget cuts had even more severe consequences than actual expenditures would show.

At the same time, the number of low income women in need of subsidized family planning services continued to increase. This trend, along with the decreased capacity of programs to serve patients, meant that program effectiveness was reduced. Nationally, the family planning program was no longer able to maintain the same level of met need. Moreover, the variation among the states in program effectiveness increased. In other words, opportunities for low income women to receive publicly subsidized family planning services became more dependent on the state in which they lived than they were before Reagan took office.

Fewer patients were served and resources were distributed less equitably across the country. Furthermore, many programs cut back their outreach services, meaning that hard-to-reach patients, such as teenagers, were no longer actively recruited (Torres, 1983; Lincoln, 1984). Established programs were more likely to continue to serve already enrolled patients than to seek new ones, and the severe cutbacks precluded many new programs from receiving public funds. Undoubtedly, some fraction of the target population (women in need) did find alternative sources for family planning services. However, other health and social services also experienced severe cutbacks (Zabin, 1983) so that overall such opportunities were not plentiful. Because teenagers enrolled in organized family planning programs are more likely than others to be effective contraceptors (Furstenberg et al., 1983), one can only conclude that the incidence of unwanted pregnancy must have increased.

The consequences of unwanted pregnancy have been widely documented. These include increased abortion rates, marital instability, and a higher incidence of child abuse. Most of the costs of unwanted fertility, however, "are not visible in the dramatic instances of abandonment or child abuse, but in the more prosaic problems of everyday family life. Family budgets can be seriously strained by the unexpected and unwanted birth of a child." Moreover, the same families that are most affected by unwanted births are the ones who most often experience them (Commission on Population Growth and the American Future, 1972, pp. 97–98).

IMPLICATIONS FOR FAMILY POLICY

These effects are ironic given the profamily stance of the Reagan administration. Planned fertility is associated with marital stability, economic self-sufficiency, and child development, all of which can enhance the family as a social unit. Perhaps the administration was unaware that the proposed structural changes would be so damaging to the national family planning program. An alternative explanation is that for the Reagan administration and much of its conservative constituency, the ends of family planning simply do not justify the means.

Was the Administration Unaware?

The impact of budget cuts and decentralized family planning policy certainly was predictable given past experience. The magnitude of the cuts along with inflation almost certainly meant that services would have to be cut. Moreover, federal block grants and state appropriations have consistently produced more variation in state spending for family planning than has categorical funding. Experience both before and during the Reagan administration has demonstrated that Title X has been the most equitable mechanism for distributing federal funds for family planning in the state. Nevertheless, the administration targeted (unsuccessfully) Title X for extinction.[5]

The claim that states would be more responsive to their own needs appears to have been little more than rhetoric, at least in the case of family planning services. Instead, the restructuring of federalism and the concomitant reduction of funds was apparently a political strategy for reducing services not favored by the administration. This maneuver is not new. Since before the New Deal, recognition of the greater reluctance of state governments to be generous toward low income persons has been the keystone of the political strategy of those at the national level who are opposed to measures that increase the well-being of the poor (Vladeck, 1980).

Ends Don't Justify Means

Although the administration purported a profamily stance, its conception of what desirable family attributes were was quite narrow compared to the range of circumstances in American society (see Chapter 2 in this volume). The White House view of the family includes or implies the following tenets:

1. intact families, with both natural mother and father present, thus requiring permanent marriage;
2. chastity before marriage and monogamy after;
3. the duty of married couples to have children;
4. an obligation to live for one's children; and
5. the undesirability of mothers working outside of the home.

Although many Americans may verbalize some or all of these tenets, the majority do not adhere to them. Divorce rates are high, and only a minority of marriages turn out to be permanent. Most men and women are not virgins when they reach the altar, and monogamy is not always practiced. Many married couples do delay childbearing, some choose not to reproduce, and nearly everyone utilizes birth control at some point during their reproductive years. Increasingly, many mothers work outside of the home in order to support their children.

The problem that Reagan and many conservatives have with family planning is that instead of being normative and prescribing certain behaviors, this service, by its very nature, recognizes the above realities. Family planning enables people, usually women, to control their fertility. By dispensing birth control, family planning services enable persons to limit the number of children that they will have. And by dispensing birth control to teens, family planning programs accept the fact that most young women are sexually active before marriage. While family planning programs do not necessarily promote behaviors that are contrary to the tenets espoused by the White House, the provision of these services inherently accepts the existence of behaviors outside of the conservative ideal. Moreover, many conservatives have been unable to separate the provision of contraceptive and sterilization services from the abortion issue, even though abortion is specifically excluded from family planning funding.

Family Planning and Family Policy

Should family planning be a component of national family policy as it may develop? Certainly, the conservative constituency that developed the Bauer Report would reject such a notion, but discussions of family policy are likely to continue in a post-Reagan White House. As explained earlier, family planning programs can deliver tangible benefits for women and their families, such as an increased likelihood of marital stability, fewer abortions, and a higher quality of life for children. Publicly subsidized family planning programs should be one of the primary vehicles in the implementation of a progressive family policy.

The incorporation of existing family planning legislation, namely Title X, into an enactment of family policy would be a mistake. To a large extent, Title X survived the Reagan years because it was visible and accountable to its supporters (Dryfoos, 1987). The future of family planning under a broader family policy is far from clear. "At this point," as Patricia Spakes says in Chapter 3, "there is no shared vision of what American family policy can and should look like, nor of how it is to be implemented" (p. 24). In spite of the benefits that birth control services provide to families, many family policy proponents feel that these services are unacceptable. In a scenario where conservatives dominate the family policy agenda, publicly supported family planning services could be lost altogether. Nearly twenty years of experience have shown that the national family planning program has a much better chance of survival with the project grant mechanism under congressional oversight than with other types of funding mechanisms, especially those administered by the states. The battle for categorically supported family planning programs has been too hard fought to relinquish it for the uncertainties of future family policy (Dryfoos, 1987).

NOTES

An earlier version of this paper was presented at the 1988 Midwest Political Science Association Annual Meeting.

1. Expenditure data for fiscal 1984 and 1986 were not collected.

2. The annual adjustment factors for medical expenses are 55.4 percent (1976), 60.5 percent (1977), 66 percent (1978), 72.4 percent (1979), 80.9 percent (1980), 90.9 percent (1981), 100 percent (1982), 107.2 percent (1983), 114.8 percent (1984), 121.7 percent (1985), 128.1 percent (1986), and 130.1 percent (1987) (U.S. Department of Commerce, 1987). In terms of purchasing power for medical care, $1 in 1982 would be worth 55 cents in 1976, and the same $1 would be worth $1.28 in 1985.

3. FY 1976 and FY 1977 expenditures are adjusted by WIN estimates for 1975. FY 1978 and FY 1979 expenditures are adjusted by 1979 estimates. FY 1980 and FY 1981 expenditures are divided by 1980 WIN estimates. FY 1982–1987 are adjusted by 1981 WIN estimates.

4. Coefficients of variation, instead of standard deviations, are used to measure the variation in dollars spent per woman in need here. The standard deviation would not be an appropriate measure because the appropriations for each of the funding sources differ greatly. The coefficient of variation is the standard deviation divided by the population mean (σ/μ), a statistic that permits comparison of the variances of different populations. The larger coefficient of variation indicates more variation than does a smaller coefficient.

5. "I regret that we do not have the votes to defeat the family planning program . . . " (President Ronald Reagan, 28 July 1981, quoted in Alan Guttmacher Institute, 1987).

12

Child Support and the Feminization of Poverty

Andrea H. Beller and Seung Sin Chung

U.S. families are undergoing a major transition: they are changing in form from predominantly two-parent families to single-parent families, usually headed by a woman. Female-headed single-parent families now comprise nearly one-fifth of all families with children under 18 present, almost double their proportion in 1970 (U.S. Bureau of the Census, 1989). The consequences of this transition are of particular concern when we consider that if recent trends continue, six out of every ten children born today will spend some time living in a single-parent family (Norton and Glick, 1986). For black children, this proportion approaches nine out of ten (Garfinkel and McLanahan, 1986, p. 8). The female-headed single-parent family is a source of stress because such families are likely to exist at relatively low levels of economic well-being. Moreover, this type of family makes up a disproportionately large share of the population living in poverty, a fact which has led to the coining of the expression "the feminization of poverty" (Pearce, 1978). An important option for support to single-parent families is child support payments.

This chapter focuses on the following topics: (1) the sources of growth in female-headed single-parent families and their economic status; (2) the situation regarding child support payments in the United States today, both in terms of levels and trends; (3) the child support enforcement system as it presently stands in the United States, its problems, and its potential for reducing poverty and welfare dependency; and (4) two alternative systems of child support. We conclude by suggesting a more comprehensive system for reducing poverty.

FEMALE-HEADED SINGLE-PARENT FAMILIES: GROWTH AND ECONOMIC STATUS

The growth of the single-parent family comes from increases in divorce rates and in the rate of children born out of wedlock. The rate of divorce increased annually from 2.2 divorces per 1,000 total population in 1962 to a peak of 5.3 per 1,000 population in 1981. The rate has dropped slightly since then, but the United States still has the highest divorce rate in the world.[1] As for illegitimacy, roughly one in four births in 1986 were to unmarried mothers, triple the rate of the mid-1960s (U.S. Bureau of the Census, 1988). Of female-headed single-parent families, divorced and separated mothers form about two-thirds of the population, while never-married mothers form about one-fifth (U.S. Bureau of the Census, 1984, p. 7). One should realize that many divorced and separated mothers eventually do remarry resulting in substantial improvement in their family's economic well-being. However, proposing remarriage is not exactly a suitable public policy treatment for the feminization of poverty, nor does it excuse a man from the obligation to support his children.

It has become widely recognized that the economic well-being of women and children deteriorates substantially following a divorce, while that of men tends to increase. According to popularly cited figures from a study by Lenore J. Weitzman (1985), after divorce, income in relation to needs decreases 73 percent for women and children but increases 42 percent for men.[2] While the dramatic magnitude of the former figure has been challenged, even the lower 30 percent figure found by Saul Hoffman and Greg Duncan (1988) affirms the fundamental point that women and children face considerable economic hardship after divorce. Many of these women and children fall into poverty.

The incidence of poverty is far greater among single-parent families headed by women than among other types of families.[3] Of the 8.8 million women with children present and father absent in 1985, 2.8 million had incomes below the poverty level.[4] Of the 3 million who were divorced, 26 percent had incomes below the poverty level (U.S. Bureau of the Census, 1987b, p. 5).

Why are families headed by women so likely to fall into poverty? The reasons concern family size, the smaller earned incomes of women with respect to men, and the failure of men to contribute to the support of their children. Family size plays a role when, after divorce, women typically get custody of the children. Thus, their incomes must be spread over more people than the man's.

Through 1979, women working full-time earned roughly 62 percent of what men earned. Recent statistics (second quarter of 1987) show this female-to-male earnings ratio reached a new high of 71 percent (U.S. Bureau of Labor Statistics, 1987). Even at these increased levels, if the woman and her children have to rely solely on her earnings, they would be substantially worse off than the man. This is because her earnings are lower and she has more mouths to feed. Of equal concern is the question of the children and related costs. If the mother works full time, expenses for child care reduce her income still further, placing her and the children at an even lower level of economic well-being relative to him.

Many absent fathers do not contribute to the support of their children, leaving this task instead to the woman and/or to the state.[5] Surprisingly, many women do not even have a child support award; among those that do, a high proportion do not receive payment.[6] According to a recent survey, although over one-third of the 3.4 million women who did not have a child support award did not want one, nearly half said they wanted but were unable to obtain one (U.S. Bureau of the Census, 1987b, p. 3).

The absence of child support is a significant contributing factor to the relatively low level of living of women and their children. The poverty rate in 1985 for women who did not have a child support award was 49 percent; for those who did, it was 21 percent. Among those women awarded child support, the poverty rate was 18 percent if they received payments and 27 percent if they did not (U.S. Bureau of the Census, 1987b, p. 11). Among women below poverty level with children from an absent father, about 40 percent had a child support award, whereas among women above the poverty line, 71 percent had an award (U.S. Bureau of the Census, 1987b, p. 5). These figures suggest that securing more child support from absent fathers should help to alleviate poverty among single-parent families.

CHILD SUPPORT PAYMENTS IN THE UNITED STATES

Interest in improving the nation's child support enforcement system has reached an all-time high for several reasons. These include: (1) alarming statistics on nonpayment rates; (2) the priority placed by the Reagan administration on reducing the welfare rolls; and (3) current social emphasis on the role of the family. In 1980, the Bureau of the Census released alarming statistics on nonpayment rates (U.S. Bureau of the Census, 1980). These statistics show that in 1979 only 59 percent of mothers with children from an absent father had a child support award. Among those with an award and due payment in 1978, only about half received full payment. About one-quarter received partial payment, and one-quarter received no payment at all. Moreover, payments that were made were often irregular. The average annual amount of child support received among those who received some was only $1,800 for an average of almost two children (U.S. Bureau of the Census, 1981, p. 5).

The situation was considerably worse than average among black mothers and never-married mothers. Only about one-third of black mothers had a child support award, and, among those that did, the award amount was about 18 percent lower than for nonblacks (Beller and Graham, 1986). Only 11 percent of never-married mothers had an award. Award amounts were less than half as much as for divorced mothers (Beller and Graham, 1986).

The Reagan administration placed a high priority on reducing the welfare rolls. Getting absent fathers to support their children was seen as one means of accomplishing this goal. Also, social emphasis on the role of the family and the place of private rather than public transfers facilitated child support payments becoming a nonpartisan issue.

Trends in Payments

In order to assess what has transpired in child support payments since that first Census report, trends through 1986 were analyzed based upon three more Census surveys comparable to the one in 1979. The data on trends in award rates, recipiency rates (the proportion of women due child support who received something), and the amounts received indicate a mixed picture.

While the child support award rate remained reasonably constant at around 59 percent from 1979 to 1984, it rose to 61 percent in 1986 (U.S. Bureau of the Census, 1985a; 1987b). This suggests that the likelihood of being awarded child support increased from 1984 to 1986. Indeed, the award rate rose for all racial and all marital status groups over this period (U.S. Bureau of the Census 1985b; 1987b). Interestingly, groups with the lowest award rates appear to have made the most progress over the entire period. Among blacks, the award rate increased continuously from 29 percent in 1979 to 36 percent in 1986. It also increased continuously among the never-married from 11 to 18 percent (U.S. Bureau of the Census, 1981; 1985a; 1985b; 1987b). In disaggregated analyses, A. H. Beller and J. W. Graham (1986) found that the trend toward a greater prevalence of child support awards had been going on throughout the 1960s and 1970s and had always been stronger among blacks than among nonblacks.

In sharp contrast to the increase in the award rate, the recipiency rate appears to have declined between 1983 and 1985. The proportion of women who actually received payment in 1985, 74 percent, was down slightly from the 76 percent who had received payment in 1983, although it was still higher than the 72 percent who had received payment in 1978 and 1981 (U.S. Bureau of the Census, 1987b; 1985a; 1985b; 1981). Again, there are racial differences. The steady increase in award rates among blacks has been accompanied by a steady increase in recipiency rates;

these rates rose from 63 percent in 1978 to 72 percent in 1985. Among the never-married, recipiency rates rose steadily from 1981 through 1985 (U.S. Bureau of the Census, 1985b; 1985a; 1987b).[7]

Along with the decline in the rate of receipt came a decline of 12 percent in the mean amount of child support received (among women who received some) in constant dollars between 1983 and 1985 (U.S. Bureau of the Census, 1987b, p. 4). This was viewed as disappointing because it followed a period of constancy between 1981 and 1983 and was deemed significant enough to warrant national headlines. The *New York Times* on 23 August 1987 quoted Nancy Ebb of the Children's Defense Fund as saying in reference to the decline in child support amounts, "That's certainly disheartening." The article also quoted the Census Bureau's expert on the data, Ruth Sanders, in saying that the Census Bureau did not know why the decline occurred (*Child support amounts*, 1987). Payments corrected for inflation had also declined by 16 percent between 1978 and 1981 (U.S. Bureau of the Census, 1985a, p. 2). That earlier decline was not terribly surprising because it occurred during a period of extremely high inflation (the Consumer Price Index rose about 40 percent), but inflation was much lower between 1983 and 1985, only about 7 percent. (During a period of high inflation, the value of child support awards made in earlier years declines because they typically do not have automatic adjustment clauses in them [Krause, 1981]. What is surprising is that the real value of new child support awards also decreased between 1978 and 1981 even more than the value of old awards [Beller and Graham, 1986, p. 241].)

One possible explanation for the recent decline in child support received is a change in the composition of the population of men with child support obligations. Since the award rate increased between 1983 and 1985, men with smaller incomes may have been added to the population owing child support. Their corresponding smaller payments would tend to reduce the average amount received. However, the award rate increased among both whites and blacks, while real child support payments fell only among whites (U.S. Bureau of the Census, 1987b, p. 4). Thus, no simple explanation appears evident. Further research on the reasons for the real decline in child support is needed; Beller and Graham (1990) explore this question.

Aside from the obvious, what benefits can be expected from the receipt of child support; in other words, why the concern about increasing its receipt? First, there is the possibility of a reduction in poverty and welfare dependency for the family. Second, according to one study, fathers who pay child support have more contact with their children (Chambers, 1979, pp. 127–128). Increased parental contact is associated with greater educational attainment in children (see, for example, Krein and Beller, 1988). Third, women who receive child support income tend to have higher incomes from other sources as well. Such women are more likely to be in the labor force and work longer hours than women who do not receive child support, although causality in this relationship has not been fully untangled.[8] Thus, considerable economic and social benefits may be gained by increased receipt of child support. Benefits are likely to accrue not only to mothers and children but also to the federal and state governments in the form of savings from Aid to Families with Dependent Children (AFDC) and other welfare programs.

Child Support Enforcement

What is the nature of our system for enforcing child support obligations? It is basically a state system, whereby each state has its own set of laws stipulating various techniques to enforce child support obligations. Federal initiatives to establish a national enforcement program began in 1975 with the passage of Title IV-D of the Social Security Act. Prior to that date, it was believed that states were not doing an effective job of enforcing child support obligations (Katz, 1983). Title IV-D established the Office of Child Support Enforcement to administer the nationwide child support enforcement (CSE) program and a federal Parent Locator Service. It required each state to develop a CSE program to assist in establishing paternity, locating absent parents, establishing obligations for child support, and enforcing such obligations. Since 1975, many states have enacted new child support laws.

As we have seen, many women do not receive the child support to which they are entitled. In our opinion, this is due in part to several problems with our child support enforcement system. First, the whole burden of obtaining and enforcing an award rests on the woman. Child support is not viewed as her right, but rather as something for which she must fight. In the past, if the man did not pay, the woman had to go back to court. This meant she had to take time off from work in addition to paying an attorney unless (after 1975) she used the state IV-D office. Second, there are a number of ways that absent fathers can escape their obligations. In the past, moving to another state, especially one with weak laws, was an effective means of escaping one's obligation. Now, it is less foolproof, but enforcing interstate obligations is still difficult. One way to escape a large award is by hiding income in self-employment. Additionally, unemployed men and men who change jobs frequently pose a particular problem for collection officials. Third, our system is anything but uniform, with individual judges making their own decisions on a case-by-case basis. Awards tend to be very small in proportion to men's income, an average of 13 percent in 1978–1983 (U.S. Bureau of the Census, 1985a, p. 2), and the proportion tends to decrease as income rises (Weitzman, 1985, p. 266). Fourth, if a woman is on welfare (or on the borderline) she has no incentive whatsoever to try to track down the man or get him to pay. This is because any income she receives (including child support) is taxed dollar for dollar by the welfare system. In other words, for each dollar of child support a woman receives, she loses a dollar of welfare, so she and her children are no better off. If the man is being helpful in nonpecuniary ways or even providing income-in-kind such as groceries or taking his child to a baseball game, we question why the woman would want to pursue him with the law and perhaps even get him thrown in jail.

To strengthen the nation's CSE system, in August 1984, Congress passed and President Reagan signed into law the Child Support Enforcement Amendments of 1984, which came into effect in 1985 and 1986. These amendments require all states to: (1) withhold wages automatically when support payments are overdue; (2) use expedited legal processes, such as administrative procedures, for obtaining and enforcing support orders; (3) provide for the collection of overdue support by intercepting state income tax refunds; (4) initiate a process for imposing liens against real and personal property; (5) maintain procedures for requiring security, bond, or other guarantee of payment; and (6) establish statewide advisory guidelines for child support award amounts. In addition, incentives are created to foster interstate enforcement.

The 1984 amendments should help to alleviate some, but not all, of the problems with the current system. First, automatic wage withholding begins if payment falls behind by one month, eliminating the need for the woman to return to court. Second, expedited legal processes allow child support awards to be established and enforced without going in front of a judge. Third, the woman may now keep the first $50 of child support payments when on welfare.

Since 1984, changes in state and federal laws have accelerated, culminating in the passage at the federal level of the Family Support Act of 1988. Among other things, Title I required states to meet stricter federal standards in paternity establishment, to make use of guidelines in setting awards, and to require automatic wage withholding in all cases. It was hoped that this would not only raise the level of awards but also ensure payments.

How effective can we expect these new state laws to be? One way to determine this is to evaluate the effectiveness of similar laws already on the books. In a study of the effects of 1981 state laws, Beller and Graham (1987) found that liens and administrative procedures were effective at increasing child support receipts. Laws for the mandatory and automatic withholding of wages in effect for at least three years were also found effective but only moderately so. The authors have concluded that federal officials need to realize that the passage of state laws alone does not guarantee their effective enforcement. Although these amendments

are certainly promising, on the basis of past experience we are not optimistic that they will revolutionize child support in the United States.

What is the potential of this present system for reducing welfare dependency? In a study that simulates its effects on welfare dependency,
P. K. Robins found the present system's potential for reducing welfare
dependency (i.e., the AFDC participation rate) and the poverty rate to
be minimal: "Part of the reason for such a relatively small impact of
child support enforcement . . . is probably low child support award
amounts, particularly among AFDC recipients. . . . Higher award
amounts and/or other sources of income (principally greater earnings)
are necessary" (1986, p. 786). However, Robins did find that child support policies could reduce AFDC costs significantly. By providing "the
full range of services to all AFDC families," child support agencies could
recover 15 to 16 percent of AFDC costs. If, in addition, child support
obligations were established for all AFDC mothers and all obligations
were fully enforced (i.e., full payment received), nearly 50 percent of
AFDC benefits now paid could be recovered. According to Robins,
"These findings suggest that a successful system of mandatory withholding coupled with greater efforts to establish obligations could recover somewhere between 15 and 20 percent of AFDC benefits" (p. 786).
However, he concluded, "even with higher award amounts, it does not
appear likely that child support enforcement would have a dramatic
effect on reducing the economic insecurity facing many single-parent
families" (p. 786).

ALTERNATIVE SYSTEMS OF CHILD SUPPORT

If the current system has minimal potential for reducing poverty, are
there any other alternatives? Two we would like to mention are the
system being tested in the state of Wisconsin and the system in effect
in Hungary, which Andrea H. Beller learned about in discussions with
a colleague (Kamarás, 1987).[9]

The child support assurance system being demonstrated and evaluated in Wisconsin is based upon a model developed by I. Garfinkel of
the Institute for Research on Poverty at the University of Wisconsin.
The demonstration is scheduled to continue until 1993. That system
provides payments to all women with children from an absent father.
A woman is guaranteed a minimum payment even if her absent coun-
terpart does not pay in that amount. The payment is smaller than the
AFDC benefit but is not reduced by a dollar for each dollar earned. The
state collects the child support from absent fathers by withholding it
from wages and other sources of income. This system relies upon the
child support enforcement system to track down reticent fathers. Obligations are determined by a simple legislated formula: 17 percent of

the noncustodial parent's gross income for one child; 25 percent, 29 percent, 31 percent, and 34 percent respectively for two, three, four, and five or more children (Garfinkel and McLanahan, 1986, p. 176). Garfinkel and S. S. McLanahan say, "By providing benefits outside the welfare system that are not taken away when poor women go to work, the child support assurance program will supplement the earnings of poor women who have children and thereby lessen dependence on AFDC" (1986, p. 137).

Hungary has had a very structured and apparently effective system of child support in place for some time. The woman can request wage withholding at divorce or at a later date if the man does not pay. The proportion of the man's income that goes to child support is legislated and is quite high by U.S. standards: 20 percent of his income for one child, 40 percent for two children, and 50 percent for three or more children. The woman also gets the dwelling at divorce, and apparently it can take as long as fifteen years to acquire one in Hungary. These features sometimes combine to force a man to go back and live with his parents, and often he cannot afford to remarry (Kamarás, 1987). Why do women in Hungary appear to do so well relative to men after a divorce? According to F. Kamarás (1987), it is because the most important consideration is the interest of the child. What does that say about *us*? Where do *we* place the interest of the child? Kamarás and his (female) interpreter were both surprised to learn that in the United States men have found various ways to escape their child support obligations, including moving to another state. Their surprise stemmed from the fact that one does not have to register with the police, as in Hungary, when they move to another state.

While the Hungarian system is apparently very effective for women and children, it appears to cause some not inconsiderable hardship among men. Moreover, when marriage is regulated, it can cause certain distortions. For example, remarriage rates are low in Hungary (Kamarás, 1987). Men are probably hesitant about marrying in the first place and are probably more likely to use birth control methods.

In all probability, the Hungarian system would not be acceptable here, but it should certainly be viewed as a model of one that appears to work, at least for the women and children.

Only time will tell how successful the Wisconsin system is. That system appears to be effective through eliminating the uncertainty associated with late and irregular payments and removing the burden of tracking down an unresponsive father from the woman. But it is unlikely that such a system would be able to transfer enough money to women who head families in all parts of our country in order to bring them out of poverty and keep them from needing welfare. Garfinkel and McLanahan estimate "that such a program could reduce the poverty gap among American families potentially eligible for child support nearly 40 percent and would reduce AFDC caseloads by nearly 50 percent" (1986, p. 176).

Garfinkel and McLanahan's speculations and Robins's estimates lead to the inevitable conclusion that eliminating, or even substantially reducing, the feminization of poverty requires that we do more than just improve the child support system. We must continue our efforts to increase women's earnings, to help women make the transition from working in the home to working for pay in the market, and to implement a better system of quality child care at affordable prices.

In her recent book, *The Economic Emergence of Women*, B. R. Bergmann (1986) proposes such a comprehensive system. Her proposal includes the method for overhauling the child support system proposed by Garfinkel, combined with a system of unemployment insurance for single parents. Such insurance would allow them a period of support while looking for their first job to help facilitate their transition from home to market. Unfortunately, Bergmann does not provide any details about how such a system would be financed or what the costs would be. Bergmann also emphasizes the importance of improving women's earnings for which she advocates pay equity. "In recognition of the special burdens of single parents," she also recommends, "a system of excellent, highly subsidized child care, and a system of free medical care" for the children (p. 253). Thus, Bergmann's proposal is a three-point program adding unemployment insurance for single parents and pay equity to reform of the child support system.

CONCLUSION

In conclusion, we have determined that while, at present, child support is limited by not enough awards being made and infrequent payments, getting all existing obligations fully paid and establishing awards for women without them will not eliminate the feminization of poverty, largely because award amounts are low. It can, however, reduce the costs of AFDC by a substantial amount. Prospects for improving the collection of existing awards seem promising following the 1984 Child Support Enforcement Amendments and 1988 welfare reform legislation. Whether the new requirement for mandatory guidelines will ensure adequate child support awards to raise women out of poverty is unclear. Only a complete overhaul of the present child support system could substantially reduce the economic insecurity facing many female-headed single-parent families.

Because the potential gains from reform of the child support system are limited, we must proceed on a number of fronts. Of utmost priority is to continue our efforts to increase women's earnings. One way of doing this is by continuing to open job opportunities in traditionally male-dominated occupations. In addition, we must provide a decent system of child care at affordable prices. Related to this goal, parental leave on the birth of a new child would also be helpful. Unfortunately, a bill proposing such leave was vetoed by President George Bush in September of 1990. As we can see, no single program can solve the entire problem of the feminization of poverty. While working to improve the child support enforcement program is desirable, multiple program efforts must be pursued.

NOTES

Andrea H. Beller is first author of this chapter, which was first delivered as a speech by her at the YMCA's Friday Forum Series on American Families in Transition, University of Illinois at Urbana-Champaign, 9 October 1987.

1. Sources for these figures are U.S. Department of Health and Human Services (1986b), table 2–1, pp. 2–5, for the period 1962 to 1982; and U.S. Bureau of the Census (1986b), table no. 124, p. 81, for 1983.

2. See Weitzman (1985), figure 3, p. 338, for more detail. This figure is based upon a weighted sample of interviews with 228 recently divorced men and women (114 men and 114 women) in Los Angeles County, California, in 1978. The sample was selected to be representative of the entire population of divorced people, stratified by length of marriage and socioeconomic status (Weitzman, 1985, pp. 407–411).

3. This point is discussed extensively in two recent books: Garfinkel and McLanahan (1986) and Rodgers (1986).

4. The poverty level is that level of income below which it is deemed that a family does not have enough money to maintain a decent level of living. The poverty level was $11,200 for a family of four in 1987.

5. It is not known to what extent absent mothers do not contribute to the support of their children. The absence of data on this situation reflects the fact that single-parent families headed by men are a relatively rare phenomenon. Moreover, they are much less likely than single-parent families headed by women to fall into poverty due to the fact that men typically earn much more than women. Thus, even if there is a problem of this nature, it does not arouse as much social concern. Nevertheless, all discussions pertaining to enforcement of child support payments can be thought of as applying to absent mothers as well as to absent fathers.

6. All women with children from an absent father are eligible for a child support award. Once an award is either voluntarily agreed to or court-ordered, there is still a question of whether the woman receives payment. There are two reasons why she may not: She either is not due payment in a particular year because, for example, the child is too old, or although she is due payment, the father does not pay.

7. The rate, however, fell substantially between 1978 and 1981 and by 1985 had not regained the initial levels (U.S. Bureau of the Census, 1981).

8. For an attempt to untangle cause and effect, see Graham and Beller (1986).

9. Kamarás is Deputy Chief, Population Statistics Section, Hungarian Central Statistical Office, Budapest, Hungary.

13
Child Care in America: Retrospect and Prospect

Sally Lubeck and Patricia Garrett

Child care has become a central issue in discussions about the relationship between employment and family life. Forty years ago most fathers were breadwinners and most mothers were homemakers. Today, however, families are experiencing conflict between the two major functions the family traditionally has fulfilled: the economic responsibility to maintain households and the social responsibility to meet children's physical and psychological needs (Morgan, 1983).

Women constitute an increasingly large percentage of the U.S. work force (Jones, 1987), and demographic estimates project that 86 percent of women age 40 to 44, 83 percent of women 35 to 39, and 76 percent of women 30 to 34 will bear children (U.S. Bureau of the Census, 1988, pp. 8–9).[1] Consequently, individuals and families will continue to contend with conflicting demands of work and child care. Social policies can enhance the ability of families to care for their members, but, to do so, policy options must be broadly considered.

In this chapter, we explore both the recent past and the current situation as a basis for delineating alternative strategies for the future care and education of young children. The chapter begins with a retrospective description of trends in the labor force participation of women and changes over time in the child care arrangements of working mothers. We then briefly review probable future trends. Finally, we describe two types of policy options: (1) policies that change the conditions under which people work; and (2) those that change the conditions under which children are reared.

Figure 13.1
Female Labor Force Participation Rates: United States, 1947–1986

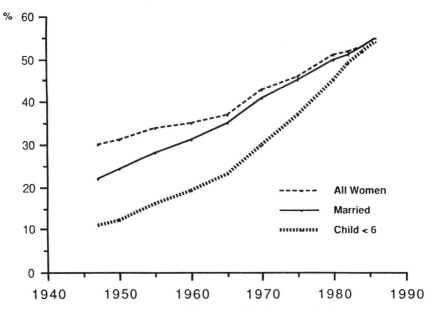

Sources: Wattenberg (1976), p. 133; U.S. Bureau of the Census, (1986c), p. 383.

A RETROSPECTIVE VIEW OF WORK AND CHILD CARE ARRANGEMENTS

Female Labor Force Participation

National data provide important insights into trends in work patterns and child care arrangements. As Figure 13.1 indicates, employment rates have risen for all women since 1945. When those married are disaggregated (the middle line), a steep rise is evident. For married women with children under the age of 6, rates increase nearly fivefold—from 11 percent in 1948 to 54 percent in 1986 (U.S. Bureau of the Census, 1986b, p. 383).

Change has been most pronounced among women with very young children (O'Connell and Bloom, 1987). Figure 13.2 illustrates that the likelihood of employment increases with the age of the child. Nonetheless, mothers of preschoolers of all ages were employed in greater numbers in 1986 than in 1970. Today, mothers with infants work in higher proportions than did mothers with 3- and 4-year-olds a decade ago.

The reasons for the increased employment of women are manifold. With new opportunities for women in business and the professions, many have elected to work. Effective contraception has allowed parents

Figure 13.2
Labor Force Participation: Married Women with Preschoolers, 1970–1987

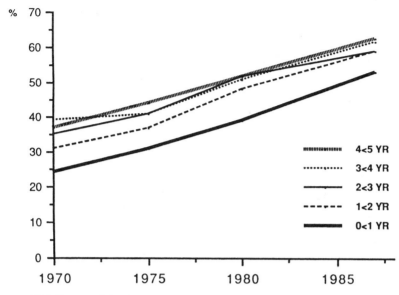

Sources: U.S. Bureau of the Census (1986c), p. 383; (1988), p. 374.

to plan their families, and many have opted to postpone childbearing and to limit family size (Cherlin, 1981). Despite these changes, however, most women are compelled to work by financial circumstances. Increasingly, couples require two incomes to maintain a family in comfort (U.S. Bureau of the Census, 1987c, p. 403). Economically active wives working full time contribute 38 percent of total family income, but women's wages are even more important if husband's income is low. For poor families with annual incomes less than $10,000 (1980), wives contribute an overwhelming 69 percent (U.S. Department of Labor, Women's Bureau, 1983, p. 17). Women's wages remain a substantial (47 percent) proportion for families with incomes between $15,000 and $19,000 a year (Reskin and Hartmann, 1986, p. 4). Finally, one-fourth of all working women with children were not married in 1985 (O'Connell and Bloom, 1987, p. 2), and these women provide the major, and frequently the sole, support for their children.

Trends in Child Care Arrangements

The principal source of information on child care arrangements is the periodic surveys conducted by the Bureau of the Census. No federal, state, or local agency collects systematic information on who cares for

Figure 13.3
Child Care Arrangements for Preschoolers of Mothers Employed Full Time,
1958–1984

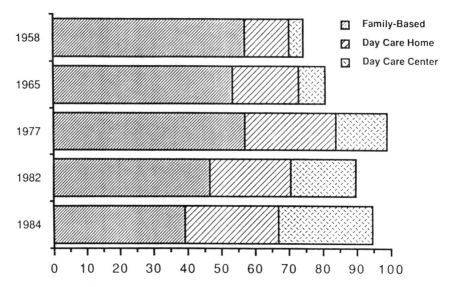

Sources: Lajewski (1959); Low and Spindler (1968); U.S. Bureau of the Census (1982; 1983a; 1987c).

children before they enter school or while classes are not in session (Papageorgiou, 1986). Consequently, it is difficult to document change over time.

By recalculating published national data on the child care arrangements of working mothers, we were able to depict basic trends.[2] It is not possible to describe child care arrangements for all subgroups in the population. Roughly comparable data could be generated only for mothers of preschoolers who work full time. Figure 13.3 illustrates the basic trend for the period 1958 through 1984 and shows the primary arrangement for the youngest child under the age of 5. The relative proportion of care provided by relatives and by others has changed over time, with family-based care decreasing and extrafamilial care increasing (Lubeck and Garrett, 1988).

The proportion of children in different types of care varies with the age of the child. Young children in nonfamilial arrangements are more likely to be cared for in homes. At age 3, higher proportions of children are in formal, center-based arrangements. Between 1965 and 1980 enrollment of 3- and 4-year-olds in such programs more than tripled (U.S. Bureau of the Census, 1986a). Nonetheless, the percentage of infants in centers as their primary arrangement increased from 5 percent to 14 percent between 1982 and 1984. The increase was from 12 percent to 17 percent for children ages 1 to 3 and from 26 to 32 percent for children 3 to 5 (U.S. Bureau of the Census, 1983a; U.S. Bureau of the Census, 1987c).[3] Change of this magnitude in only two years is noteworthy. Currently the primary child care arrangement for nearly one in four children ages 0–4 (1.9 million) is a preschool or daycare center; another 22 percent are cared for in family daycare homes (U.S. Bureau of the Census, 1987c, Table 3).

Despite the attention currently directed at group-based alternatives, family-based care by parents, grandparents, older children, or extended kin remains important. A majority (62 percent) of mothers of preschool children who work part time depend on family-based child care and a substantial minority (39.4 percent) of children whose mothers are employed full time are also in family-based arrangements (Lubeck and Garrett, 1988).

A PROSPECTIVE VIEW OF WORK AND CHILD CARE ARRANGEMENTS

American women are expected to increase their labor force participation rates (O'Connell and Bloom, 1987) and to approach higher levels such as those in Europe (Kamerman, 1980; McMahon, 1986). By the year 2000, 47 percent of the work force is projected to be female (Jones, 1987).

In order to predict the percentage of children with mothers in the work force, S. Hofferth and D. Phillips (1987) use a simple linear model, noting a "straightline increase" in the proportion of children with employed mothers since 1972. Their equations predict the proportion of children with employed mothers in 1990 and in 1995. Estimates suggest that 65 percent of preschoolers and 77 percent of school-age children will have mothers in the work force by 1995. If these projections are correct, 14.6 million preschoolers (ages 0 to 6) and 34.4 million school-age children (ages 6 to 18) will have employed mothers by 1995 (Hofferth and Phillips, 1987, Table 1, but note caveats, footnotes 1 and 2 of that table).

Since the 1950s and 1960s, there has been a gradual decrease in family-based arrangements and an increase in child care external to the family. Although the proportion of children cared for in family daycare homes has remained relatively constant, the proportion of young children in centers appears to be expanding at a rapid rate.

POLICY OPTIONS TO ADDRESS EMERGING ISSUES OF WORK AND FAMILY

High levels of maternal employment and increased reliance on extra-familial child care raise important questions for social policy. In the industrial market economies and centrally planned economies of Europe, public provisions have been made for both familial and extrafamilial forms of care (Lubeck, 1989a). In the United States, however, no such provisions are available to all, and, for many parents, responsibilities for work and child care are increasingly difficult to reconcile. New initiatives can enhance the ability of parents and family members to care for children, but it is imperative to consider what practices should change and what types of policies would foster those changes.

Facilitating the Care of Children by Working Parents

Some policies that have the potential to make it easier for parents both to work and to care for their children involve restructuring the conditions of employment. These policies to varying degrees have now been implemented in Europe and in some large American corporations. Government policies and employer-sponsored benefit plans directed at the changing needs of families include maternity benefits, paid job-protected leaves, and supplementary unpaid leaves (Kamerman, 1983b). Innovative scheduling has also been suggested: flextime, compressed work weeks, flexyear contracts, permanent part-time work, and job splitting (Best, 1982).

Maternity Benefits. Only since the passage of the Pregnancy Discrimination Act (PDA) in 1978 has the law against sex discrimination been expanded to encompass discrimination based on pregnancy and childbirth, defining pregnancy as a "temporary disability" that should be covered by existing sickness and medical plans (Kamerman, 1991). Maternity benefits in the United States are now granted through disability payments that some employers provide or through the temporary disability insurance benefits available in California, Hawaii, New York, New Jersey, and Rhode Island (Kamerman, Kahn, and Kingston, 1983). Although the government requires that pregnant women be treated the same as any employee with a disability, only those women whose employers provide disability benefits or who live in a state with specific legislation are eligible for coverage.

It has been estimated that no more than 40 percent of American women are eligible for employer-provided disability insurance, sick leave, or paid leave, and most of the employers who do provide it limit eligibility to six to eight weeks (Kamerman, Kahn, and Kingston, 1983; Kamerman, 1991).

Parental Leave. Some form of parental leave, typically maternity leave, is available to those having children in all developed nations, and many developing nations of the world (Lubeck, 1989a; Garrett, Lubeck, & Wenk, 1988). In the United States, a parental leave bill has still failed to pass at the federal level. The Family and Medical Leave Act (S 249 and

HR 925), which would have provided job guarantees in the event of a medical emergency, childbirth, adoption, or the need for dependent care, passed both houses of Congress in 1990 but was subsequently vetoed by the president in June.

At the state level, there is a growing movement to establish parental leave policies (Lenhoff and Stoneback, 1989). California, Montana, Iowa, Rhode Island, Minnesota, and Oregon, among others, now have unpaid leave. The number of employees a company must have to be required to grant leave varies, as does the amount of time allotted. Tennessee and Louisiana exclude fathers from their leave legislation, although they do offer maternity leave. Maryland has leave policies for state employees only, while Connecticut offers parental leave for state employees and employees of private firms (Trzcinski and Finn-Stevenson, 1990). Twenty additional states are now considering parental leave in some form (Kamerman, 1991). Additionally, parental or "childrearing" leaves are increasingly being negotiated through labor contracts (e.g., AFSCME, 1988).

Flexible Benefits. Despite the changes that have occurred in the composition of the work force, most fringe-benefit packages have changed little since the 1940s and 1950s (Kamerman, 1983b). With the increasing heterogeneity of the labor force, however, has come pressure to meet the needs of specific subgroups (Bloom and Martin, 1983). Married couples do not need two health insurance policies, single persons do not need life insurance, and parents may prefer family benefits and dental policies over other options. As the numbers of women in the work force continue to expand, benefit plans that include options for maternity coverage and child care are increasingly desirable.

Innovative Scheduling. A 1980 Gallup Poll asked employees to select the types of programs that would be of most help to them in dealing with conflicting demands of job and family. More than half indicated the need for more flexible schedules (Rothman and Marks, 1987, p. 471). Flextime allows employees to decide, within a two-hour span morning and evening, when they will arrive and depart. Most plans retain a "core time" from 9:30 to 3:00 when all employees must be present. The principal advantage of this arrangement is that it increases employees' ability to minimize conflicts between personal/family obligations and job requirements (Kuhne and Blair, 1978).

Other plans now provide flexweek and flexyear options. These include compressed time (e.g., four ten-hour days; three and a half eleven to twelve hour days) and plans whereby employees voluntarily reduce work time with a percentage cut in pay (5 percent for 10.5 days, etc.). Free time can be especially desirable during the summer months when children are home from school. Some flexyear plans are built on full-time work during the academic year and part-time during the summer so that parents can more easily care for out-of-school children. This option is available in some European countries, but it is virtually untried in the United States.

Another set of innovations involves part-time work. The principal alternatives are "permanent part-time" positions that provide fringe benefits, career advancement, and "job sharing" or "job splitting," which enables two or more workers to share one job.

Each of these policies has the potential to decrease the disjuncture between work and family life. Nonetheless, implementation of such measures is not unproblematic. Without a national policy, benefits and options are being inequitably distributed across sectors and occupations. To date, even innovative firms seem most willing to accommodate women at the coporate executive level, leaving those with fewer resources to fend for themselves, and general acceptance of a "mommy track" could permanently bifurcate work and family roles (Ehrlich, 1989). In addition, the corporate culture now seems to discourage men from taking parental leave, even when such leaves ostensibly are available (Catalyst, 1986, p. 38). One goal of a national policy, available to most, should be to guarantee both equity and choice.

Nonparental Child Care

Family-based Care. Child care within the family comes in a variety of forms, including arrangements that can be made with family members and close friends or neighbors ("kin," broadly considered). Nearly half (47.9 percent) of the preschool children of working mothers are cared for by a parent or other family member as their primary arrangement (U.S. Bureau of the Census, 1987c, Table 3). From a policy standpoint, however, family-based care has several characteristics that make it different from other options. First, it is a type of care unlikely to be regulated by the government. Second, it has generally been nonmonetized and unsupported through public funds (Morgan, 1985).

Because of this, government support of extrafamilial options may well have the effect of accelerating the decline in the amount of care provided by families. If, however, an important objective of child care policy is to support families, it is imperative to define a policy agenda supportive of both family-based and extrafamilial forms of care.

In a survey designed to study employment patterns and child care arrangements of 1,000 parents of 4-year-olds in three "representative" counties in North Carolina, it was found that two-parent families tended to rely on group-based care, while single parent families used family or family in combination with group care (p < .001). Blacks used family-based care more heavily than whites, lower income families used family-based or a combination of services, and higher income families used group-based services (p < .001) (Garrett, Wenger, Lubeck, and Clifford, 1990). It is not known whether many parents currently using family-based care prefer it or select it because they cannot afford group-based alternatives.

Family Daycare Homes. Group-based child care takes two principal forms: family daycare homes and daycare centers. A hybrid of these is the large daycare home or "mini-center."

Family daycare homes constitute a regulated, if informal, form of care in most states (Morgan, 1985). Generally, a caregiver is responsible for no more than six children. A recent Census Bureau report, based on data collected in 1984–1985, found 22.3 percent of the preschool children of working mothers in this form of care (U.S. Bureau of the Census, 1987c, Table D). Information was not available on the percentage of children in regulated homes.

Child Care Centers. Child care centers can be categorized as for-profit centers, not-for-profit centers, and public (government-sponsored) centers. For-profit centers are locally owned and operated ("Mom and Pop") operations or national franchises, such as Kinder Care or La Petite. The primary arrangement for 23.1 percent of preschool children is in organized facilities, daycare centers, or preschools. About 15 percent are in a daycare/group care center (U.S. Bureau of the Census, 1987c, Figure 1).

Both family daycare homes and daycare centers share certain commonalities. The success of each is predicated on the low wages of the women who care for children (Nelson, 1987; Zinsser, 1986), itself a cause of frequent turnover. Low wages, the inability of clients to pay more, funding cutbacks, expensive liability insurance, overcrowding, and the scarcity of trained teachers have created problems for both those who work in and count on homes and centers.

Much of the recent activity at the federal level has focused on improving care in homes and centers. Many child care bills have been introduced in Congress in recent years, but bipartisan support has now been forged for the Act for Better Child Care Services, commonly known as the ABC bill.[4]

Employer-supported Child Care. A study conducted by the Bureau of Labor Statistics found employer-supported provisions for child care to vary depending on the size of the company and whether it was a public or private facility. Large companies and government agencies were most likely to provide child care benefits and services to their employees (U.S. Department of Labor, Bureau of Labor Statistics, Table 3).

There are numerous ways in which businesses assist employees in providing quality child care. F. Glasser (1981) describes options by which a company can directly assist employees with child care, either by establishing a daycare center at the work site (onsite model) or by joining with other businesses in the area to establish a joint center (consortium model). Currently, only about 2 percent of American firms with ten employees or more sponsor child care centers for employees' children (U.S. Department of Labor, Bureau of Labor Statistics, 1988, p. 1). Companies do have other options, however. They can contract with existing centers in order to reserve places for employees' children (vendor program) or provide vouchers that can be used in the setting of a parent's choice (voucher program). Less directly, the company can offer a referral service to help parents find child care or arrange for sick child care. They can also establish some of the polices (parental leave, flextime, flexweek, etc.) discussed above.

Policies currently in place have served to encourage some firms to assist working parents with their child care needs. The Economic Tax Recovery Act of 1981 (ERTA) allows companies to treat child care costs as business expenses when the purpose is to improve employee retention rates. Employers who establish child care centers receive several benefits. Startup and operating costs are deductible, and capital costs (building, renovation, and equipment) can be depreciated over five years. Finally, if the center has an open admissions policy, it is exempt from federal income tax (O'Brien, 1987, p. 10).

Under the Dependent Care Assistance Plan (DCAP), several benefits accrue to employees. Costs for child care can be deducted as business expenses and, therefore, excluded from taxable gross income. Parents can also claim tax credits for one or two children on a sliding scale based on their gross income.

School-based Child Care. Public schools are the principal providers of child care services to school-age children. Approximately 75 percent (13.8 million) of the children of working mothers are in school during the time when their mothers work (U.S. Bureau of the Census, 1987, p. 2).

Since public schools already provide child care services to a large segment of the population, many of the reforms proposed to address child care needs are extensions of this universally available institution (Lubeck, 1989b; Schultz and Lombardi, 1989; Zigler, 1987b). Before- and after-school programs (Seligson, 1986) and programs for special populations of prekindergarten children (Morado, 1989) are now being offered or proposed in public school systems throughout the nation.

Public schools have already witnessed a downward extension of services. More 5-year-olds are attending kindergarten and for longer periods of time (Robinson, 1987), and public school-based programs for 3- and 4-year-olds appear to be increasing (Mitchell, 1987; Marx and Seligson, 1988). Suggestions have recently been made to further extend school-based prekindergarten programs with supplementary child care provided either at school or in neighboring daycare centers (Blank, 1985; Zigler, 1987a; Schweinhart et al., 1987).

Edward Zigler recommends that public schools provide universal child care services (Zigler, 1987b; Zigler and Finn-Stevenson, 1989). Current school-based programs for preschool children, however, continue to be for special populations of 3- and 4-year-olds and those who are handicapped (Bailey, 1989) or considered to be "at risk" (Morado, 1989; Marx and Seligson, 1988). No state offers universal preschool education for children of any age.

SUMMARY AND CONCLUSION

This chapter has illustrated retrospective and prospective trends in the labor force participation of women and the child care arrangements of working parents. Two broad types of policy options were identified to address the disjuncture between work and family life. One approach focuses on parents and involves initiatives that change the terms of employment through the provision of parental leave, maternity benefits, flexible benefit plans, and innovative scheduling. Another, potentially complementary approach involves support for nonparental care primarily through improving the availability and quality of child care services.

A demographic perspective provides insight into the changing nature of employment patterns and changes in the arrangements made for the care of children. Some have interpreted broad trends to mean that American parents, and kin generally, are no longer able or willing to care for children (e.g., Coleman, 1987). A closer analysis suggests that this is not the case. Rather than blame individuals, it is necessary to address the structural constraints that make it difficult for parents to perform dual roles. This paper has presented the argument that broad-based reforms are needed to support parents specifically and families generally in their efforts to nurture the next generation.

NOTES

1. American women expect to have at least one child during their childbearing years. In 1988, 10 percent expected to be childless. In 1976, 10.1 percent had such an expectation (U.S. Bureau of the Census, 1988, pp. 1, 9).

2. Data were recalculated following the suggestions of Martin O'Connell of the Bureau of the Census. Available studies of child care arrangements sometimes provided information on all preschoolers; alternately, information was provided only for the youngest child. Recalculations were restricted to tables concerning the youngest child under age 5 (U.S. Bureau of the Census, 1983a, pp. 4–5; U.S. Bureau of the Census, 1987c, p. 15). Missing data and "don't knows" were then excluded from analysis, and percentages were recalculated. Further problems were encountered because data were collected during different seasons. In 1977 and 1982, data were collected in June when most school-based

programs were closed, so these results may have underreported the number of children in group-based care (Kamerman, 1983a). The 1984 data, by contrast, were collected during winter 1984–1985 when a combination of holidays and poor weather may have influenced child care arrangements. Data are as comparable as possible, given these factors and differences in the original research designs and sampling frames.

3. "Preschoolers" refers to the youngest child under 5 (1982) and all children under 5 (1984/1985). Because average family size is small, this distinction has no dramatic consequences. Nevertheless, the data are not strictly comparable.

4. In fall 1990 this legislation was enacted after years of work and countless reformulations. The new policy targets low and moderate income working families. It authorizes $2.5 billion (over three years) in block grants to states to subsidize care and to improve and expand the supply of care, both for preschool-age and school-age children. It authorizes $1.5 billion (over five years) for child care for low income working families. It provides $50 million to states to improve standards, train providers, and monitor compliance. Finally, it expands the Earned Income Tax Credit and establishes a refundable tax credit for low income families. During fall 1990 the act reauthorizing Head Start was also passed, permitting wraparound funds for full-day programs and ensuring that all eligible children can be served by 1994.

14
Rethinking Joint Custody Policy: Option or Presumption?

Clifton P. Flynn

Since the late 1970s, the United States has witnessed the adoption of joint custody legislation in two-thirds of the states (Freed and Walker, 1986; Weitzman, 1985). In some states, not only is joint custody available as a custody option, it is presumed to be in the "best interests of the child." Ideologically, joint custody laws stress the importance of the child maintaining a relationship with both parents following divorce and, at the same time, acknowledge the equal parental rights of both the father and the mother.

Not surprisingly, the issue of joint custody has generated much debate among social scientists, legal professionals, and policy makers. Unfortunately, this debate has been hampered by the limited amount of reliable data on the effects of joint custody.

What is the best policy regarding joint custody? Is joint custody always in the child's best interests? The purpose of this chapter is to argue for joint custody but against laws that establish a presumption in favor of joint custody. After a brief discussion of the legal aspects of joint custody, the major arguments in the joint custody debate are summarized. Next, the literature on joint custody arrangements and their effects on children is reviewed. Finally, it is argued that legislation that makes joint custody available as *an* option, but not *the* best option, is the best policy.

LEGAL ASPECTS OF JOINT CUSTODY

Joint Custody Laws

Thirty-three states have adopted some form of joint custody legislation (Freed and Walker, 1986). Four types of joint custody statutes have been identified (Schulman and Pitt, 1984; Weitzman, 1985):

1. *Joint custody as an option.* These laws allow courts to consider joint custody equally along with other custody alternatives.
2. *Joint custody when parents agree.* This type of statute permits the courts to order joint custody only when requested by both parents.
3. *Joint custody at one party's request.* Under this form of legislation, courts may award joint custody when only one parent has asked for it.
4. *Joint custody preference or presumption.* A joint custody preference statute requires judges to consider joint custody not as an equal option but as the preferred custody arrangement. "Even more forceful is a joint custody presumption. This is a legal presumption that joint custody is in the child's best interests. In order to overcome this presumption, the party who does not want joint custody has to prove that joint custody would be detrimental to the child" (Weitzman, 1985, p. 247).

Joint Custody Awards

Joint custody awards may take one of two forms: joint legal custody and joint physical custody (Charnas, 1983; Frankel, 1985; Miller, 1979; Weitzman, 1985). Joint legal custody recognizes the rights of both parents to make major decisions affecting their child's life. Judges may award joint legal custody without awarding joint physical custody and often do. Although a variety of living arrangements are possible under joint legal custody, physical custody is typically awarded to the mother. In this way, joint legal custody closely resembles sole maternal custody with liberal visitation for the father. Much of the increase in joint custody awards can be attributed to an increase in awards of joint legal custody (Coller, 1988; Racusin et al., 1989; Weitzman, 1985).

Under joint physical custody, not only do parents share decision making, they also share in the physical care of their child. Though the division of responsibilities may not be equal, the child lives alternately for major periods of time with each parent (Charnas, 1983; Frankel, 1985). In effect, both parents participate in the day-to-day care of the child and make minor as well as major decisions in the child's life (Miller, 1979).

THE JOINT CUSTODY DEBATE

L. G. Katz notes that "in any field in which the data base is unreliable—especially in terms of its validity—the vacuum generated by such data weakness is filled by ideologies" (1975, p. 268). The limited empirical evidence on joint custody has resulted in such a phenomenon. After an extensive review of the joint custody literature, W. G. Clingempeel and N. D. Reppucci concluded that "the available studies are egregiously inadequate, and for the most part the debates have been nourished solely by opposing ideologies" (1982, p. 124).

Two opposing ideologies in the joint custody debate are represented by M. Roman and W. Haddad (1978) and by J. Goldstein, A. Freud, and A. J. Solnit (1979). In their book, *The Disposable Parent*, Roman and Haddad argue passionately and persuasively for a legal presumption of joint custody: "Unlike sole (generally maternal) custody, it does not banish the father or overburden the mother, and, just as important, it does not sever ties between one parent and the children" (1978, p. 104).

On the other hand, Goldstein et al., in *Beyond the Best Interests of the Child*, argue strongly for insuring the stability and the continuity of the child's relationship with one psychological parent.

Once it is determined who will be the custodial parent, it is that parent, not the court, who must decide under what conditions he or she wishes to raise the child. Thus, the noncustodial parent should have no legally enforceable right to visit the child, and the custodial parent should have the right to decide whether it is desirable for the child to have such visits. What we have said is designed to protect the security of an ongoing relationship—that between the child and the custodial parent (1979, p. 38).

The advantages and disadvantages of joint custody have been thoroughly and thoughtfully discussed and summarized by legal and mental health professionals (Benedek and Benedek, 1979; Charnas, 1983; Derdeyn and Scott, 1984; Frankel, 1985; Miller, 1979; Nehls and Morgenbesser, 1980; Raines, 1985–1986; Robinson, 1982–1983; Skoloff, 1984). Most arguments are based on joint physical custody, but many apply to joint legal custody as well. These arguments can be organized around five issues: (1) adjustment of the child; (2) the coparental relationship; (3) parental adjustment; (4) flexibility; and (5) decision making.

Child's Adjustment: Two Parents versus One Parent

Those who favor joint custody believe that a continuing relationship with both parents is in the child's best interests. Shared parenting, proponents argue, largely negates the detrimental effects that absence of the father can have on the child. The child's deep sense of loss will be significantly lessened or eliminated. The benefits of both parents as role models, as well as exposure to two different environments and two different philosophies, will broaden the child's experience in a beneficial way.

Opponents counter these arguments by insisting that joint custody undermines the continuity and stability that are essential to the child's postdivorce adjustment. Children need a sense of finality and certainty after divorce, and shuffling back and forth between two parents can be extremely unsettling. Opponents stress the importance of the child's continuing relationship with one psychological parent and view loyalty conflicts as inevitable in joint custody arrangements. Finally, living in two homes, with different authority figures who may hold different values, is seen as a major source of confusion for the child.

Coparental Relationship

Advocates suggest that joint custody leads to an improved relationship between exspouses. Joint custody requires cooperation, and parents who are able to put their children's interests above their own are likely to reduce the level of conflict in their relationship. Less relitigation and reliable payment of child support are two positive outcomes that may result from reduced conflict in the coparental relationship.

Many argue, however, that it is unrealistic to expect a couple to suddenly put aside their differences and to cooperate in childrearing. If the divorce was bitter and hostile, and if parents differ considerably on how to raise their children, "forced cooperation" may lead to an increase, rather than a decrease, in conflict. In those circumstances, the child is kept in the middle of a conflict-ridden relationship that was supposed to be terminated by divorce.

Parental Adjustment

Proponents also believe that parents' postdivorce adjustment is enhanced by the joint custody arrangement. With joint custody, there is no "winner" or "loser." The sense of loss often felt by the noncustodial parent is alleviated. Fathers, for example, can feel like parents and not visitors to their children, and mothers can be relieved from the role of sole caretakers of the children.

This ongoing and frequent interaction, however, may make it difficult for the couple to resolve their marital relationship. Spouses need to accept the fact that the marriage is over, and involvement in a joint custody arrangement could foster confusion and uncertainty. Though joint custody might be psychologically appealing to fathers, opponents warn that existing social realities will not change and that child care responsibilities will remain with the mother.

Flexibility

Both parents and children will experience changes in their lives, and joint custody can best accommodate those changes. Parents may change jobs, children may change schools, and other social and economic circumstances may require adjustments. A joint custody arrangement allows families flexibility to adapt to change.

Opponents, however, point out that the demands of joint custody may restrict the mobility of a parent. Parents may forego career advancement if taking a new job entails moving to a new city or involves other changes that might interfere with the shared parenting arrangement. In addition, the logistics problems created by maintaining two homes for the child, and the related transition difficulties, suggest that the flexibility of joint custody has its drawbacks.

Decision-Making

Finally, proponents argue that joint custody is appealing to those involved in the decisionmaking process. Judges can avoid the painfully difficult choice of awarding custody to one parent over another. The number of contested custody cases is likely to decrease as parents realize that there will be no winner or loser in joint custody.

For opponents, parents and judges who choose joint custody are being evasive. For parents who cannot agree on custody, and for judges with difficult custody decisions, joint custody is seen as an easy out. Parents may enter into a joint custody arrangement for the wrong reasons, perhaps trying not to hurt the other parent's feelings, rather than making a decision based on what is best for the child.

This summary of arguments for and against joint custody reveals the underlying ideological conflicts. But what is known about actual joint custody arrangements and their effects on children and parents? Who chooses joint custody and on what basis? Are joint custody parents satisfied with the arrangement? Answering these questions, by examining the relevant research literature, can move us beyond the ideological debate.

JOINT CUSTODY RESEARCH

Most studies have focused on joint physical custody arrangements that were chosen by the parents. With joint physical custody, the child lives in two homes and spends at least 25 to 33 percent of his or her time with one parent (Abarbanel, 1979; Irving et al., 1984; Luepnitz, 1986; Rothberg, 1983; Steinman, 1981). A few studies have examined the effects of joing legal custody (Bowman and Ahrons, 1985; Ilfeld, et al., 1982), an arrangement that may include a variety of shared parenting patterns (Ahrons, 1980). Virtually all research has been done on white middle- and upper-middle-class men and women. These individuals, often well-educated professionals, are typically in joint custody arrangements by choice, not by a court-imposed order (see, for example, Racusin et al., 1989).

Most joint custody parents report that the arrangement was mutually agreed upon and that the idea originated with the couple. In one study (Irving et al., 1984) of 201 Canadian parents involved in a shared parenting arrangement, 85.3 percent said the arrangement was suggested by one of the spouses. C. R. Ahrons (1980) found that a majority of the 41 parents with joint legal custody in her study had mutually chosen that option.

Often the husband may initiate the discussion of joint custody. B. Rothberg (1983) asked thirty joint physical custody parents (fourteen men, sixteen women) why they chose joint custody. A total of 57 percent of the women said that they agreed to joint custody because their husbands asked for it. The remaining 43 percent indicated that both parents had wanted joint custody. Since sole custody is usually awarded to mothers, it is not surprising that many fathers initially suggest joint custody.

Parents' Attitudes Toward Joint Custody

Most couples appear to be satisfied with their joint custody arrangements. H. H. Irving et al. (1984) found that 77.4 percent of their sample of 201 parents said they were "satisfied" or "extremely satisfied" with the overall arrangement. Further, 79.6 percent were satisfied with the process of selecting joint custody, while 86.2 percent expressed satisfaction with the schedule that had been worked out. The source of satisfaction centered on the childrearing benefits derived from the arrangement, including shared responsibility and parental involvement. Uncertainty about the developmental effects of joint custody on children and concern about the lack of time spent with children contributed to the parents' feelings of dissatisfaction. Several factors were shown to affect the parents' level of satisfaction. First, those in court-ordered arrangements were significantly less satisfied than those who had reached an informal agreement. Second, the greater the guilt over the marital breakup, the lower the satisfaction with the arrangement. Third, the higher the level of preseparation conflict, the lower the level of satisfaction. Fourth, as the duration of the shared parenting arrangement increased, so did the level of satisfaction.

Rothberg (1983) reported that 67 percent of her sample of thirty parents had generally good feelings about the joint physical custody arrangement. Of the remaining subjects, 13 percent had negative feelings, and 20 percent expressed ambivalence. Difficulties in the children's adjustment to two homes and the necessary interaction with the former spouse were the two main reasons given for negative and ambivalent feelings.

Rothberg asked the parents to identify the greatest problem and the greatest benefit in joint custody. The four major problems reported (and the percent who said it was the greatest problem) were: (1) transitions (logistics problems, stress on children) (50 percent); (2) dealing with the exspouse (23 percent); (3) geography (necessity of parents living close together) (10 percent); and (4) finances (maintaining two homes) (7 percent). No major problems were reported by 10 percent of the respondents. The three major benefits of joint physical custody identified by the parents (and the percent who said each was the greatest benefit) were: (1) children having both parents (50 percent); (2) children having a "real father" (expressed primarily by men) (30 percent); and (3) free time for parents (cited exclusively by women) (17 percent).

Among Ahron's (1980) sample of forty-one individuals with joint legal custody, 84 percent indicated they were satisfied with the arrangement. The two most common reasons for satisfaction were that the children had access to both parents and that the arrangement provided greater flexibility for child care. A majority of the respondents were "satisfied" or "very satisfied" with the amount of coparental sharing and with the relationship with the former spouse. The greatest source of dissatisfaction was the quality of involvement of the nonresidential parent, the parent without joint physical custody. Over one-third of the sample expressed this concern, and most were nonresidential parents.

In summary, it seems that parents are generally satisfied with their joint custody arrangements, largely because of the benefits that their children gain from continued relationships with both parents. Sources of dissatisfaction for joint physical custody parents include problems of transition and concern about children's adjustment, while joint legal custody parents are dissatisfied with the limited involvement of the nonresidential parent.

Parents' Recommendations. In two studies, parents were asked if they would recommend joint custody to other separating parents. In the Rothberg (1983) study, 24 out of 30 parents (80 percent) said they would recommend joint custody. Irving et al. (1984) reported that out of the 201 parents in their sample, 87.6 percent would recommend shared parenting, 3.2 percent were ambivalent, and 9 percent were against it. Yet, in both studies, virtually all of those who favored joint custody warned that it is not for everyone. They felt that those who were unable to put their children first and to cooperate with their exspouse would not be good candidates for joint custody.

Child Adjustment

D. A. Luepnitz (1986) compared the postdivorce adjustment of ninety-one children, matched by age and sex, in sixteen families with sole maternal custody, sixteen with sole paternal custody, and eleven with joint physical custody. She concluded that child adjustment (measured both by the Piers-Harris Self-Concept Test for Children and by parents' ratings of the child's self-esteem, psychosomatic problems, and behavior problems) was not related to custody type. Luepnitz also found that a majority of joint custody children liked their arrangement and experienced little confusion. In fact, 75 percent of the children saw having two homes as an advantage.

Similar findings were reported by S. Steinman (1981). She studied thirty-two children from twenty-four families in joint physical custody arrangements and found, as did Luepnitz, that these children had relationships with two psychological parents. Children were aware of the differences between their two homes, their relationship with each parent, and the differences between each parent's personality and values, and they were accepting of these differences. Most of these children experienced no major loyalty conflicts. However, about one-third of the sample were particularly sensitive to their parents' feelings and worried about being fair to their parents. Steinman referred to this reaction as "hyper-loyalty." Similarly, living in two homes did not result in feelings of confusion or insecurity for most children, with only one-fourth of the children having problems in this area. Thus, the criticism that joint physical custody produces confusion and loyalty conflicts in children is not supported by the evidence.

The encouraging findings of Luepnitz and of Steinman are reinforced by the research of R. J. Glover and C. Steele (1988–1989), who compared twenty-four children in matched triplets from two-parent, joint custody, and single custody families. The children were from middle- to upper-middle-class white families and were matched according to gender and age at time of assessment. The results revealed no significant differences between the three groups on locus of control, self-concept, or relations with father or mother. In addition, a comparison of children in joint and single custody arrangements also yielded no differences in their adjustment to divorce. Further descriptive analysis of individual triplets indicated that the responses of joint custody children on the above measures were often as positive or more positive than those of children in single custody or two-parent families.

Three factors are particularly important in understanding children's adjustment to divorce: (1) parent-child relationships; (2) parental conflict; and (3) parents' adjustment.

Parent-Child Relationships. One of the most significant correlates of children's postdivorce adjustment is a continuing relationship with both parents (Hess and Camara, 1979; Wallerstein and Kelly, 1980). The findings from several studies support joint custody as an arrangement that facilitates the continued involvement of both parents in the child's life after divorce.

In the Luepnitz (1986) study, half of the sole custody children never saw the other parent, while all joint physical custody children maintained regular contact with both parents. Observers have been particularly concerned about the disappearance of the noncustodial father from the child's life (e.g., Hetherington et al., 1976). Three studies reveal increased parental involvement by joint custody fathers (Ahrons, 1980; Bowman and Ahrons, 1985; Grief, 1979). M. E. Bowman and Ahrons (1985) compared twenty-eight legal custody fathers with fifty-four noncustodial fathers on three aspects of parental involvement one year after divorce: physical contact with their children, parental involvement, and parental interaction. Joint custody fathers had significantly more contact with their children, rated themselves as more involved in activities with their children, and as more fully sharing parental responsibilities with their exspouses than did noncustodial fathers. Ahrons (1980) found that sixty-five percent of seventeen fathers with joint legal but not joint physical custody saw their children at least once a week or more, several on a daily basis. About half of this group reported that they were more involved in their children's lives than at any point previously.

J. B. Grief (1979) examined the parental involvement of thirty-two noncustodial fathers and eight fathers with joint custody. Compared to the noncustodial fathers, joint custody fathers had greater contact with their children, saw themselves as more involved in their children's lives, were more satsified with the degree of their parental involvement, and felt they had more influence over their child's emotional development. These studies suggest that even in joint legal custodial arrangements where the mother has physical custody, the involvement of fathers in their children's lives is greater than that of noncustodial fathers.

A word of caution is in order regarding a causal interpretation of these findings. All of these studies share the problem of self-selection, which suggests that people who choose joint custody may be different from those who do not. "Whether fathers who are more involved choose joint custody or whether the divorced joint-custodial family arrangement encourages more involvement of fathers after divorce, or some combination of these factors, remains unanswered by this research" (Bowman and Ahrons, 1985, p. 487).

Parental Conflict. Postdivorce conflict between parents is likely to have negative consequences for children's adjustment (Lowery and Settle, 1985; Wallerstein and Kelly, 1980). The limited evidence provides support for the notion that joint custody parents experience less conflict in their relationships than spouses in traditional sole custody arrangements (Ilfeld et al., 1982; Irving et al., 1984; Luepnitz, 1986).

Relitigation of custody has been used as an objective measure of parental conflict. Researchers "assume that relitigation of custody means that parents are in conflict with one another and that parental conflict strong enough to bring them to the courts has adverse effects on the children" (Ilfeld et al., 1982, p. 63). F. W. Ilfeld et al. (1982) compared the relitigation rates of 414 custody cases in California over a 2-year period. They found that the relitigation rate for joint legal custody cases was half that of exclusive custody cases. A total of 32 percent of the exclusive custody cases were relitigated (87 out of 276) compared with only 16 percent (22 out of 138) of the joint custody cases.

Included in the 138 joint custody cases was a subsample of 18 in which joint custody was awarded without the consent of one parent. The relitigation rate for these parents was about the same as that of sole custody parents (33 percent versus 32 percent).

Luepnitz (1986) also investigated relitigation of custody. None of her eleven joint physical custody families returned to court, while 50 percent of the thirty-two single custody families had relitigated. If relitigation is a valid indicator of parental conflict, then joint custody parents appear to experience significantly less conflict than parents with sole custody.

The failure to pay child support may also be associated with parental conflict. Several studies show that joint custody fathers are more likely to fulfill their financial obligations reliably (Irving et al., 1984; Luepnitz, 1986; Steinman, 1981).

Although many joint custody couples have maintained good relations with each other, their relationships are by no means free of conflict. Couples may employ strategies designed to minimize conflict, such as restricting conversation and interaction to "safe" areas (Ahrons, 1980; Irving et al., 1984). Regardless of the nature of the coparental relationship, joint custody parents, for the most part, are able to put their children first. Research findings support the idea that parents can separate their marital problems from their responsibilities as parents and that they can continue a parental relationship after the marital relationship has ended.

Once again, one must be careful not to conclude that the joint custody arrangement "causes" less conflict between parents. An alternative explanation may be that parents who choose joint custody tend to have lower levels of pre- and postseparation conflict than sole custody parents. These parents may also be self-selected for their ability to communicate and negotiate effectively (Luepnitz, 1986).

Parents' Adjustment. Children's adjustment following divorce has been linked to the adjustment of their parents (Pett, 1982). Joint physical custody has a positive effect on parents' emotional adjustment after divorce (Rothberg, 1983; Steinman, 1981). For many of the twenty-four couples in her study, Steinman noted that "coparenting helped to mute their sense of loss and disruption, and allowed them gradually to reorganize their lives" (1981, p. 407). Rothberg (1983) also found that joint custody fathers and mothers felt that the arrangement contributed to their adjustment, but she discovered sex differences in their explanations. Joint custody made the separation easier for men because it provided their lives with continuity and structure. Women valued joint custody for the time it allowed them to spend on their own lives.

In summary, research on joint custody has revealed several positive outcomes for both children and parents. Certain attractive features of joint custody families—heightened paternal involvement, reduced parental conflict, and enhanced parental adjustment—are also correlates of children's postdivorce adjustment. Further, parents have favorable attitudes toward joint custody and feel that such an arrangement has benefits for their children as well as for themselves.

On the surface, these findings provide strong support for statutes that establish a joint custody presumption. However, closer scrutiny of the data and a more careful consideration of the issues indicate that such a conclusion is premature and that a policy of joint custody presumption may be unwise.

JOINT CUSTODY POLICY: OPTION, NOT PRESUMPTION

Several joint custody advocates have argued strongly for a legal presumption in favor of joint custody (Miller, 1979; Robinson, 1982–1983; Roman and Haddad, 1978). J. S. Wallerstein and J. B. Kelly (1980) appear to support a presumption of joint legal custody but not joint physical custody. Although joint custody is an attractive arrangement that has much to offer many children and parents, a joint custody presumption (particularly joint physical custody) is inappropriate.

First, a joint custody presumption lacks empirical support (Benedek and Benedek, 1979; Clingempeel and Reppucci, 1982; Derdeyn and Scott, 1984; Marafiote, 1985). The evidence on the consequences of j 'nt custody for children and for parents is far too limited (McKinnon and Wallerstein, 1988). Only a few studies have been done, and most of these have had very small, homogeneous samples. Most of the studies did not employ a control group. Although many of the findings may be seen as encouraging, the existing data do not warrant the establishment of a legal presumption favoring joint custody. In the words of E. P. Benedek and R. S. Benedek,

Without corroborative research that is far more extensive and convincing than that which is currently available, the arguments of the proponents of joint custody are not sufficiently persuasive to justify a legal presumption favoring joint custody or any predisposition to award joint custody in preference to traditional dispositions (1979, p. 1543).

Those who call for the adoption of presumption statutes go far beyond the available evidence. As A. P. Derdeyn and E. Scott note, "There is a marked disparity between the power of the joint custody movement and the sufficiency of evidence that joint custody can accomplish what we expect of it" (1984, p. 207).

Second, research on joint custody is characterized by self-selection bias. Almost all research on joint custody arrangements and their effects on children and parents has involved couples who wanted and chose joint custody and who were committed to making it work. Further, the studies have looked almost exclusively at middle-class, well-educated parents. It is these individuals who are most likely to have the money, communication skills, and other resources needed to make joint custody work. Their willingness to participate in these studies suggests that they may be the most successful joint custody families. Clearly, one cannot claim that they are representative.

Due to self-selection bias, it is not possible to conclude that joint custody leads to fathers' greater parental involvement and to reduced conflict between parents. An alternative explanation is that fathers who are more involved with their children, and parents who have lower levels of conflict, are more likely to choose joint custody. In other words, the postdivorce behavior of joint custody parents in these areas is a continuation of behavioral patterns established within marriage. "The limited empirical data we have to date suggests that, for those parents who *choose* the option of joint custody, it appears to be a workable and satisfactory arrangement which permits both parents to continue their parenting roles and relationships after divorce" (Bowman and Ahrons, 1985, p. 487).

Studies of joint custody parents who did not voluntarily choose the arrangement can shed light on the self-selection problem. Only two studies have included information of court-ordered joint custody (Ilfeld et al., 1982; Irving et al., 1984). Ilfeld et al. (1982) reported that relitigation rates of court-imposed joint custody cases and sole custody cases were virtually identical. Irving et al. (1984) found that parents in court-imposed joint custody arrangements were less satisfied than parents that had reached a joint custody agreement on their own. These findings cannot be used to support a legal presumption in favor of joint custody.

Third, joint custody presumption legislation is coercive (Benedek and Benedek, 1979; Derdeyn and Scott, 1984; Weitzman, 1985). Under such legislation, many parents will feel compelled to "agree" to joint custody, even when doing so violates their beliefs about what is best for their children. A parent who is strongly opposed to joint custody should not be forced into that arrangement. In the words of one attorney, "joint custody is not a panacea for every case and certain parents should not be compelled to enter into an arrangement that is counterproductive to them and counterproductive to their children's best interests" (Skoloff, 1984, p. 54).

Fourth, this coercive policy seems destined to perpetuate conflict between exspouses (Derdeyn and Scott, 1984; Weitzman, 1985). The vast majority of divorcing couples are able to negotiate and agree on custody settlements out of court. Cases in which parents cannot reach an agreement and custody is contested comprise only about 10 percent of all divorces involving children. Yet it is these parents, those with the greatest degree of interpersonal conflict and hostility toward each other, to whom the joint custody presumption laws will be applied. This court-imposed custody arrangement is likely to result in the perpetuation of conflict between the couple.

Thus, those who are least likely to succeed at joint custody will become likely candidates for joint custody. L. J. Weitzman discusses the implications of this situation for children:

Since joint custody requires an extraordinary level of cooperation, communication, and goodwill between parents, it is surprising to see courts ask this of parents who may still be antagonistic and who can not—and do not wish to—cooperate on a daily basis. If these couples are pressured into a joint custody agreement, it may turn out to be a prescription for exacerbating and prolonging the tensions of divorce for children (1985, p. 247).

Fifth, joint custody presumption could also mean that exwives have less protection from abusive husbands (Luepnitz, 1986). Clearly, sole custody is the preferred arrangement in cases involving spouse abuse.

Sixth, presumption statutes imply that joint custody should be the norm and discourage the assessment of each case on an individual basis (Marafiote, 1985). Each case is unique, and the needs of every child and of every family are different. Because of the critical importance of custody decisions, a careful, thoughtful, case-by-case evaluation is essential.

All of these objections also apply to statutes that make joint custody the preferred option or that permit joint custody at the request of one party. Although statutes that permit joint custody only when both parents agree appear reasonable and harmless, they contain the potential for subtle coercion:

Assume, for example, that one parent does not want joint custody but is afraid of losing sole custody if a judge learns that he or she was "uncooperative" and refused joint custody. This parent may feel she or he has to agree to joint custody to avoid the risk of losing custody altogether (Weitzman, 1985, p. 246).

Based on the available evidence, the best policy seems to be legislation that makes joint custody an *option*. Such legislation minimizes the opportunities for coercion and the perpetuation of conflict. Joint custody, as one custody option among several, enables judges to assess carefully each individual case and thereby best determine which custody arrangement is in the best interests of the child. Finally, this policy encourages the sensible application of scientific knowledge to the custody decision-making process. Research findings can be used to guide individual custody decisions and not generalized to cover all custody cases.

GUIDELINES FOR JOINT CUSTODY

Judges, lawyers, counselors, mediators, and parents need guidelines when considering joint custody. Drawing on the recommendations made in the literature by legal scholars and mental health professionals (Abarbanel, 1979; Benedek and Benedek, 1979; Irving et al., 1984; Miller, 1979; Steinman, 1981; Steinman et al., 1985), I have compiled the following list of conditions or requirements to be met by joint custody parents. The first five features apply to joint legal custody, and all seven are important for joint physical custody. Both parents should:

1. be "fit" parents;
2. desire joint custody and be committed to making it work;
3. enter the joint custody agreement in good faith and trust each other to honor it;
4. be willing and able to cooperate with each other;
5. be supportive of each other's relationship with the child;
6. have the flexibility to organize and coordinate schedules and responsibilities and to adapt to changes that may arise; and
7. live close to each other in order to minimize disruption for the child.

When deciding on joint custody, parents and professionals should also consider the age, number, and age range of the children; the financial means of the parents; and the potential impact of remarriage.

CONCLUSION

Joint custody is undoubtedly the best custody arrangement for many children and their parents. However, it is not for everyone. A legal presumption in favor of joint custody is coercive and is based on an inaccurate reading of current knowledge of the consequences of joint custody for children. Children and parents will be better served through policies that make joint custody an available option after divorce.

NOTE

I gratefully acknowledge the contribution of Hyman Rodman for his helpful comments on an earlier version of this chapter.

15

Policy Implications of Involving Parents in Head Start

Robert K. Leik, Mary Anne Chalkley,
and Nancy J. Peterson

The Head Start Family Impact Project was designed to address the effects of Head Start participation on families and children. Significant long-term benefits of children's participation in a variety of preschool programs have been documented, leading some investigators to posit explanations for those effects on the parent's response to the child's participation in such programs (Lazar, 1983). Yet although family involvement has been a central aspect of Project Head Start since its inception (Condry, 1983), little attention has been given to family factors.

Assuming that parental involvement is important is not sufficient for creating an informed policy aimed at maximizing the benefits of preschool experience. It is still necessary to determine just what constitutes optimal parental involvement and how benefits from that involvement are derived. Without the ability to demonstrate the mechanisms whereby preschool intervention and parental involvement have positive long-term consequences, one cannot evaluate the effectiveness of ongoing programs appropriately nor advise policy makers in which directions change and innovation would be most beneficial. The project reported here provides some initial evidence regarding how parental and family factors interact with the Head Start experience to increase benefits for the child.

The emergence of project Head Start in 1965 reflected a major change in federal social policy regarding families. A sense of social activism and concern for the poor of that era was given focus by research evidence that deficits in academic (and other) skills could be offset by changing the individual's environment. It was argued that children of poverty would benefit academically from preschool enrichment programs. Initial research findings supported large academic gains for children who participated in preschool programs, and Head Start received substantial support. Later, however, the Westinghouse report (Westinghouse Learning Corporation, 1969) concluded that these gains virtually vanished by the fourth or fifth grade, and support for Head Start was cut. Only with the development of the Consortium for Longitudinal Studies and their more recent finds of long-term advantages for poor children who participated in preschool programs (Consortium for Longitudinal Studies, 1983; Lazar and Darlington, 1982) has Head Start again received significant support (see Condry [1983] for a detailed discussion of the history of Head Start, its funding, and the role played by the Consortium for Longitudinal Studies).

Yet, support for Head Start has never reached levels where all eligible and interested families can participate. Much of the current willingness to fund Head Start is based on the fact that the long-term benefits documented by the Consortium (Lazar and Darlington, 1982; Royce et al., 1983) are ones that reduce the ultimate cost of educating children from poor families. Compared with children who did not participate in preschool programs, Head Start children from poor families were less likely to be retained in grade or to need special education during their schooling careers. While these results are indeed gratifying, they are limited in two major ways. First, they focus on purely academic costs without measures of other potential costs and benefits for society. Second, there is little evidence that variation in the specific preschool curriculum content has significant impact on the long-term advantages of the preschool experience.

The one pattern of intervention that may be most efficacious includes services for parents as well as for children, involvement of parents in the instruction of the child, and home visits (Royce et al., 1983). Fostering an environment is apparently more important than providing specific skills. Clearly, the family provides the primary environment for preschoolers.

Whether to foster systematic involvement of parents or other family members in Head Start is a policy question. Data from the Head Start Family Impact Project, a one-year demonstration and research project focused on the consequences of involving family members in the Head Start program, suggest that such involvement can indeed be beneficial. Yet there are indications that optimal involvement is not a simple matter. In particular, there appear to be important cultural differences that interact with certain parent and family variables in the Head Start context.

The Head Start Family Impact Project was conducted at Parents in Community Action (PICA), the Head Start program for Hennepin County, Minnesota, in conjunction with a research team from the University of Minnesota. The project's theoretical basis derives from family systems theory. Specific hypotheses include:

1. The child's participation in Head Start should have beneficial effects on his or her feelings of competence, social acceptance, and independence, which are essential to enable optimal learning.
2. Parental involvement in Head Start will allow parents and children both to observe and interact with each other in a structured context involving other adults and children. That experience, in turn, will enable more accurate perceptions and more favorable evaluations of each other.
3. Parental involvement in Head Start, especially for the economically disadvantaged, should foster a sense of parental self-efficacy, hence greater self-esteem and feelings of personal control of one's life.
4. Higher parental evaluation of the child and higher parental self-esteem will both generate closer parent-child relations, fostering greater family cohesion, a greater sense of togetherness.
5. Higher parental sense of personal control will allow less rigid family attempts to control, hence greater family adaptability (that is, greater flexibility in assigning responsibilities, changing rules, and dealing with discipline).
6. Both the parent variables and the family variables cited above will feed back on the child's ability to benefit from the educational environment, fostering greater advances than would occur without involvement of the parents in Head Start.

DESIGN

Before and After Design

The PICA Head Start program is an all-day program that meets two or three days a week from 1 October to the first week in May. Assessments of all families studied were made at two time points: mid-October 1986 and late April 1987. Consequently we have the opportunity to assess change over the program year. It should be noted, however, that the actual elapsed time between assessments was just six months, which may be too little time for some types of effects to become apparent.

Samples

Three comparison groups were selected for study: two samples of Head Start families and one control sample. Head Start families were divided into the *regular group*, which had the usual menu of opportunities for parental participation in PICA Head Start, and the *enriched group*, which was expected to take part in specially designed experiences. Being in the enriched group did not preclude participation in the usual menu of activities available to the regular group. PICA Head Start makes an unusually strong effort to involve all parents in the program. The *control group* was selected from families who had applied for Head Start but were not accepted because of space limitations.

Initial sampling plans called for selecting fifty cases per group, but that number proved to be unattainable for a variety of reasons. Families were eliminated because (1) they did not meet the established criteria of single-parent, female-headed families with a child between 3.6 and 5.1 years of age; (2) they were not fluent in English (recent Asian immigrants); (3) they dropped out of Head Start; or (4) they failed to respond to numerous recruiting attempts including telephone calls, mail, and notes sent with their children. Our enormous sampling difficulties are instructive for those studying this type of population. Details are available from the authors.

The final count of Head Start families was eighty-one, originally divided equally between the regular and enriched groups. However, because a number of the families initially assigned to the enriched group indicated at the outset that they were unable to meet the schedule of special activities, they were reassigned for analysis purposes to the regular group. Final frequencies for the two groups were thirty enriched and fifty-one regular.

Sampling for the control group was even more problematic. Substantial proportions of the pool were two-parent families, had only younger children, or were non-English speaking. Of the families that fit our criteria, only twenty-seven finally agreed to participate, and only twenty-one came in for both assessments. The control sample may be nonrepresentative because it was only about 2 percent of the pool from which we assumed we could draw.

Assessment

Assessments consisted primarily of a self-report questionnaire completed by the mother. Additionally, a pictorial self-report task was completed by each child. We will focus only on the family and child variables suggested above. (For a complete description of assessments and other procedures see Leik, Peterson, and Chalkley [1987].) Specific variables of interest are:

a. FACES III (Family Adaptability and Cohesion Scales) (Olson, et al., 1985). Two measurements result from FACES: family cohesion and family adaptability. D. H. Olson's circumplex theory suggests that extreme scores in either direction on either dimension inhibit family functioning.

b. Mother's self-esteem (Rosenberg, 1965).

c. Mother's locus of control (Rotter, 1966).

d. Child's independence (Chalkley, 1986).

e. Mother's satisfaction with child's independence (Chalkley, 1986).

f. Child's perceived competence and acceptance (child is respondent) (Harter and Pike, 1984).

g. Mother's perception of child's competence and acceptance (mother responds about the child) (Harter and Pike, 1984).

h. Selected demographic variables.

With the exception of the independence measures, all of the scales used are well-established, existing scales. For the two independence scales created by M. A. Chalkley for this project, reliability (Cronbach's alpha) was .56 for the behavioral report and .75 for the parental satisfaction. For the other scales reliability ranged from .75 to .83. No attempt to assess the child's perception of the parent was made, although that is a very important question for future research.

The Enrichment Activities

Seven enrichment activities were designed specifically to foster the parent-child relationship in the context of the Head Start program. There were three support groups, three computer games, and a role-playing session. Two of the support groups were for the mothers only, whereas the other five activities involved both the mothers and their children. The support sessions focused on (1) what the mothers wanted for their families, (2) sharing and playing with children, and (3) preparing the families for the child's entry into school.

Role-playing sessions were organized into sets of three or four parent-child pairs (six to eight participants per session). The activity called for the parent and child to switch roles and act out resolving some problem they identified. Role playing of each pair was observed by the rest of the group so that all could benefit from the experience.

The three computer sessions involved: (1) a simple color sketching game in which the child, with mother's help, created a drawing on the monitor; (2) a birthday party planning game emphasizing that each decision one makes constrains future decisions; and (3) a treasure hunt emphasizing systematic search procedures for obtaining resources. The majority of the mothers found all seven activities to be enjoyable and useful, according to responses to a questionnaire administered at the end of the study. In particular, the mothers strongly endorsed adopting such activities in all Head Start programs.

DESCRIPTION OF THE PARTICIPANT FAMILIES

This presentation emphasizes the eighty-one Head Start families which participated in the project. Data regarding the control group families are presented only in those instances where these families differ from the Head Start families on some important variable. Similarly, all Head Start families are combined except in those instances when differentiating between the regular and enriched groups reveals important differences between the groups.

Demographic Data

Head Start mothers averaged 28 years of age with a median income of $531 per month. Of all our sample mothers, 74 percent had either a high-school diploma or GED certificate. Of the eighty-one Head Start mothers studied, 39.8 percent were white, 42.2 percent black, 15.7 percent American Indian, and 2.4 mixed. Two-thirds of these mothers were never married, yet the households were atypically large, with a mean of 3.95 and a median of 3.66 members. One-third had three or more children, and nearly half had two or more adults. A total of 23 percent of the mothers reported some type of male partner residing with them.

Typical family composition differed somewhat from sample to sample. Less than one-tenth (9.5 percent) of the control group families had only one child; almost a quarter (24.7 percent) of the Head Start families had only one child. Furthermore, none of the families in the enriched sample had more than three children, but 19.6 percent of the regular families had four or more children.

Parent Variables (Self-Esteem and Locus of Control)

The Head Start mothers showed no essential differences from available norms for either self-esteem or locus of control despite the fact that divorce typically increases locus of control scores temporarily (Hetherington, Cox, and Cox, 1982). Higher locus of control scores imply more external control, whereas lower scores imply more internal control.

Child Variables (Independence, Competence, and Acceptance)

The child's independence behavior, as rated by the mother, averaged 37.18 for the Head Start families, compared to a mean of 38.08 for children in a University of Minnesota preschool program. The difference approaches significance, indicating a tendency for Head Start mothers to see their children as slightly less independent ($t = 1.14$, $p < .20$).

When the mothers' satisfaction with their children's independence behavior is examined, however, Head Start mothers were more satisfied than were the mothers in the university preschool (25.04 v. 23.00; $t = 2.85$, $p < .01$).

The pictorial procedure for assessing a child's perceived competence and acceptance does not distinguish the Head Start children from known scale norms (Head Start mean equals 76.54 compared to a norm mean of 76.20) (Harter and Pike, 1984). Using identical items, the Head Start mothers rated their children somewhat lower (73.33). The difference of 3.21 points is statistically significant ($t = 2.3$, $p < .02$).

Even more noteworthy is the fact that the mean discrepancy between mothers and their children differs across the treatment groups: enriched $= 2.54$, regular $= 4.81$, and control $= 6.04$. Since so few variables showed important differences in the fall assessment, it should be noted that these scores were obtained in November, over a month after the Head Start year began and families had been assigned to treatment groups. It is possible that some effects of the differential treatment were already underway. As will be seen, the difference between Head Start and control families became even greater over the balance of the year.

Family Variables (Cohesion and Adaptability)

One set of scale scores remains; the cohesion and adaptability scores from FACES III (Olson et al., 1985). To interpret the findings correctly, it is necessary to recognize that Olson's circumplex model specifies both high and low extreme scores as detrimental. That is, too much cohesion or too much adaptability poses a problem for family functioning, just as too little of either would be problematic. On both scales, the Head Start families showed far more extreme scores than did the normative sample data from Olson. A total of 42 percent of the Head Start families were in either extreme of the cohesion dimension, compared to only 29.9 percent based on available norms. For adaptability, 50.6 percent of the Head Start families fell into one of the extreme categories compared to only 32.3 percent of the normative sample. These data are shown in Figure 15.1.

Although the Head Start population differed considerably from reported norms, the control group was not as extreme as were the Head Start samples. Combining the percentages that fell in either extreme reveals that unlike both Head Start samples, the control group was not noticeably different from Olson's norms in terms of adaptability (35 percent v. 32.3 percent). For cohesion, Olson reports that 29.9 percent of his sample fell into the extreme range. By comparison 37.7 percent of the regular Head Start sample were extreme on cohesion, and 50 percent of the enriched group and the control sample were extreme on

Figure 15.1
Percentage Distribution of Head Start Families According to Olson's Typology, Fall 1986

FAMILY COHESION

FAMILY ADAPTABILITY	Disengaged	Separated	Connected	Enmeshed	
Chaotic	6.2 (3.0)	6.2 (5.0)	8.6 (4.0)	7.4 (4.0)	28.4 (16.0)
Flexible	0.0 (4.5)	8.6 (10.0)	7.4 (12.9)	2.5 (5.0)	18.5 (29.4)
Structured	9.6 (7.0)	18.5 (13.9)	2.5 (13.9)	1.2 (3.5)	30.9 (38.3)
Rigid	12.3 (1.0)	0.0 (8.0)	6.2 (3.0)	3.7 (1.5)	22.2 (16.3)
	27.2 (16.3)	33.3 (33.8)	24.7 (36.3)	14.8 (13.6)	

Summary percentages by family type

Balanced (white)	37.0	(50.7)
Mid-range (single line)	33.3	(40.0)
Extreme (double line)	29.6	(9.5)

Olson's norms are shown in parentheses

Summary percentages by family type: Balanced (white): 37.0 (50.7); Mid-range (boxed): 33.3 (40.0); Extreme (shaded): 29.6 (9.5). Olson's norms are shown in parentheses.

that dimension. Thus, the control group reflected family patterns closer to those described by Olson than did the Head Start groups, but all three groups were more extreme than Olson's norms in at least one dimension.

When the two dimensions—adaptability and cohesion—are plotted jointly, following Olson, it is apparent that the four most extreme family types (extreme on both dimensions) were three times as likely among the Head Start families compared to the norms: 29.6 percent v. 9.5 percent (regular sample, 29.4 percent; enriched sample, 30.0 percent). By con-

Table 15.1
Predicted v. Observed Proportions of Extreme Family Types

Extreme Type	Group	Predicted	Observed
'rigid-disengaged'	Enriched	6.0%	10.0%
	Regular	6.0%	13.7%
	Control	4.5%	5.0%
'chaotic-enmeshed'	Enriched	6.7%	10.0%
	Regular	3.0%	5.9%
	Control	4.0%	15.0%

Predictions are based on marginal distribution of the relevant cohesion and adaptability types.

trast just 20 percent of the control group families fell into the four extreme family types. Balanced families, having intermediate scores on both dimensions, were underrepresented among the Head Start sample (37.3 percent) and among the control group sample (35 percent; norm = 50.7 percent). The most striking difference occurs in the single extreme category of "disengaged–rigid," representing twelve times the percentage of Head Start families compared to normative (Olson) sample families.

The high percentages of the four extreme family types in the Head Start samples are not merely an independent function of the fact that more of these families were extreme on either cohesion or adaptability. Examination of Table 15.1 reveals that the percentage of families of the extreme types was not only considerably higher in the Head Start sample than in Olson's sample, but the co-occurrences of extremity on both dimensions that define those family types were higher than would be expected if adaptability and cohesion are independent dimensions.

DOES INVOLVEMENT IN HEAD START MAKE A DIFFERENCE?

Amount of Mother's Participation in Head Start

Setting aside the 15 or 20 hours required for the enrichment activities, mothers in the enrichment group invested a mean of 25.9 hours in Head Start activities over the 6-month period, with a median of 17.3 hours. The range was from only 2 hours to an impressive 153 hours. When time spent in the enrichment activities is added to the other time spent, enriched sample mothers averaged about 1.6 hours per week involved in Head Start activities.

In contrast, the regular Head Start sample had a mean time investment of 19.4 hours, with a median of 13.6 and a range of 0 to 154. Overall, the regular sample mothers averaged less than 1 hour per week throughout the 6 months of study, or about half the time put in by the enriched sample.

It is possible, of course, that the enriched sample was willing to be in that treatment group because they had more time available. However, we doubt that such an explanation covers the very large difference documented. It would appear that committing themselves to the enrichment treatment induced these mothers to take a much more active part in the entire Head Start program. If so, this is a very important finding.

Cohesion and Adaptability

The Head Start families made significant changes in family cohesion and adaptability during the six months of study (see Figure 15.2). In particular, at the final assessment, the proportion of disengaged (low cohesion) families had dropped to 18.5 percent from the initial 27.2 percent. Similarly, the proportion of rigid (extreme lack of adaptability) families dropped to 17.3 percent compared to the initial 22.2 percent. Overall, the four extreme family types dropped to only 13.5 percent from the initial 29.6 percent. Although there were still fewer "balanced" families than the norms would imply, many previously extreme families moved into more intermediate types.

One possible explanation of the changes in cohesion and adaptability is the well-known problem of regression to the mean of extreme scores. Although this could explain some of the observed change, it is unlikely that regression is a complete answer. Earlier test-retest reliability checks on FACES (a fifty-item version of FACES II rather than FACES III) produced a reliability coefficient of .84 over a five-week period, which is certainly indicative of stability of the scores. Not only did substantial change occur in the Head Start family scores, but the change was not symmetric. For cohesion, the percentage of disengaged families dropped 8.0 percent whereas the percentage of enmeshed families dropped 5.6 percent compared to only a 0.7 percent drop in the percentage of chaotic families.

Changes in the number of extreme family types highlight differences among the three groups studied. For the control group all four families that were initially classified as an extreme family type were not so classified in the spring; but three other control families became extreme-type families by spring. Thus, the net reduction of families of the extreme types was only 25 percent for the control group. For the regular group, ten out of the fifteen families initially identified as extreme were not so classified in the spring, while four families moved into the extreme classification, giving a 40 percent net reduction of extreme family types for the regular Head Start group. For the enriched families, eight out of nine families moved out of an extreme family type, and only one family

Figure 15.2
Percentage Distribution of Head Start Families According to Olson's Typology, Spring 1987

FAMILY COHESION

FAMILY ADAPTABILITY	Disengaged	Separated	Connected	Enmeshed	
Chaotic	3.7 (3.0)	13.6 (5.0)	7.4 (4.0)	3.7 (4.0)	28.4 (16.0)
Flexible	3.7 (4.5)	16.0 (10.0)	3.7 (12.9)	3.7 (5.0)	27.2 (29.4)
Structured	6.2 (7.0)	13.6 (13.9)	4.9 (13.9)	2.5 (3.5)	27.2 (38.3)
Rigid	4.9 (1.0)	7.4 (8.0)	3.7 (3.0)	1.2 (1.5)	17.3 (16.3)
	18.5 (16.3)	50.6 (33.8)	19.8 (36.3)	11.1 (13.6)	

Summary percentages by family type

Balanced (white)	38.2	(50.7)
Mid-range (single line)	48.2	(40.0)
Extreme (double line)	13.5	(9.5)

Olson's norms are shown in parentheses

Summary percentages by family type: Balanced (white): 38.2 (50.7); Mid-range (boxed): 48.2 (40.0); Extreme (shaded): 13.5 (9.5). Olson's norms are shown in parentheses.

became an extreme type, resulting in a 78 percent drop in the extreme type for the enriched group. If percent reduction in the enriched family type is considered a random variable, then percent reduction in the enriched families is significantly different from both the control families and the regular families ($p < .01$ for both comparisons). The control and the regular families do not differ significantly ($p = $ about .20).

If change in cohesion and adaptability scores is purely a statistical artifact, then the probability of change should not be affected by treatment. All three groups showed high probabilities of initially extreme scores becoming less extreme during the period of study (control, 100 percent; regular, 66.7 percent; enriched, 89 percent). However, the probability of cases initially classified as less extreme becoming more extreme differed greatly and systematically by treatment. For control group families, 17.7 percent (three out of the seventeen that were initially intermediate or balanced) became extreme by the time of the spring assessment. For the regular sample, only 11.4 percent (four out of thirty-five) of the originally nonextreme families became extreme. For the enriched sample, a surprisingly small 4.8 percent (one out of twenty-two) of the families moved into the extreme types.

It seems likely that participation in an enriched Head Start program may provide a "buffer" or special resource that helps to prevent deterioration of family functioning. Of course, small sample sizes prevent apparently sizeable differences from reaching statistical significance. Nevertheless, the data justify further research into the question of how Head Start participation, and participation in enrichment activities in particular, might serve to enhance family functioning and possibly prevent its decline.

Competence and Acceptance

The next intriguing finding concerns the competence and acceptance scores (Harter and Pike, 1984). From the fall to the spring assessment, the children's own scores increased slightly for both treatment groups and for the control group. Increases averaged 3.2 points for the enriched group ($p < .05$), 2.8 for the regular group ($p < .005$), and 2.2 (n.s.) for the controls. The parents' assessments of their children's competence and acceptance, however, shows a very different pattern. Parents in both Head Start samples increased their scores more than the children did (4.2 for the enriched, 6.6 for the regular; p for both $< .0005$), with the result that the earlier discrepancies between parent and child scores almost disappeared. The mean parent-child difference was only .89 in the spring assessment.

In contrast, control group parents' discrepancies from their children's scores in the fall did not decrease during the six months of the study. In fact they increased slightly, from a mean difference of 6.16 at the beginning of the study to a mean difference of 6.28 at the end. Both differences are significant at $p < .025$. It appears that involvement in Head Start, regardless of enriched or regular participation, allowed parents' assessments of their children, at least on this dimension, to become more accurate reflections of how the children see themselves.

A Qualification Regarding Assessing Change

At the end of the school year, both Head Start and control mothers were asked to respond to a questionnaire regarding specific changes they had noticed in their children, in themselves, or in their relationship with their children over the past nine months. In general, there were few items that differentiated between the two groups. Control group mothers did see their relationships with other adults as having improved more than did Head Start mothers ($t = 2.29$, $p < .02$), while Head Start mothers reported that their children were happier ($p < .05$). Further analysis of these data revealed no systematic pattern of change that favored either Head Start or control families. It became apparent, however, that the parents' reports on such simplified items were suspect. The control parents, for example, reported increased independence for their children, yet no such difference occurred when they were actually asked to rate their children's behavior (that is, there were no fall-spring differences on the independence measures). Similarly, items related to competence failed to obtain differential responses despite the marked difference between the Head Start and control parents on the competence and acceptance scale. Clearly, merely asking parents what they may have noticed or how their attitudes may have changed is not a sensitive enough measure of how they are actually affected by the Head Start program. Better articulated measures of change are necessary in order to capture the impact of Head Start upon parental and family variables.

We do have evidence that involving mothers in Head Start can have favorable impact on their perception of their children and on family functioning. Other data are less clearly indicative of advantages for the Head Start families compared to the control families. In certain respects, control families indicated more favorable initial circumstances compared to Head Start families. Consequently, we may assume that any differences occurring over the Head Start year that favor the Head Start families are to that extent more convincing than if the samples were equal at the outset.

A Cautionary Note

The involvement scores (or time spent in Head Start activities) provide an intriguing finding that suggests certain problems for getting parents involved in Head Start. There is a negative correlation between involvement and the family pride scale of $-.21$ for all Head Start mothers. Thus, those mothers who spent more time in Head Start activities had lower family pride scores. The most immediate explanation, suggested by informal conversation between the mothers and both the research staff and the PICA Head Start staff, is that getting involved in activities outside the home often causes friction between the mothers and their partners. Of course, not all of the mothers had partners at home, and we do not have anecdotal evidence relating to other family members' (e.g., grandparents') reactions. However, investing time outside the home is evidently risky for some relationships. A most important question for future research is whether involving the friend or partner as well as the mother can strengthen the whole family rather than threaten the adult relationship.

A POSSIBLE THEORETICAL MODEL

As interesting as the preceding findings are, they remain idiosyncratic observations. To provide theoretical context for our work, we have been exploring a simple causal model relating child, mother, and family variables. The mode is shown in Figure 15.3. In general, mother's self-esteem, child's acceptance/competence, mother's perception of child's acceptance/competence, and family cohesion are seen as one set of closely linked variables, while mother's locus of control, child's independence, mother's satisfaction with child's independence, and family adaptability are seen as another closely linked set. There are a few cross-over effects hypothesized between these sets.

As indicated in Figure 15.3, we hypothesize that mother's factors influence child's factors, which in turn influence mother's perception of and satisfaction with child, resulting in impacts on family factors. The family factors, then, impact on possible changes as a result of involvement in Head Start, especially on changes in the child factors. It is not the purpose of this chapter to pursue the reasons for this particular model. However, if evidence supports such a causal structure, then there are clear implications for involving mothers, or, more generally, adults from the families of Head Start children, in the Head Start programs.

It would be convenient to report a solution to the model and stop at that point. Unfortunately, a single solution would be grossly misleading. Exploration of the model began with a more detailed examination of discrepancies between children's perception of their acceptance/competence and mothers' perception of their children's acceptance/competence at the spring assessment.

It immediately became obvious that race had a major impact on the discrepancy data. Mean mother-child discrepancies were: white $=$ -2.25; black $= 6.37$; and native American $= 9.17$. The differences between white and either of the other two groups are significant at the .05 level. Other major differences between the three groups also ap-

Figure 15.3
Proposed Causal Model Linking Parent, Child, and Family Factors

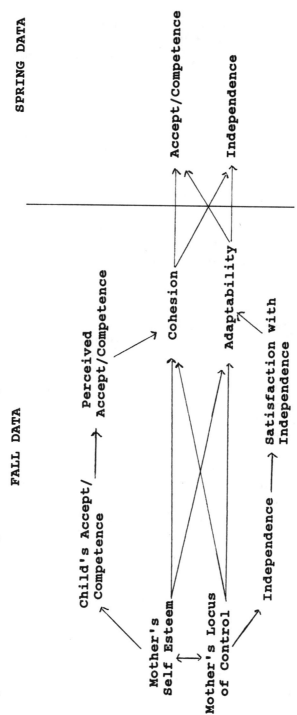

peared. For example, mean locus of control scores were: white = 8.53; black = 10.58; and native American = 9.07. The white-black difference is significant at the .01 level. Finally, mean stress levels differed: white = 14.81; black = 10.65; and native American = 14.05. Again, the white-black difference is significant at the .01 level, and the black–native American difference approaches .05 significance.

Those differences suggested that perhaps relevant covariances were also different between the racial samples. Indeed, examination of the separate correlation matrices indicated some major effects of race on the interrelationships of the relevant variables. Painfully aware of the restrictions posed by having only forty-two white, forty black, and twenty native American families, we nevertheless concluded that it would be necessary to estimate the proposed model separately for each racial group. Table 15.2 contains the path coefficients, by race, along with multiple R^2 values for all variables predicted by other variables in the model. The table is an unusual form for path model results, but it makes comparison of racial groupings easier.

Detailed commentary on Table 15.2 is not warranted, but it is relevant to point out a few major features. First, the overall predictability (R^2) of the child variables is virtually nonexistent in the fall data (except for child's independence in the white sample) but is consistent and of reasonable strength for the spring data (multiple correlations are on the order of .4 to .5). Since the spring predictions rely on the family variables as well as the mother's perception and satisfaction variables, it is reasonable to conclude that those variables are particularly important. Second, note that both magnitude and sign of the various path coefficients change from one racial group to the other. For example, the path from mother's self-esteem to family adaptability is .40 for whites but −.03 for blacks. The path from mother's locus of control to independence is −.50 for whites but .28 for native Americans. Other similar shifts can be observed throughout the table.

It is inescapable, then, that the cultural differences represented by the label "race" create different and in some instances opposite effects for the variables under study. No single strategy for maximizing the benefits of Head Start would appear appropriate for these three cultures. Without further data, we must conclude that other cultures not included in our sample (e.g., Asian, Hispanic) may also show important differences in the way the parent, child, and family variables are linked.

Caution is necessary in determining why parental involvement has the benefits indicated. We have sketched a relatively simply causal model linking parental factors, family functioning, and child factors. However, the relationships among those variables differ in important ways depending upon cultural context.

Table 15.2
R^2 Values and Path Coefficients by Race, for the Model in Figure 15.3[1]

	White (n = 42)	Black (n = 40)	Native American (n = 20)
Mother's Self-Esteem			
Child's Accept/Comp	.21	.03	-.02
Cohesion	.63	.12	.42
Adaptability	.40	-.03	.16
Mother's Locus of Control[2]			
Independence	-.50	-.02	.28
Cohesion	-.04	-.25	.03
Adaptability	.05	-.32	.31
Child's Accept/Comp	(.043)	(.001)	(.000)
Perceived Accept/ Comp	.27	.30	.51
Child's Independence	(.246)	(.001)	(.082)
Satisfaction with Indep	.61	.20	.03
Perceived Accept/Comp	(.075)	(.089)	(.261)
Cohesion	.00	.34	-.12
SPRING Child's Accept/Comp	.27	.46	.37
Satisfaction with Independence	(.375)	(.042)	(.001)
Adaptability	-.01	.15	.34
SPRING Child's Independence	.26	-.13	-.20
Cohesion	(.419)	(.214)	(.200)
SPRING Child's Accept/Comp	-.42	.05	-.25
SPRING Child's Independence	.45	.58	-.26
Adaptability	(.145)	(.110)	(.249)
SPRING Child's Accept/Comp	.21	.13	.31
SPRING Child's Independence	-.27	-.22	-.08
SPRING Child's Accept/Comp	(.215)	(.252)	(.251)
SPRING Child's Independence	(.294)	(.223)	(.141)

1. R^2 values are shown in parentheses.

2. High locus of control scores imply external control whereas low scores imply internal control.

POLICY CONSIDERATION

Given the cultural variation in our findings, it may be that no single policy for parental involvement will be equally satisfactory for all cultural groups. Of course we need much more evidence before drawing extensive policy conclusions. However, our data do speak to several policy issues.

1. A fundamental premise of this research was that Head Start affects families, not just children. We were fortunate to work with a Head Start program that places high importance on family involvement. Given the change in Head Start mothers' perceptions of their children's competence and acceptance reported here, it is apparent that Head Start does affect the parent as well as the child.

2. An obvious corollary of the significance of parental involvement is that not all types of involvement are equally significant. Our theoretical model focuses on the importance of the parent and child interacting in a setting where each would have the opportunity to perceive the other as competent. Our enrichment activites were designed to meet this special need. Those families that participated in these activities were the ones that evidenced the most significant positive changes in family functioning. Although the parents in the regular Head Start program had some similar opportunities (e.g., to work as an aid in the classroom), systematic efforts to offer this special kind of parental involvement need to be encouraged.

3. Parental involvement may not be the only type of involvement that is appropriate for Head Start programs. B. Brown (1987) has argued that involvement in Head Start of other extended family members could have beneficial effects for both the child and the family. Indeed, if such involvement would enhance family pride, then it could offset our finding that parental involvement may involve a cost in family pride.

4. Another important policy problem is to determine how best to capitalize on cultural variations to maximize benefits to all children in Head Start. Our evidence regarding possible models of change clearly indicates that one cannot ignore racial/cultural variation. While our data are not adequate to generate specific program proposals, we would argue that greater effort must be made to be sensitive to the cultural context in which these families live.

5. Finally, it is apparent that more research of the type outlined here is needed. Even the members of the Consortium for Longitudinal Studies expressed concern that the only criterion used for measuring "success" was academic in nature (Royce et al., 1983). Without expanded definitions of success and without further research to investigate them, Head Start could lose much of what it was intended to offer. Merely asking parents if they thought things have improved is also not enough (as

witnessed by our data). A concerted effort must be made to develop methods to evaluate the broad range of Head Start goals. Only when one can consider the impact on the family, the social and emotional impact on the child, and the effect within the various cultural communities, as well as the impact on the child's academic success can one begin to evaluate program effectiveness and assess the true social cost of excluding children of the poor from programs like Head Start. At this point, there is good reason to believe that involving parents in Head Start as coparticipants with their children, rather than simply as home-based teachers, fosters the type of family environment that helps the children most in the long run.

NOTE

Without the tireless efforts of Dr. Bernard Brown, Social Research Analyst, Administration on Children, Youth and Families, this project would never have come to pass. Not only was Dr. Brown instrumental in obtaining funding, he contributed many of the ideas upon which this research is based.

We would like to acknowledge the efforts of Alyce Dillon, director of PICA (Parents in Community Action) Head Start of Minneapolis, in establishing this project. Special thanks go to Lori Holmberg who served as the project coordinator at PICA. Her diligence and good humor were essential to the effective creation and implementation of the enrichment activities and to the successful completion of the data collection. We are also grateful to PICA staff who assisted us both directly and indirectly. This project could not have happened without the generosity of the parents and children who allowed us a glimpse into their personal lives.

We also wish to thank all of the researchers who allowed us to use (and in some cases modify) their various assessment instruments. Thanks also go to Lisa Tahti who as project secretary kept us organized and up to date.

This project was funded through a subcontract with PICA Head Start. Primary funding was provided by the Administration on Children Youth and Families/ Department of Health and Human Services (ACYF/DHHS). Additional funding was provided by the Center for Urban and Regional Affairs, University of Minnesota. Some computer equipment was made available through Project Woksape and Project Minnemac, University of Minnesota.

16

The Future of Family Policy: A Postscript

Elaine A. Anderson

Throughout its history the United States has had an ambivalent approach to social policy, vacillating between a belief in rugged individualism and a belief in proactive social reform. During the 1980s, many of the accomplishments brought about by the New Deal were dismantled as the federal government attempted increasingly to rely on market forces to respond to social ills (Anderson, 1989, pp. 191–192).

In spite of political verbiage to the contrary, there has been a lack of governmental concern about the well-being of families and, hence, a lack of governmental or bureaucratic structures that focus primarily on family needs. Many governmental programs have been developed to deal with the consequences of dysfunction in families, but rarely have these social programs been directed toward the family as a unit. Although most countries have found it difficult to establish a cohesive and comprehensive family policy, the United States lags far behind the efforts of others.

From the early years of this country, the relationship between family and government has been uneasy. Unlike most Western democracies, the Constitution of the United States does not assume protection of family life. In fact, the founding fathers chose not to mention the family in that document. The reigning philosophy of that time celebrated individualism, and the focus was on removing constraints on individual freedom. To this day, political quarrels about family policy can be traced to a conflict between concern for the individual and concern for the well-being of the family group.

Under the 10th Amendment to the U.S. Constitution, powers not assigned to the federal government were delegated to the various states.

Issues related to family matters, such as marriage, divorce, property distribution, and child welfare, were relegated to the individual states. Thus, state laws and judicial actions, differing from state to state, created the structure that regulated families and were, in effect, the first family policies.

When state regulation failed to resolve certain family problems, the federal government has been willing to step in on occasion. Government began, for example, to assume responsibility for the care of children and dependents who could not be cared for properly by their own families. However, once again, social policy emphasizing concern for the individual rather than for the total family dominated governmental activity until recent years.

By the mid-1970s, there was a small but significant press for government policy to focus more directly on the well-being of the American family and its members. American demographics were beginning to indicate that family life was changing, and many were concerned that the family was being destroyed. Efforts were made to develop policies to accommodate such family trends as women's growing presence in the work place, the need for child care services, divorce, teenage single parenthood, and elderly dependents, as well as problems such as teenage suicide, substance abuse, and family violence. The 1980 White House Conference on Families focused on the relationship between government and family life. It seemed for a time that the groundswell needed to form an American consensus on family policy had begun.

The 1980s did not witness the development of any cohesive and comprehensive family policy. However, political dialogue increasingly included a discussion of the potential impact of proposed legislation on family life. Social service reform, industrial benefits, and child welfare legislation were some of the legislative areas to consider the needs of families. The pluralism of families began to be accepted and ethnic diversity to be understood. A recognition was developing that the American government should promote the stability and well-being of American families; that the social programs of the federal government should be formulated and administered with family stability in mind; and finally that the president, or some person so designated by him (Rue, 1973), should report to the Congress on the condition of the American family—reflecting the great range of American families in terms of regions, national origins, and economic status. Thus, we have entered the 1990s with heightened awareness but little substantive policy change.

The decade of the 1990s brings social problems of unprecedented magnitude since the Depression. Although public programs have successfully curtailed poverty among the aged, poverty rates for children have sharply increased. Children in single-parent families are particularly at risk (Martin and Bumpass, 1989). A growing number of children—now almost one in four—are born to unmarried women. Children in female-headed households have a poverty rate of 55 percent (Evans et al., 1984). This percent is five times the poverty rate of children in families who are not headed by single mothers.

R. Reischauer has demonstrated that in terms of income distribution by age and family composition, we are becoming more unequal: "The average adjusted family income of people in the bottom fifth—or quintile—of the population was 11 percent lower in 1987 than for their counterparts in 1973, while that of the top fifth was 24 percent higher" (1989, p. 130). Single mothers with children fared the worst. Scholars are now studying whether or not family structure has become the major determinant of class structure.

There is no doubt to many that issues of family must be addressed by the federal government. However, in order to address the issue of what family policy should be in the 1990s requires several activities. The federal budget irresponsibilities of the last decade must be remedied. Without such budgetary solutions, we cannot finance policies to develop and improve programs that will change the condition of families. Without fiscal resources, it will be difficult at best to generate support for addressing the major family issues.

The domain of family policy, as T. Ooms and S. Preister (1988) have discussed, should be confined to four basic areas of family functioning, namely policies that directly and explicitly concern the nation's investment in *family composition and structure* (policies that affect childbirth, marriage, divorce, parenting, adoption, and foster care); *economic support* (policies that affect families' ability to provide for their dependents' basic needs); *childrearing* (policies that concern parents' ability to nurture and rear their children); and *family care* (policies that concern families' ability to care for their chronically ill, frail, or disabled members and relatives of all ages). Family policy should design programs directed at the major family social conditions that attempt to address and support the aforementioned family issues and responsibilities.

Currently, most public policymaking continues to focus on individuals with specific needs or problems. Once again, we would argue that policymaking needs to broaden its focus to include individuals' family context. The family is often a part of an individual's problem (Ooms, 1984), it is affected by the problem, and usually needs to be involved in the solution to the problem. Thus a family perspective, which keeps families as a policy priority, acknowledges family in the role of the individual's well-being and keeps policy makers informed about the changes in family demographics needed in public policy today. Families' lives and government are not independent of each other, if they ever were, but they are inextricably intertwined.

The chapters in this book offer us the opportunity to explore further how family is affected by government and how government affects families. We believe these chapters provide specific examples of some of the theoretical, research, and programmatic challenges facing decision makers in their attempt to maintain a family perspective toward the reconstruction of public policy.

References

Abarbanel, A. (1979). Shared parenting after separation and divorce: A study of joint custody. *American Journal of Orthopsychiatry, 49,* 320–329.

Abramovitz, M. (1989). *Regulating the lives of women.* Boston: South End Press.

Abramowitz, M. (1985). The family ethic and the female pauper: A new perspective on public aid and social security programs. *Journal of Education for Social Work, 21*(2), 15–26.

Adams, C. T., & Winston, K. T. (1980). *Mothers at work: Public policies in the United States, Sweden, and China.* New York: Longman.

Adler, N. E. (1975). Emotional responses of women following therapeutic abortion. *American Journal of Orthopsychiatry, 45,* 446–454.

Adler, N. E. (1976). Sample attrition in studies of psychological sequelae of abortion: How great a problem? *Journal of Applied Social Psychology, 6*(3), 240–259.

Adler, N. E., David, H., Major, B., Roth, S., Russo, N., & Wyatt, G. (1990). Psychological responses after abortion. *Science, 248,* 41–44.

Ahrons, C. R. (1980). Joint custody arrangements in the postdivorce family. *Journal of Divorce, 3,* 189–205.

Alan Guttmacher Institute (AGI). (1983). *Current functioning and future priorities in family planning services delivery.* New York: AGI.

Alan Guttmacher Institute (AGI). Domestic and international family planning under fire. *Issues in Brief.* New York: AGI.

Alan Guttmacher Institute (AGI). (1988). *Women at risk: The need for family planning services, state, and county estimates.* New York: AGI.

Aldous, J. (1982). American families in the 1980s: Individualism run amok? *Journal of Family Issues, 8,* 422–425.

Aldous, J. (1987). Individualism run amok? *Journal of Family Issues, 8,* 422–425.

American Federation of State, County, and Municipal Employees (AFSCME). (1988). *AFL-CIO, leading the way: Parental leave arrangements in AFSCME contracts*. Washington, DC: AFSCME.

American Psychiatric Association. (1987). *Diagnostic and statistical manual of mental disorders* (3rd ed.). Washington, DC: American Psychiatric Association.

Anderson, C. (1975). Systems and strategy in comparative policy analysis. In W. B. Gwyn & G. E. Edwards (Eds.), *Perspectives on public policymaking* (pp. 225–227). New Orleans: Tulane University Press.

Anderson, E. A. (1989). Implications for public policy: Towards a pro-family AIDS social policy. In E. D. Macklin (Ed.), *AIDS and families* (pp. 187–228). New York: The Haworth Press.

Anhui Ribao. (1980, 20 February). *Anhui Ribao* Ridicules Old Way of Arranged Marriages. Trans. in *JPRS 75169*, p. 53.

Athanasiou, R., Oppel, W., Michelson, L., Unger, T., & Yager, M. (1973). Psychiatric sequelae to term birth and induced early and late abortion: A longitudinal study. *Family Planning Perspectives, 5*, 227–231.

Atkenson, B., Calhoun, K., Resick, P., & Ellis, E. (1982). Victims of rape: Repeated assessment of depressive symptoms. *Journal of Consulting and Clinical Psychology, 50*, 96–102.

Austin, C. (1987). Nutrition programs. In G. L. Maddox (Ed.), *The encyclopedia of aging* (pp. 495–496). New York: Springer Publisher Company.

Average child support payment drops by 12 percent. (1987, August). *New York Times*, p. 26.

Bailey, D. (1989, Winter). Early schooling for children with special needs. *Theory into Practice*, pp. 64–68.

Baillargeon, D. L. (1987). *Dependency: Economic and social data for New York City*. New York: New York City Human Resources Administration, Offices of Policy and Economic Research.

Baldus, D. C. (1973). Welfare as a loan: An empirical study of the recovery of public assistance payments in the U.S. *Stanford Law Review, 25*, 123–125.

Baluk, U., & O'Neill, P. (1980). Health professionals' perceptions of the psychological consequences of abortion. *American Journal of Community Psychology, 8*(1), 67–75.

Bauer, G. L. (Ed.). (1986). *The family: Preserving America's future*. Washington, DC: White House Working Group on the Family.

Beck, A., Ward, C., Mendelson, M., Mock, J., & Erbaugh, J. (1961). An inventory for measuring depression. *Archives of General Psychiatry, 4*, 561–571.

Beijing couple suffers economic sanctions for fourth child. (1980, 21 April). *FBIS (Foreign Broadcast Information Service), Beijing City Service*.

Beijing officials describe divorce procedures in city. (1980, 5 February). *Beijing Xinhua*, trans. in *FBIS* (7 February 1980).

Beller, A. H., & Graham, J. W. (1986). Child support awards: Differentials and trends by race and marital status. *Demography, 23*(2), 231–245.

Beller, A. H., & Graham, J. W. (1987). *The effect of child support enforcement on child support payments*. Paper presented at the meeting of the American Sociological Association, Chicago.

Beller, A. H., & Graham, J. W. (1990). *Trends in the value of child support awards*. Paper presented at the meeting of the Population Association of America.

Belsky, J. (1985). The science and politics of day care. In R. L. Shotland & M. M. Mark (Eds.), *Social science and social policy* (pp. 237–262). Newbury Park, CA: Sage Publications.

Benedek, E. P., & Benedek, R. S. (1979). Joint custody: Solution or illusion? *American Journal of Psychiatry, 130,* 1540–1544.

Bengtson, Y., & DeTerre, E. (1980). Aging and family relations. *Marriage & Family Review, 3*(112), 51–75.

Berger, B., & Berger, P. (1984). *The war over the family: Capturing the middle ground.* Garden City, NY: Anchor Press.

Bergmann, B. R. (1986). *The economic emergence of women.* New York: Basic Books.

Berk, R. A., & Berk, S. F. (1979). *Labor and leisure at home: Content and organization of the household day.* Beverly Hills: Sage Publications.

Best, F. (1982). Flexible life scheduling. In J. O'Toole, J. L. Schuber, & L. C. Wood (Eds.). *Working, changes, and choices* (pp. 307–314). New York: Human Sciences Press.

Bird, G., Bird, G., & Scruggs, M. (1984). Determinants of family task sharing: A study of husbands and wives. *Journal of Marriage and the Family, 46*(2), 345–355.

Blank, H. (1985, May). Early childhood and the public schools. *Young Children,* pp. 52–55.

Blenkner, M. (1965). Social work and family relationship in later life with some thoughts on filial maturity. In E. Shanas & G. F. Streib (Eds.), *Social structure and the family* (pp. 46–59). Englewood Cliffs, NJ: Prentice-Hall.

Block, F., & Noakes, J. (1988). The politics of new-style workfare. *Socialist Review, 18*(8), 31–60.

Bloom, D., & Martin, M. (1983). Fringe benefits a la carte. *American Demographics, 5,* 22–25.

Blumberg, B., & Golbus, M. (1975). Psychological sequelae of elective abortion. *The Western Journal of Medicine, 124,* 188–193.

Bogue, D. J. (1970). *Family planning improvement through evaluation,* Family Planning Research and Evaluation Manual, no. 1 (pp. 27–28). Chicago: University of Chicago Press.

Booth, A. (1987). The state of the American family. *Journal of Family Issues, 8,* 429–430.

Boulding, K. E. (1985). *Human betterment.* Newbury Park, CA: Sage Publications.

Bowman, M. E., & Ahrons, C. R. (1985). Impact of legal custody status on fathers' parenting postdivorce. *Journal of Marriage and the Family, 47,* 481–488.

Bracken, M. (1978). A causal model of psychosomatic reactions to vacuum aspiration abortion. *Social Psychiatry, 13,* 135–145.

Bradley, C. F. (1984). Abortion and subsequent pregnancy. *Canadian Journal of Psychiatry, 29*(6), 494–498.

Brody, E. (1986). Parent care as a normative family stress. In L. E. Troll (Ed.), *Family issues in current gerontology* (pp. 97–122). New York: Springer.

Bronfenbrenner, U., & Crouter, A. C. (1982). Work and family through time and space. In S. B. Kamerman & C. D. Hayes (Eds.), *Families that work: Children in a changing world* (pp. 39–83). Washington, DC: National Academy Press.

Brooks, E., & Hurley, B. (1988). *For mommy and me: Toward a child development policy for welfare recipients.* New York: Robert Sterling Clark Foundation.

Brown, B. (1987). Personal communication.

Brown, C. (1986). Mothers, fathers and children: From private to public patriarchy. In L. Sargent (Ed.), *The unhappy marriage of Marxism and feminism* (pp. 239–267). London: Pluto Press.

Bulcroft, K., Leynseele, J. V., & Borgatta, E. F. (1989). Filial responsibility laws. *Research on Aging, 2,* 374–393.

Burke, G. C., & Koren, M. J. (1984). Home care: An industry on the horizon. *Business and Health, 2,* 8–12.

Burnell, G. M., & Norfleet, M. A. (1979). Women who place their infant up for adoption: A pilot study. *Patient Counseling and Health Education, 1,* 169–172.

Butterfield, F. (1979, 11 November). In the new China, 1 + 1 = 4 no more. *New York Times,* section 4, p. E7.

Byrd, C. D. (1988). Relative responsibility extended: Requirement of adult children to pay for their indigent parent's medical needs. *Family Law Quarterly, 22,* 87–102.

Cain, V. S., & Hofferth, S. L. (1989). Parental choice of self-care for school-age children. *Journal of Marriage and the Family, 51,* 65–77.

Cantor, M. H. (1983). Strain among caregivers—A study of experiences in the United States. *The Gerontologist, 2,* 597–603.

Catalyst. (1986). *Report on a national study of parental leaves.* New York: Catalyst.

Cates, W., Jr., Schulz, K., & Grimes, D. (1983). The risks associated with teenage abortion. *New England Journal of Medicine, 309,* 621–624.

Chalkley, M. A. (1986). *Measuring independence.* Unpublished manuscript. Minneapolis: University of Minnesota.

Chambers, D. L. (1979). *Making fathers pay.* Chicago: University of Chicago Press.

Chamie, M., & Henshaw, S. K. (1981). The costs and benefits of government expenditures for family planning programs. *Family Planning Perspectives, 13*(3), 117–124.

Charnas, J. F. (1983). Joint child custody counseling—Divorce 1980s style. *Social Casework, 64,* 546–554.

Cherlin, A. (1981). *Marriage, divorce, remarriage.* Cambridge, MA: Harvard University Press.

Cherlin, A. (1983). Family policy: The conservative challenge and the progressive response. *Journal of Family Issues, 4,* 427–438.

Cherlin, A. (1984). Family policy and family professionals. *Journal of Family Issues, 5,* 155–159.

Cherlin, A. (1989). *The changing American family and public policy.* Washington, DC: The Urban Institute.

Chesler, P. (1986). *Mothers on trial: The battle for children and custody.* New York: McGraw Hill.

Child support amounts. (1987, August). *New York Times,* p. 37.

China Daily. (1981, 4 August). Extravagant wedding parties bring burdens, p. 4.

Chinese women discuss life and work. (1979, 8 March). *Beijing Review,* pp. 19–27.

Cicirelli, Y. G. (1983). Adult children and their elderly parents. In T. H. Brubaker

(Ed.), *Family relationships in later life* (pp. 31–47). Beverly Hills: Sage Publications.

Clingempeel, W. G., & Reppucci, N. D. (1982). Joint custody after divorce: Major issues and goals for research. *Psychological Bulletin, 91,* 102–127.

Cohen, T., & Roth, S. (1984). Coping with abortion. *Journal of Human Stress, 18*(3), 140–145.

Cole, C., & Rodman, H. (1987). When school-age children care for themselves: Issues for family life educators and parents. *Family Relations, 36,* 92–96.

Coleman, J. (1987, August/September). Families and schools. *Educational Researcher,* pp. 32–38.

Coller, D. R. (1988). Joint custody: Research, theory, and policy. *Family Process, 27,* 459–469.

Commission on Population Growth and the American Future. (1972). *Population and the American future.* Washington, DC: U.S. Government Printing Office.

Condry, S. (1983). History and background of preschool intervention programs and the Consortium for Longitudinal Studies. In the Consortium for Longitudinal Studies, *As the twig is bent . . . Lasting effects of preschool programs* (pp. 1–31). Hillsdale, NJ: Erlbaum.

Consortium for Longitudinal Studies. (1983). *As the twig is bent: Lasting effects of preschool programs.* Hillsdale, NJ: Erlbaum.

Contributions of rural women. (1980, 9 March). *Beijing Xinhua,* trans. in *JPRS* 75386 (27 March), p. 44.

Corder, J., & Stephan, C. W. (1984). Females' combination of work and family roles: Adolescents' aspirations. *Journal of Marriage and the Family, 46*(2), 391–402.

Council of State Governments. (1982). *Book of the states, 1981–82.* Lexington, KY: Council of State Governments.

Dahl, T. S. (1984). Women's right to money. In H. Holter (Ed.), *Patriarchy in a welfare society* (pp. 46–66). Oslo: Universitetsforlaget.

Daniels, N. (1988). *Am I my parent's keeper?* An essay on justice between the young and the old. New York: Oxford University Press.

David, H. P. (1985). Post-abortion and post-partum psychiatric hospitalization. In R. Porter & M. O'Connor (Eds.), *Abortion: Medical progress and social implications,* Ciba Foundation Symposium No. 115 (pp. 150–161). London: Pitman.

David, H. P., & Matejcek, Z. (1981). Children born to women denied abortion: An update. *Family Planning Perspectives, 13*(2), 32–34.

Davis, J. A., & Smith, T. (1972–1986). General Social Surveys (machine-readable data file). Principal Investigator, James A. Davis; Senior Study Director, Tom W. Smith. NORC ed. Chicago: National Opinion Research Center, producer, 1986. Storrs, CT: The Roper Center for Public Opinion Research, University of Connecticut, distributor. One data file (20,056 logical records) and one codebook (619 pp.).

Davis, K., & Rowland, D. (1986). *Medicare policy: New directions for health and long-term care.* Baltimore: Johns Hopkins University Press.

Dempsey, J. (1981). *The family and public policy: The issue of the 1980s.* Baltimore: Brookes Publishing Company.

Denny, E., Poleka, J., Jackson, J., & Matava, M. (1989). Influencing child welfare policy. *Child Welfare*, 68(3), 275–287.

Derdeyn, A. P., & Scott, E. (1984). Joint custody: A critical analysis and appraisal. *American Journal of Orthopsychiatry*, 54, 199–209.

Deykin, E. Y., Campbell, L., & Patti, P. (1984). The postadoption experience of surrendering parents. *American Journal of Orthopsychiatry*, 54, 271–280.

Diamond, I. (1983). *Families, politics, and public policy: A feminist dialogue on women and the state*. New York: Longman.

Divorce. (1981, 4 May). *Beijing Review*, p. 26.

Domestic Policy Council Low Income Opportunity Working Group. (1987). *Up from dependency: A new national public assistance strategy*. Washington, DC: U.S. Government Printing Office.

Doring-Bradley, B. (1977). *Financial resources for organized medical family planning services in the United States: A historical interview*. New York: Alan Guttmacher Institute, unpublished.

Dornbusch, S. M., & Strober, M. H. (Eds.). (1988). *Feminism, children and new families*. New York: Guilford Press.

Downtown Welfare Advocate Center. (1979). *Some facts and figures about New York's basic grant*. New York: Downtown Welfare Advocate Center.

Dryfoos, J. G. (1973). A formula for the 1970's: Estimating need for subsidized family planning services for the United States. *Family Planning Perspectives*, 5(2), 145–174.

Dryfoos, J. G. (1975). Women who need and receive services: Estimates at mid-decade. *Family Planning Perspectives*, 7(4), 172–179.

Dryfoos, J. G. (1987). Whither family planning. *American Journal of Public Health*, 77(11), 1393–1395.

Dye, T. (1966). *Politics, economics, and the public: Policy outcomes in the American states*. Chicago: Rand McNally & Co.

Edwards, J. N. (1987). Changing family structure and youthful well-being: Assessing the future. *Journal of Family Issues*, 8, 355–372.

Ehrenreich, B., Hess, E., & Jacobs, G. (1986). *Re-making love: The feminization of sex*. New York: Anchor.

Ehrlich, E. (1989, 20 March). The mommy track: Juggling kids and careers in corporate America takes a controversial turn. *Business Week*, pp. 126–134.

Eisenstein, Z. R. (1982). The sexual politics of the new right: Understanding the crisis of liberalism for the 1980s. In N. O. Keohane, M. Z. Rosaldo, & B. C. Gelpi (Eds.), *Feminist theory: A critique of ideology* (pp. 77–98). Chicago: University of Chicago Press.

Eisenstein, Z. R. (1984a). *Feminism and sexual equality*. New York: Monthly Review Press.

Eisenstein, Z. R. (1984b). The patriarchal relations of the Reagan state. *Signs*, 10(2), 329–337.

Elazar, D. (1986). Marketplace and commonwealth and the three political cultures. In M. Gittell (Ed.), *State politics and the new federalism* (pp. 172–179). New York: Longman.

Ellwood, D. T. (1988, 17 July). Reforming welfare: Treat the cause, not the symptoms. *New York Times*, p. F2.

Engels, F. (1972). *The origins of family, private property and the state.* New York: International Publishers.

Estes, C. L., Newcomer, R. J., & Associates. (1983). *Fiscal austerity and aging.* Beverly Hills: Sage Publications.

Etaugh, C. (1980). Effects of nonmaternal care on children: Research evidence and popular views. *American Psychologist, 35,* 309–319.

Evans, V., Hofferth, S., & Radish, E. (1984). *Family and household structure fact sheet.* Prepared for the Demographic and Behavioral Sciences Branch, Center for Population Research, National Institute of Child Health and Human Development, National Institutes of Health.

Executive Committee of sixth Zhejiang provincial women's federation. (1980, 12 December). *FBIS,* p. O–4.

Extravagant wedding parties bring burdens. (1981, 4 August). *China Daily,* p. 4.

Extravagant weddings criticized. (1981, 19 January). *Beijing Review,* p. 8.

Family Research Council. (1987). *Family research today.* Washington, DC: Family Research Council.

Family Protection Act. (1981). 97th Congress, 1st Session. H.R. 311 (Rep. Hanson); S. 1378 (Sen. Jepson and Sen. Laxalt).

Federal Register. (1988). Statutory prohibition statement of appropriated funds in programs where abortion is a method of family planning; standard of compliance for family planning services projects. *53,* pp. 2922–2946.

Feinstein, K. W. (1984). Directions for day care. In P. Voydanoff (Ed.), *Work and family: Changing roles of men and women* (pp. 298–309). Palo Alto, CA: Mayfield.

Finch, J., & Mason, J. (1990). Filial obligations and kin support for elderly people. *Aging and Society, 10,* 151–175.

Fingerer, M. (1973). Psychological sequelae of abortion: Anxiety and depression. *Journal of Community Psychology, 3,* 221–225.

Firestone, S. (1970). *The dialectic of sex.* New York: Morrow.

Fisher, D., & Rosoff, J. I. (1972). How states are using Title iv-a to finance family planning services. *Family Planning Perspectives, 4*(4), 31–43.

Ford, D. (1989). Translating the problems of the elderly into effective policies: An analysis of filial attitudes. *Policies Studies Review, 8,* 704–716.

Ford Foundation. (1989). *Work and family responsibilities: A balance.* A program paper of the Ford Foundation. New York: Ford Foundation.

Forrest, J. (1987). Unintended pregnancy among American women. *Family Planning Perspectives, 19*(2), 76–77.

Francoeur, R. T. (1983). Religious reactions to alternative lifestyles. In E. D. Macklin & R. H. Rubin (Eds.), *Contemporary families and alternative lifestyles* (pp. 379–399). Beverly Hills: Sage Publications.

Frankel, S. A. (1985). Joint custody awards and children: A theoretical framework and some practical considerations. *Psychiatry, 48,* 318–327.

Freed, D. J., & Walker, T. B. (1986). Family law in the fifty states: An overview. *Family Law Quarterly, 39,* 331–441.

Freedman, A. E. (1983). Sex equality, sex differences, and the Supreme Court. *Yale Law Journal, 92*(6), 913–968.

Freeman, E. (1977). Influence of personality attributes on abortion experiences. *American Journal of Orthopsychiatry, 47*(3), 503–513.

Friedman, C. M., Greenspan, R., & Mittleman, F. (1974). The decision-making process and the outcome of therapeutic abortion. *American Journal of Psychiatry, 131,* 1332–1337.

Furstenberg, F. F., Jr., Shea, J., Allison, P., Herceg-Baron, R., & Webb, D. (1983). Contraceptive continuation among adolescents attending family planning clinics. *Family Planning Perspectives, 15*(5), 211–217.

Galambos, N. L., & Garbarino, J. (1983, July-August). Identifying the missing links in the study of latchkey children. *Children Today* (2–4), 40–41.

Garfinkel, I. (1987, 20 February). *Welfare: Reform or replacement? Child support enforcement.* Testimony before the Subcommittee on Social Security and Family Policy, U.S. Senate Committee on Finance, Washington, DC.

Garfinkel, I., & McLanahan, S. S. (1986). *Single mothers and their children.* Washington, DC: The Urban Institute.

Garrett, N. E. (1979–1980). Filial responsibility laws. *Journal of Family Law, 8,* 793–818.

Garrett, P., Lubeck, S., & Wenk, D. (1988, September). *Parental leave: Comparative and empirical perspectives.* Paper presented at the Wingspread Conference on Parental Leave, Racine, WI, pp. 1–22.

Garrett, P., Wenger, M., Lubeck, S., & Clifford, D. (1990, Fall). Child care arrangements for 4-year-olds: A state-level view. *Dimensions, 6,* 32.

Gecas, V. (1987). Born in the USA in the 1980s: Growing up in difficult times. *Journal of Family Issues, 8,* 434–436.

Genovese, R. (1984). *Families and change: Social needs and public policies.* New York: Praeger.

Gilbert, N. (1983). *Capitalism and the welfare state: Dilemmas on social benevolence.* New Haven: Yale University Press.

Gilliland, N. (1986, July). Mandating family responsibility for elderly members, cost and benefits. *Journal of Applied Gerontology,* pp. 26–36.

Gimenez, M. E. (1980). Feminism, pronatalism and motherhood. *International Journal of Women's Studies, 3*(3), 215.

Glasser, F. (1981). *Helping working parents: Child care options for business.* Raleigh, NC: Office of the Governor.

Glover, R. J., & Steele, C. (1988–1989). Comparing the effects on the child of post-divorce parenting arrangements. *Journal of Divorce, 12,* 185–201.

Gold, R. B., & Guardado, S. (1988). Public funding of family planning, sterilization, and abortion services, 1987. *Family Planning Perspectives, 20*(5), 228–233.

Gold, R. B., & Nestor, B. (1985). Public funding of contraceptive, sterilization, and abortion services, 1983. *Family Planning Perspectives, 17*(1), 25–30.

Goldstein, J., Freud, A., & Solnit, A. J. (1979). *Beyond the best interests of the child.* New York: The Free Press.

Goodin, R. E. (1986, September). Defining the welfare state. *American Political Science Review,* pp. 952–954.

Googins, B., & Burden, D. (1987, July-August). Vulnerability of working parents: Balancing work and home roles. *Social Work,* pp. 295–299.

Graham, J. W., & Beller, A. H. (1986). *The effect of child support payments on the labor supply of female family heads.* Unpublished paper, University of Illinois at Urbana-Champaign.

Greenhalgh, S., & Bongaarts, J. (1987). Fertility policy in China: Future options. *Science, 235*(6), 1167.

Grief, J. B. (1979). Fathers, children, and joint custody. *American Journal of Orthopsychiatry, 49*, 311–319.

Gueron, J. M. (1988, Spring). State welfare employment initiatives: Lessons from the 1980s. *Focus, 11*, 17–23.

Gui, S. (1980, 25 April). Population control and economic policies. *Shanghai Shifan Daxue Xuebao (Zhexue Shehui Kexueban), 2*, 16–21.

Guizhou couple punished for having third child. (1980, 25 March). *FBIS*, p. Q–1.

Guizhou Ribhao. (1980, 27 June). Guizhou officials punished for birth control failures. Trans. in *FBIS*, p. Q–1.

Gusfield, J. R. (1984). On the side: Practical action and social constructivism in social problems theory. In J. W. Schneider & J. I. Kitsuse (Eds.), *Studies in the sociology of social problems* (pp. 31–51). Norwood, NJ: Ablex.

Hagestad, G. O. (1987). Able elderly in the family context: Changes, chances, and challenges. *The Gerontologist, 27*, 417–421.

Hagestad, G. O. (1987). Family. In G. L. Maddox (Ed.), *The encyclopedia on aging* (pp. 247–249). New York: Springer.

Hall, R. (1982). The classroom: A chilly climate for women. *Project on the status and education of women.* Washington, DC: Association of American Colleges.

Hall, R., & Sandler, B. (1984). Out of the classroom: A chilly climate for women? *Project on the status and education of women.* Washington, DC: Association of American Colleges.

Hamon, R. (1986, 30 April). *Filial responsibility: Implications for caregiving aging parents.* Paper presented at the meeting of The Southern Gerontological Society, Norfolk, VA.

Hamon, R., & Blieszner, R. (1990). Filial responsibility expectations among adult child–older parent pairs. *The Journal of Gerontology, 45*, 110–112.

Handler, J. F. (1988, Spring). State welfare employment initiatives: Lessons from the 1980s. *Focus, 11*, 29–34.

Handy, J. (1982). Psychological and social aspects of induced abortion. *British Journal of Clinical Psychology, 21*, 29–41.

Hanke, S. H. (1987). *Prospects for privatization.* New York: Academy of Political Science.

Hanson, R. (1988, 28 October). *Mean seasons and warm business climates in the American states: The political economy of welfare policy.* Paper presented at the 10th Annual Research Conference of the Association for Public Policy Analysis and Management, Seattle, WA.

Hao, L., & Liu, J. (1984). Local laws and regulations concerning protecting the legitimate rights and interests of women and children. *Faxue, 11*, 28–31.

Harrington, C., Estes, C., Lee, P., & Newcomer, R. (1985). State policies on long-term care. In C. Harrington, C. L. Estes, R. J. Newcomer, et al. (Eds.), *Long-term care of the elderly, public policy issues* (pp. 67–88). Beverly Hills: Sage Publications.

Harter, S., & Pike, R. (1984). The pictorial scale of perceived competence and acceptance for young children. *Child Development, 55*, 1969–1982.

Hassinger, E. E. (1982). *Rural health organization: Social networks and reorganization.* Ames: Iowa University Press.

Hayslip, B., Ritter, M. L., Ottman, R. M., & McDonnel, C. (1980). Home care services and the rural elderly. *Gerontologist, 20,* 192–198.

Health Care Financing Administration. (1987). *Annual Medicare program statistics: Medicare enrollment, reimbursement, and utilization, 1983.* Baltimore: Bureau of Data Management and Strategy.

Hendricks, J., & Calasanti, T. (1986). Social policy on aging in the United States. In C. Phillipson & A. Walker (Eds.), *Aging and social policy: A critical assessment* (pp. 237–262). London: Gower Publishing Company.

Henshaw, S., Forrest, J., & Van Vort, J. (1987). Abortion services in the United States, 1984–1985. *Family Planning Perspectives, 19*(2), 63–70.

Henshaw, S., & Silverman, J. (1988). The characteristics and prior contraceptive use of U.S. abortion patients. *Family Planning Perspectives, 20*(4), 158–168.

Hernes, H. M. (1984). Women and the welfare state: The transition from private to public dependence. In H. Holter (Ed.), *Patriarchy in a welfare society* (pp. 26–46). Oslo: Universitetsforlaget.

Hess, R. D., & Camara, K. A. (1979). Post-divorce family relationships as mediating factors in the consequences of divorce for children. *Journal of Social Issues, 35,* 79–96.

Hetherington, E. M., Cox, M., & Cox, R. (1976). Divorced fathers. *The Family Coordinator, 25,* 417–428.

Hetherington, E. M., Cox, M., & Cox, R. (1982). Effects of divorce on parents and children. In M. E. Lamb (Ed.), *Nontraditional families: Parenting and child development* (pp. 233–288). Hillsdale, NJ: Erlbaum.

Hobbs, B., & Rodman, H. (1987, November). *The politics of numbers: Inflating the number of latchkey children.* Paper presented at the meeting of the National Council on Family Relations, Atlanta, GA.

Hofferth, S., & Phillips, D. (1987, August). Child care in the United States, 1970 to 1995. *Journal of Marriage and the Family,* pp. 559–571.

Hoffman, S. D., & Duncan, G. J. (1988, November). What are the economic consequences of divorce? *Demography, 25,* 641–645.

Hollings, Ernest F. (1970). *The case against hunger: A demand for a national policy.* New York: Cowles Book Company.

Holter, H. (Ed.). (1984). *Patriarchy in a welfare society.* Oslo: Universitetsforlaget.

Honig, E., & Hershatter, G. (1988). *Personal voices: Chinese women in the 1980s.* Stanford, CA: Stanford University Press.

Hopkins, J., Marcus, M., & Campbell, S. B. (1984). Postpartum depression: A critical review. *Psychological Bulletin, 95,* 498–515.

Horn, J., & Turner, R. (1976). Minnesota multiphasic personality inventory profiles among subgroups of unwed mothers. *Journal of Consulting and Clinical Psychology, 44*(1), 25–33.

House Committee on Education and Labor. (1984). *School facilities child care act: Hearings before a subcommittee on elementary, secondary, and vocational education.* Washington, DC: U.S. Government Printing Office.

Howard, R. (1981). *A social history of American family sociology.* Westport, CT: Greenwood Press.

How is property divided on divorce? (1987, February). *Women of China,* p. 42.

Hudson, R. (1987). Policy analysis: Issues and practices. In G. L. Maddox (Ed.), *The encyclopedia of aging* (pp. 526–528). New York: Springer.

Huttenen, E., & Tamminen, M. (1989, 6–9 April). *The Finnish day care system and the needs of families*. Paper presented at the Association for Childhood Education International Study Conference, Indianapolis.

Ilfeld, F. W., Ilfeld, H. Z., & Alexander, J. R. (1982). Does joint custody work? A first look at outcome data of relitigation. *American Journal of Psychiatry, 139*, 62–66.

Illsley, R., & Hall, M. (1976). Psychological aspects of abortion: A review of issues and needed research. *Bulletin of the World Health Organization, 53*, 83–103.

Indest, G. F., III. (1988). Legal aspects of HCFA's decision to allow recovery from children for Medicaid benefits delivered to their parents through state financial responsibility statutes: A case of bad rulemaking through failure to comply with the administrative procedure act. *Southern University Law Review, 15*, 225–352.

Irving, H. H., Benjamin, M., & Trocme, N. (1984). Shared parenting: An empirical analysis utilizing a large data base. *Family Process, 23*, 561–569.

Jencks, C., & Edin, K. (1990, April). The real welfare problem. *The American Prospect, 1*(1), 31–50.

Jewell, K. S. (1988). *Survival of the black family: The institutional impact of U.S. social policy*. New York: Praeger.

Johnson, A. (1987). The family: The need for sound policy, not rhetoric and ideology. *Public Administration Review, 47*(3), 280–284.

Johnson, M., & Hess, B. (1984). Missing links: Notes on an impossible mission. *Marriage and Family Review, 7*(3/4), 203–215.

Jones, C. O. (1970). *An introduction to the study of public policy*. Belmont, CA: Wadsworth Publishing Company.

Jones, R. (1987). Employment and training policy: The next steps. *Policy Studies Review, 6*(4), 777–781.

Kamarás, F. (1987, 24 July). Interview with author (A. H. Beller), Budapest, Hungary.

Kamerman, S. (1979, Summer). Work and family in industrialized societies. *Signs*, pp. 632–650.

Kamerman, S. (1989). Toward a child policy decade. *Child Welfare, 63*(4), 371–390.

Kamerman, S. (1983a, December). Child care services: A national picture. *Monthly Labor Review*, pp. 35–39.

Kamerman, S. (1983b). *Meeting family needs: The corporate response*. New York: Pergamon Press.

Kamerman, S. (1984). Women, children and poverty. *Signs, 10*(2), 249.

Kamerman, S. (1985). Child care services: An issue for gender equity and women's solidarity. *Child Welfare, 64*, 259–271.

Kamerman, S. (1988, November). Child care and family benefits: Policies of industrialized countries. *Monthly Labor Review*, pp. 23–28.

Kamerman, S. (1980, November). Child care and family benefits: Policies of industrialized countries. *Monthly Labor Review*, pp. 23–28.

Kamerman, S. (1991). Parental leave and infant care: U.S. and international trends and issues (1978–1988). In J. Hyde (Ed.), *Parental leave and child care*. Philadelphia: Temple University Press.

Kamerman, S., & Kahn, A. (1981). *Child care, family benefits and working parents*. New York: Columbia University Press.

Kamerman, S., & Kahn, A. (1989, Spring). Family policy: Has the U.S. learned from Europe? *Policy Studies Review, 8*(3), 581–598.

Kamerman, S., & Kahn, A. (Eds.). (1978). *Family policy: Government and families in fourteen countries*. New York: Columbia University Press.

Kamerman, S., Kahn, A., & Kingston, P. (1983). *Maternity policies and working women*. New York: Columbia University Press.

Kane, N. M. (1989). The home care crisis of the nineties. *The Gerontologist, 29*, 24–31.

Kasten, R. A., & Todd, J. E. (1980, October 24–25). *Transfer recipients and the poor during the 1970s*. Paper presented at the 2nd Annual Research Conference of the Association for Public Policy Analysis and Management, Washington, DC.

Katz, L. G. (1975). Early childhood programs and ideological disputes. *The Educational Forum, 39*, 267–271.

Katzner, D. W. (1979). *Choice and the quality of life*. Newbury Park, CA: Sage Publications.

Kelman, S. (1978, November). Regulation that works. *The New Republic, 25*, 16–20.

Keniston, K. (1977). *All our children*. New York: Harcourt, Brace, Jovanovich.

Kerschner, P. A., & Hirschfield, I. S. (1975). Public policy and aging: Analytic approaches. In D. S. Woodruff & J. E. Birren (Eds.), *Aging: Scientific perspective and social issues* (pp. 352–373). New York: D. Van Nostrand Company.

Klerman, G. L., & Weissman, M. M. (1980). Depressions among women: Their nature and causes. In M. Guttentag, S. Salasin, & D. Belle (Eds.), *The mental health of women* (pp. 484–513). New York: Academic Press.

Kong, Y. (1981, 4 May). Changes in marriage conventions. *Beijing Review, 18*, 22.

Koop, C. E. (1989a, 9 January). Letter to President Reagan.

Koop, C. E. (1989b, 21 March). *Surgeon general's report: The public health effects of abortion*. In Congressional Record, E906–E909.

Kosterlitz, J. (1989, 2 December). Devil in the details. *National Journal*, pp. 2942–2946.

Kotz, N. (1969). *Let them eat promises: The politics of hunger in America*. Englewood Cliffs, NJ: Prentice-Hall.

Kotz, N., & Kotz, M. L. (1977). *A passion for equality*. New York: W. W. Norton and Company.

Krach, P. (1990). Filial responsibility and financial strain: The impact on farm families. *The Journal of Gerontological Nursing, 16*, 38–41.

Krause, H. D. (1981). *Child support in America*. Charlottesville, VA: The Michie Company.

Krein, S. F., & Beller, A. H. (1988, 2 May). Educational attainment of children from single-parent families: Differences by exposure, gender and race. *Demography, 25*, 221–234.

Kristof, N. (1987, April 21). China's birth rate on rise again as official sanctions are ignored. *New York Times*, pp. 1, 6.

Kuhne, R., & Blair, C. (1978, April). Flexitime. *Business Horizons*, pp. 39–44.

Lajewski, H. (1959). *Child care arrangements of full-time working mothers: 1958.* Children's Bureau Publication No. 378. Washington, DC: U.S. Government Printing Office.

Lalinec-Michaud, M., & Engelsmann, F. (1984). Depression and hysterectomy: A prospective study. *Psychosomatics, 25,* 550–558.

Lamb, M. (Ed.). (1982). *Nontraditional families: Parenting and child development.* Hillsdale, NJ: Erlbaum.

Lammers, W. W. (1987). Government programs: State. In G. L. Maddox (Ed.), *The encylcopedia of aging* (pp. 294–296). New York: Springer.

Laslett, P., & Wall, R. (Eds.). (1972). *Household and family in past time.* Cambridge: Cambridge University Press.

LaVor, J. (1979). Long-term care: A challenge to service system. In V. LaPorte & J. Rubin (Eds.), *Reform and regulation in long-term care* (pp. 17–63). New York: Praeger Publishers.

Lazar, I. (1983). Discussion and implications of the findings. In the Consortium for Longitudinal Studies, *As the twig is bent . . . Lasting effects of preschool programs* (pp. 461–466). Hillsdale, NJ: Erlbaum.

Lazar, I., & Darlington, R. (1982). Lasting effects of early education: A report from the consortium for longitudinal studies. *Monographs of the Society of Research in Child Development*, Whole Serial No. 195, 47(2–3).

Leik, R. K., Peterson, N. J., & Chalkley, M. A. (1987). *The impact of Head Start on family dynamics and structure.* Paper presented at Positive Approaches to Child and Adolescent Development, an Interagency Panel of Research and Development on Children and Adolescents, Washington, DC.

Lemkau, J. (1988). Emotional sequelae of abortion: Implications for clinical practice. *Psychology of Women Quarterly, 12,* 461–472.

Lenhoff, D., & Stoneback, S. (1989, August). *Review of state legislation guaranteeing jobs for family or medical needs.* Washington, DC: Family and Medical Leave Act Coalition.

Lerner, R. M., & Spanier, G. B. (1978). A dynamic view of interactional child and family development. In R. M. Lerner & G. B. Spanier (Eds.). *Child Influences on marital and familial interaction* (pp. 1–22). New York: Academic Press.

Levine, E. M. (1987). The realities of daycare for children. *Journal of Family Issues, 8,* 451–454.

Lewis, K., & Carr, T. (1986). *Abortion: Judicial and legislative control.* Washington, DC: Congressional Research Service.

Li Chang (1981, 9 December). Building a socialist spiritual civilization. *Beijing Review, 10,* 16–17.

Lihui, H., & Jie, L. (1984, 10 November). Local laws and regulations concerning protecting the legitimate rights and interests of women and children. *Faxue, 11,* 28–31.

Lincoln, R. (1984). Too many teen pregnancies. *Family Planning Perspectives, 16,* 1.

Littlewood, T. B. (1977). *Politics of population control*. Notre Dame, IN: University of Notre Dame Press.

Long, L., & Long, T. J. (1983). *The handbook for latchkey children and their parents*. New York: Arbor House.

Long, T. J., & Long, L. (1982). *Latchkey children: The child's view of self care*. Washington, DC: Catholic University of America, ERIC Document Reproduction Service No. ED 211 229.

Lopes, J. L. (1975). Filial support and family solidarity. *Pacific Law Review, 6*, 508–535.

Low, S., & Spindler, P. (1968). *Child care arrangements of working mothers in the United States: 1965*. Children's Bureau Publication No. 461. Washington, DC: U.S. Government Printing Office.

Lowery, C. R., & Settle, S. A. (1985). Effects of divorce on children: Differential impact of custody and visitation patterns. *Family Relations, 34*, 455–463.

Lowi, T. J. (1964). American business, public policy, case studies, and political theory. *World Politics, 16*, 677–715.

Lowi, T. J. (1970). Decision making vs. policy making. *Public Administration Review, 30*, 324–325.

Lowi, T. J. (1972). Four systems of policy, politics and choice. *Public Administration Review, 32*, 298–310.

Lubeck, S. (1989a). A world of difference: American child care policy in cross-national perspective. *Educational Policy, 3*(4), 331–354.

Lubeck, S. (1989b, Winter). Four-year-olds and public schooling? Framing the question. *Theory into Practice*, pp. 3–10.

Lubeck, S. (1989, December). A world of difference: America child care policy in cross-national perspective. *Educational Policy*, pp. 331–354.

Lubeck, S. (forthcoming). Lessons from abroad: A cross-national survey of policies supporting childbearing and rearing. In B. Persky & L. Golubchick (Eds.), *Early childhood education*. New York: University Press of America.

Lubeck, S., & Garrett, P. (1988, Spring). Child care 2000: Policy options for the future. *Social Policy*, pp. 31–37.

Luepnitz, D. A. (1986). A comparison of maternal, paternal, and joint custody: Understanding the varieties of post-divorce life. *Journal of Divorce, 9*, 1–12.

Lundberg, C. J. (1984). Home health care: A logical extension of hospital services. *Topics in Health Care Financing, 10*(3), 22–23.

Luo Qiong. (1985, 1 March). Women and reform. *Hongqi, 5*, 16–19.

Luttrell, W. (1984). Beyond the politics of victimization. *Socialist Review, 77*, 42–47.

Lyons, J., Larson, D., Huckeba, W., Rogers, J., & Mueller, C. (1988). Research on the psychosocial impact of abortion: A systematic review of the literature 1966 to 1985. In P. Uhlenberg, L. Wardle, E. Worthington, W. Bennett, S. Clinton, J. Lyons, R. Strom, V. Mark, A. Evans, & R. Marker (Eds.), *Values and public policy* (pp. 77–89). Washington, DC: Family Research Council of America.

Macklin, E. D., & Rubin, R. H. (Eds.). (1983). *Contemporary families and alternative lifestyles*. Beverly Hills: Sage Publications.

Major, B. (1987, 2 December). Testimony to the U.S. Surgeon General. Unpublished.

Major, B., Mueller, P., & Hildebrandt, K. (1985). Attributions, expectations and coping with abortion. *Journal of Personality and Social Psychology, 48*, 585–599.

Malitz, D. (1984). The costs and benefits of Title XX and Title XIX family planning services in Texas. *Evaluation Review, 8*(4), 519–536.

Mao Zedong. (1970). Miss Chao's Suicide. In S. Schram (Ed.), *The political thought of Mao Tse-tung* (pp. 334–337). New York: Praeger.

Marafiote, R. A. (1985). *The custody of children: A behavioral assessment model*. New York: Plenum Press.

Maret, E., & Finlay, B. (1984). The distribution of household labor among women in dual career families. *Journal of Marriage and the Family, 46*(2), 357–364.

Marriage advertisements in China and new wedding trends. (1985, November). *Women of China*, pp. 13–14.

Marriage Law. (1980). *Main documents of third session of fifth National People's Congress* (pp. 209–224). Beijing: Foreign Languages Press.

Martin, T., and Bumpass, L. (1989). Recent trends in marital disruption. *Demography, 26*(1), 37–51.

Marx, F., & Seligson, M. (1988). *The public school early childhood study: The state survey*. New York: Bank Street College of Education.

McDonald, M. (1977). *Food, stamps, and income maintenance*. New York: Academic Press.

McDowell, I., & C. Newell. (1987). *Measuring health: A guide to rating scales and questionnaires*. New York: Oxford Press.

McFarlane, D. R. (1985). Are block grants more responsive to state health needs? The case of the federal family planning program (FY 76–81). *Journal of Health and Human Resources Management, 8*(2), 147–167.

McFarlane, D. R. (1988, Winter). Family planning needs: An empirical study of federal responsiveness before and during the Reagan administration. *Journal of Primary Prevention*, pp. 41–56.

McKinnon, R., & Wallerstein, J. S. (1988). A preventive intervention program for parents and young children in joint custody arrangements. *American Journal of Orthopsychiatry, 58*, 168–178.

McMahon, P. (1986, May). An international comparison of labor force participation, 1977–84. *Monthly Labor Review*, pp. 3–12.

Mead, L. (1987, 23 February). *Principles for welfare reform*. Testimony before the Subcommittee on Social Security and Family Policy, U.S. Senate Committee on Finance, Washington DC.

Mead, L. (1990, Summer). Should workfare be mandatory? What research says. *Journal of Public Policy Analysis and Management, 9*, 400–404.

Miller, D. J. (1979). Joint custody. *Family Law Quarterly, 13*, 345–412.

Mindel, O. H. (1979). Multigenerational family households: Recent trends and implications for the future. *Gerontologist, 19*, 456–463.

Mirowsky, J., & Ross, C. (1989). *The social causes of psychological distress*. New York: Aldine DeGruyter.

Mitchell, A. (1987, 20–24 April). *Public schools and young children: A report of the first national survey of public school districts regarding their early childhood programs*. Paper presented at the meeting of the American Educational Research Association, Washington, DC.

Mizio, E. (1974, February). Impact of external systems on the Puerto Rican family. *Social Casework*, pp. 76–83.

Moffitt, R. (1987, June). *Work and the U.S. welfare system: A review*. Paper presented at the Institute for Research on Poverty, University of Wisconsin-Madison.

Moffitt, R. (1988). *Has state redistribution policy grown more conservative? AFDC, Food Stamps, and Medicaid 1960–1984*. Institute for Research on Poverty Discussion Paper #851–88.

Moore, J. T., & Tolley, D. H. (1976). Depression following hysterectomy. *Psychosomatics, 17*, 86–89.

Morado, C. (1989, Winter). The roles taken by state government to provide schooling for 4-year-olds. *Theory into Practice*, pp. 34–40.

Morgan, G. (1983). Child day care policy in chaos. In E. Zigler, S. Kagan, & Klugman (Eds.), *Children, families, and government: Perspectives on American social policy* (pp. 249–265). New York: Cambridge University Press.

Morgan, G. (1985, February). *Child care and early education: What legislators can do*. Paper presented at the Advanced Legislative Program Services in Education Meeting, Austin, TX, pp. 1–20.

Moroney, R. (1986). *Shared responsibility: Families and social policy*. New York: Aldine Publishing.

Moseley, D., Follingstad, D., Harley, H., & Heckel, R. (1981). Psychological factors that predict reaction to abortion. *Journal of Clinical Psychology, 37*, 276–279.

Moynihan, D. (1986). *Family and nation*. New York: Harcourt, Brace, Jovanovich.

Mueller, P. M. (1986). *Causal attributions, perceived self-efficacy, and coping with a negative life event*. Unpublished doctoral dissertation, University of New York at Buffalo.

Mueller, P. M., & Major B. (1989). Self-blame, self-efficacy, and adjustment to abortion. *Journal of Personality and Social Psychology, 57*, 1059–1068.

Murray, C. (1984). *Losing ground: American social policy, 1950–1980*. New York: Basic Books.

Murray, C. (1986, Summer). No, welfare isn't really the problem. *The Public Interest, 84*, 3–11.

Myles, J. (1984). *Old age in the welfare state: The political economy of public pensions*. Boston: Little, Brown.

Naisbitt, J. (1984). *Megatrends*. New York: Warner Books.

National Center for Health Statistics. (1972). *Home care for persons 55 and over*. DHEW Publication No. (HSM) 72–1062. Washington, DC: U.S. Government Printing Office.

National Center for Health Statistics. (1987). *Advance report, final mortality statistics, 1985*. DHHS Publication No. (PHS) 87–1120. Hyattsville, MD: Public Health Service.

National Coalition for Women and Girls in Education. (1989). Women, illiteracy and employment. *Journal of Employment Counseling, 26*(1), 16–18.

National Conference of State Legislatures. (1987). *The 1987 state legislative summary: Children, youth, and family issues*. Denver: National Conference of State Legislatures.

Nationwide demographic science discussion held in Chengdu. (1979, 15 December). *Guangming Ribao*, p. 1.

Nehls, M., & Morgenbesser, M. (1980). Joint custody: An exploration of the issues. *Family Process, 19*, 117–125.

Nelson, M. (1987, September). *Providing family day care: An analysis of home-based work.* Paper presented at the meeting of the American Sociological Association, Chicago.

Nestor, B. (1972). Public funding of contraceptive services 1980–82. *Family Planning Perspectives, 14*(4), 198–203.

New York City Human Resources Administration. (1987). *Shelter policy options.* New York: New York City Human Resources Administration.

Noble, J., & Sussman, M. (1987). *Government and the family.* New York: Haworth.

Nock, S. (1987). The symbolic meaning of children. *Journal of Family Issues, 8*, 373–393.

Nolen-Hoeksema, S. (1987). Sex differences in unipolar depression: Evidence and theory. *Psychological Bulletin, 101*, 259–282.

Norton, A. J., & Glick, P. C. (1986, January). One parent families: A social and economic profile. *Family Relations, 35*(1), 9–17.

Novak, M., et al. (1987). *The new consensus on family and welfare: A community of self-reliance.* Washington, DC: American Enterprise Institute.

Nye, P. (1979). Relationship between abortion and child abuse. *Canadian Journal of Psychiatry, 24*(7), 610–620.

O'Brien, P. (1987). *How to select the best child-care option for your employees.* Binghamton, NY: Almar Press.

O'Connell, M., & Bloom, D. (1987, February). *Juggling jobs and babies: America's child care challenge*, No. 12. Washington, DC: Population Reference Bureau, Inc.

Offe, C. (1972). *Structural problems of the capitalist state.* London: Macmillan.

Olson, D. H., Portner, J., & Lavee, Y. (1985). FACES III. See Olson, D. H. FACES III—Family Adaptability and Cohesion Scales. In D. H. Olson, H. I. McCubbin, H. Barnes, A. Larsen, M. Muxen, & M. Wilson, *Family inventories* (pp. 1–42). St. Paul: University of Minnesota, rev. ed.

Olson, L. K. (1982). *The political economy of aging: The state, private power, and social welfare.* New York: Columbia University Press.

Ooms, T. (1984, June). The necessity of a family perspective. *Journal of Social Issues, 5*(2), 160–181.

Ooms, T., & Preister, S. (Eds.). (1988). *A strategy for strengthening families: Using family criteria in policymaking and program evaluation.* A consensus report of the Family Criteria Task Force. Washington, DC: The Family Impact Seminar, the American Association for Marriage and Family Therapy Research and Education Foundation.

Orr, M. T. (1983). The family planning program and cuts in federal spending: Impact on state management of family planning. *Family Planning Perspectives, 15*(4), 176–191.

Osofsky, J., & Osofsky, H. (1972). The psychological reaction of patients to legalized abortion. *American Journal of Orthopsychiatry, 42*(1), 48–60.

Osofsky, J. D., Osofsky, H. J., & Rajan, R. (1973). Psychological effects of abortion: With emphasis upon immediate reactions and follow-up. In H. J.

Osofsky & J. D. Osofsky (Eds.), *The abortion experience: The psychological and medical impact* (pp. 188–205). Hagerstown, MD: Harper & Row.

Page, B., Shapiro, R., & Dempsey, G. (1987, March). What moves public opinion? *American Political Science Review*, pp. 23–43.

Papageorgiou, M. (1986). *The national preschool data base*. Position paper prepared for the National Preschool Data Base Planning Conference, Washington, DC.

Parish, W., & Whyte, M. K. (1978). *Village and family in contemporary China*. Chicago: University of Chicago Press.

Pascall, G. (1986). *Social policy: A feminist analysis*. London: Tavistock Publications.

Pearce, D. (1978, February). The feminization of poverty: Women, work and welfare. *The Urban and Social Change Review, 11*(1), 28–36.

Peck, A., & Marcus, H. (1966). Psychiatric sequelae of therapeutic interruption of pregnancy. *Journal of Nervous and Mental Disease, 143*(5), 417–425.

Peden, J., & Glahe, F. (1986). *The American family and the state*. San Francisco: Pacific Institute for Public Policy Research.

Pennsylvania Abortion Control Act of 1988. (1988). Act 21, Harrisburg, PA.

Perry, E., & Wong, C. (1985). *The political economy of reform in post-Mao China*. Cambridge, MA: Harvard University Press.

Peterson, P. E. (1984). Federalism and the states: An experiment in decentralization. In J. L. Palmer & I. V. Sawhill (Eds.), *The Reagan record* (pp. 217–259). Cambridge, MA: Ballinger Publishing.

Peterson, P. E., et al. (1986). *The Reagan block grants: What have we learned?* Washington, DC: The Urban Institute Press.

Peterson, P. E., & Rom, M. C. (1987). Federalism and welfare reform: Determinants of interstate differences in poverty rates and benefit levels. *Brookings Discussion Papers in Governmental Studies*, No. 14. Washington, DC: The Brookings Institution.

Peterson, P. E., & Rom, M. C. (1988, Winter). The case for a national welfare standard. *The Brookings Review*, pp. 24–32.

Peterson, P. E., & Rom, M. (1989, September). American federalism, welfare policy, and residential choices. *American Political Science Review, 83*, 711–728.

Pett, M. G. (1982). Correlates of children's social adjustment. *Journal of Divorce, 5*, 25–39.

Phillips, E., Fisher, M. E., Macmillan-Scattergood, D., Baglioni, A. J., & Troner, J. C. (1987, June). Home health care: Who's where? *American Journal of Public Health*, pp. 733–734.

Phillipson, C., & Walker, A. (1986). *Aging and social policy: A critical assessment*. London: Gower Publishing Company.

Pirie, M. (1988). *Privatization: Theory, practice and choice*. London: Wildwood Press.

Piven, F. F., & Cloward, R. A. (1977). *Poor people's movements*. New York: Pantheon Books.

Planned Parenthood—World Population. (1981). Family planning funds spent by state health, welfare agencies increased 15% in FY 79. *Family Planning/Population Reporter, 10*(2), 28–31.

Polit, D. (1980). *The one-parent/one-child family: Social and psychological consequences*.

Cambridge, MA: American Institute for Research, Institute on Women and Families.

Popenoe, D. (1987). Beyond the nuclear family: A statistical portrait of the changing family in Sweden. *Journal of Marriage and the Family, 49,* 173–184.

Population policy key to China's future. (1987, 20 July). *Beijing Review,* 5.

Quinn, J. L. (1987). Home health care. In G. L. Maddox (Ed.), *The encyclopedia of aging* (pp. 324–325). New York: Springer.

Racusin, R. J., Albertini, R., Wishik, H. R., Shnurr, P., & Mayberry, J. (1989). Factors associated with joint custody awards. *Journal of the American Academy of Child and Adolescent Psychiatry, 28,* 164–170.

Raines, P. M. (1985–1986). Joint custody and the right to travel: Legal and psychological implications. *Journal of Family Law, 24,* 625–656.

Rainwater, L. (1965). *Family design: Marital sexuality, family size and contraception.* Chicago: Aldine.

RAM v. Blum, 77 Appellate Division 2nd 278, 1st Dept. (1980). Appeal Withdrawn 54 NY 2nd 834.

Rapoport, R., Rapoport, R. N., & Strelitz, Z. (Eds.). (1977). *Fathers, mothers, and society: Toward new alliances.* New York: Basic Books.

Reischauer, R. D. (1987, Summer). Welfare reform: Will consensus be enough? *The Brookings Review,* pp. 3–8.

Reischauer, R. (1989). *Long-term strategies for programs and issues within the jurisdiction of the committee: National savings rate of the United States and its trading partners.* In hearing testimony before the Committee on Ways and Means, House of Representatives, 101st Congress, 1st session, Serial 101–21. Washington, DC: U.S. Government Printing Office.

Renmin Ribao. (1979, 11 August). Beijing, to realize the four modernizations, it is necessary to control population increase in a planned way. *Beijing,* p. 1.

Renmin Ribao. (1980, 4 January). *Beijing,* p. 5.

Renmin Ribao. (1980, 8 March). Commemorating March 8—international women's day. *Beijing,* p. 5.

Renmin Ribao. (1980, 16 September). A code for marriage and family life. *Beijing,* p. 1.

Renmin Ribao. (1980, 28 November). Elimination of feudalism. *Beijing,* p. 5.

Renmin Ribao. (1986, 9 March). Chinese women courageously shoulder the "double responsibility." *Beijing,* p. 4.

Report on 5th Xinjiang Regional People's Congress: Draft Supplement to the Marriage Law. (1980, 15 December). *FBIS,* p. T-9.

Reskin, B., & Hartmann, H. (Eds.). (1986). *Women's work, men's work: Sex segregation on the job.* Washington, DC: National Academic Press.

Retirement in the countryside. (1981, 26 October). *Beijing Review,* p. 28.

Rice, R. (1977). *Family policy in the United States.* New York: Family Service Association.

Rich, S. (1987, 6 February). Number of "latch-key" children overstated, census suggests. *Washington Post,* p. 18.

Rich, S. (1988, 24–30 October). Helping those who help themselves: The new welfare law stresses education. *The Washington Post National Weekly Edition,* pp. 33–34.

Ritzdorf, M. (1986). Women and city: Land use and zoning issues. *Journal of Urban Affairs, 7*(1), 15–25.

Ritzdorf, M. (1990). Whose American dream? *Journal of the American Planning Association, 56*(3), 386–389.

Robbins, J. M. (1979). Objective versus subjective responses to abortion. *Journal of Consulting and Clinical Psychology, 47*, 994–995.

Robbins, J. M., & DeLamater, J. (1985). Support from significant others and loneliness following induced abortion. *Social Psychiatry, 20*(2), 92–99.

Robins, P. K. (1986, September). Child support, welfare dependency, and poverty. *The American Economic Review, 76*(4), 768–788.

Robinson, H. L. (1982–1983). Joint custody: An idea whose time has come. *Journal of Family Law, 21*, 641–685.

Robinson, J. (1982, May-July). Interviews in People's Republic of China, Shandong Province.

Robinson, J. (1985, March). Of women and washing machines: Employment, housework and the reproduction of motherhood in socialist China. *The China Quarterly, 101*, 32–57.

Robinson, S. (1987, March). Kindergarten in America: Five major trends. *Phi Delta Kappan*, pp. 529–530.

Rodgers, H. (1986). *Poor women, poor families. The economic plight of America's female headed households.* Armonk, NY: M. E. Sharpe, Inc.

Rodman, H. (1984, May). *Do self-care (latchkey) arrangements have negative consequences for children's development?* Paper presented at the First National Conference on Latchkey Children, Boston, MA.

Rodman, H. (1990). The social construction of the latchkey children problem. *Sociological Studies of Child Development, 3*, 163–174.

Rodman, H., & Cole, C. (1987). Latchkey children: A review of policy and resources. *Family Relations, 36*, 101–105.

Rodman, H., Pratto, D. J., & Nelson, R. S. (1985). Child care arrangements and children's functioning: A comparison of self-care and adult-care children. *Developmental Psychology, 21*, 413–418.

Rodman, H., Pratto, D. J., & Nelson, R. S. (1988). Toward a definition of self-care children: A commentary on Steinberg (1986). *Developmental Psychology, 24*, 292–294.

Roman, M., & Haddad, W. (1978). *The disposable parent: The case for joint custody.* New York: Holt, Rinehart, & Winston.

Rosado v. Wyman. (1970). 397 U.S. 412–414.

Rosen, A. (1988). State anxiety and abortion. *Anxiety Research, 1*, 115–125.

Rosenberg, M. (1965). *Society and the adolescent self-image.* Princeton, NJ: Princeton University Press.

Rosenmayer, L. (1984). Socio-cultural change in the relation of the family to its older member. In *Proceedings from Xth International Conference of Social Gerontology* (pp. 49–63). Paris: International Center of Social Gerontology.

Rosoff, J. I. (1973). Can state-administered programs achieve the national goal? *Family Planning Perspectives, 5*(4), 209–212.

Rosoff, J. I. (1981). Blocking family planning. *Family Planning Perspectives, 13*(3), 125–131.

Ross, C. M., & Danziger, S. (1987, Fall). Poverty rates by state, 1979 and 1985: A research note. *Focus, 10,* 1–4.

Rothberg, B. (1983). Joint custody: Parental problems and satisfactions. *Family Process, 22,* 43–52.

Rothman, S., & Marks, E. (1987). Adjusting work and family life: Flexible work schedules and family policy. In N. Gerstel & H. Gross (Eds.), *Families and work* (pp. 469–477). Philadelphia: Temple University Press.

Rotter, J. B. (1966). Generalized expectancies for internal vs. external control of reinforcement. *Psychological Monographs, 80* (whole no. 609).

Roybal, E. R. (1987). Making home care a workable alternative. *Business and Health, 4,* 11–13.

Royce, J. M., Darlington, R. B., & Murray, H. W. (1983). Pooled analyses: Findings across studies. In Consortium for Longitudinal Studies, *As the twig is bent . . . Lasting effects of preschool programs.* Hillsdale, NJ: Erlbaum.

Rue, V. (1973, November). A U.S. department of marriage and the family. *Journal of Marriage and the Family,* pp. 689–699.

Rynearson, E. K. (1982). Relinquishment and its maternal complications: A preliminary study. *American Journal of Psychiatry, 139,* 338–340.

Sacks, K. (1974). Engels revisited: Women, the organization of production and private property. In M. Rosaldo & L. Lamphere (Eds.), *Women, culture and society* (pp. 207–222). Stanford, CA: Stanford University Press.

Safilios-Rothschild, C. (1974). *Women and social policy.* Englewood Cliffs, NJ: Prentice-Hall.

Salisbury, R. H. (1968). Analysis of public policy: A search for theories and roles. In A. Ranney (Ed.), *Political science and public policy* (pp. 151–175). Chicago: Markham.

Sandler, B. (1986). The campus climate revisited: Chilly for women faculty, administrators, and graduate students. *Project on the status and education of women.* Washington, DC: Association of American Colleges.

Scanzoni, J. (1975). *Sex roles, life-styles and childbearing: Changing patterns of marriage and family.* New York: The Free Press.

Scanzoni, J. (1981). Reconsidering family policy: Status quo or force for change? *Journal of Family Issues, 3*(3), 277–300.

Scanzoni, J. (1982). *Shaping family policy for the 21st century.* Beverly Hills: Sage Publications.

Scanzoni, J. (1983). *Shaping tomorrow's family: Theory and policy for the 21st century.* Beverly Hills: Sage Publications.

Scanzoni, J. (1987). Families of the 1980s—time to refocus our thinking. *Journal of Family Issues, 8,* 394–421.

Scanzoni, J. (1989, Spring). Alternative images for public policy: Family structure versus families struggling. *Policy Studies Review, 8*(3), 599–609.

Scanzoni, J., & Arnett, C. (1987). Policy implications derived from a study of rural and urban marriages. *Family Relations: Journal of Applied Family and Child Studies, 36,* 430–436.

Scanzoni, J., Polonko, K., Teachman, J., & Thompson, L. (1989). *The sexual bond: Rethinking families and close relationships.* Newbury Park, CA: Sage Publications.

Scarr, S. (1984). *Mother care/other care.* New York: Basic Books.

Scharlach, A. E. (1987). Role strain in mother-daughter relationships in later life. *The Gerontologist, 27*, 627–631.

Schorr, A. L. (1960). *Filial responsibility in the modern family*. Washington, DC: U.S. Department of Health, Education, and Welfare, Social Security Administration.

Schorr, A. L. (1980). *Thy father and thy mother: A second look at filial responsibility and family policy*. Social Security Publication 13–1153. Washington, DC: Department of Health and Human Services.

Schulman, J., & Pitt, V. (1984). Second thoughts on joint child custody: Analysis of legislation and its implications for women and children. In J. Folberg (Ed.), *Joint custody and shared parenting* (pp. 209–222). Washington, DC: Bureau of National Affairs.

Schultz, T., & Lombardi, J. (1989). Right from the start: A report on the NASBE task force on early childhood education. *Young Children*, pp. 6–10.

Schwarz, V. (1981). Ruminations of a feminist in China. *Quest 3*, 33–35.

Schweinhart, L., Koshel, J., & Bridgman, A. (1987, March). Policy options for preschool programs. *Phi Delta Kappan*, pp. 524–529.

Seligson, M. (1986, May). Child care for the school-age child. *Phi Delta Kappan*, pp. 637–640.

Senate Committee on Labor and Human Resources. (1984). *School Facilities Child Care Act: Hearings Before a Subcommittee on Education, Arts, and Humanities*. Washington, DC: U.S. Government Printing Office.

Shanas, E. (1977). *National survey of the aged. Final report to the Administration on Aging*. AOA Grant no. 90-A–369.

Shehan, C. L., & Scanzoni, J. (1988). Gender patterns in the United States: Demographic trends and policy prospects. *Family Relations: A Journal of Applied Research, 37*, 444–450.

Sheppard, A. (1982). Unspoken premises in custody litigation. *Women's Rights Law Reporter, 7*(3), 229–234.

Sheridan, M. (1976). Young women leaders in China. *Signs, 2*(1), 59–88.

Sidel, R. (1986). *Women and children last: The plight of poor women in affluent America*. New York: Viking Press.

Simon, W. (1983, Fall). Legality, bureaucracy and class in the welfare system. *Yale Law Journal, 92*, 1198–1286.

Sixth Gansu provincial women's federation. (1980, 5 December). *FBIS*, p. T-1.

Skoloff, G. (1984). Joint custody: A jaundiced view. *Trial, 20*, 52–54.

Smith, M. P. (1988). *City, state and market: The political economy of urban society*. New York: Basil Blackwell.

Smith, S. (1988, March 16). Whole truth isn't being told about aftermath of abortion. *Argus-Champion Newspaper* (Newport, NH), p. 6.

Solving family conflicts. (1985, October). *Women of China*, pp. 1–3.

Sommers, A. R. (1985). Long-term care for the elderly and disabled: An urgent challenge to new federalism. In B. D. Dunlop (Ed.), *New federalism and long-term health care of the elderly* (pp. 43–61). Millwood, VA: Center for Health Affairs, Project Hope.

Spakes, P. (1985). The Supreme Court, family policy, and alternative family lifestyles: The clash of interests. *Lifestyles: A Journal of Changing Patterns, 7*(3), 171–186.

Spakes, P. (1988, Spring). A feminist case against national family policy: View to the future. *Policy Studies Review, 8*(3), 610–621.

Spakes, P. (1989). *National family policy and the Supreme Court: Issues and directions.* Work in progress.

Speckhard, A. (1987a). *Post abortion counseling: A manual for Christian counselors.* Falls Church, VA: PACE.

Speckhard, A. (1987b). *Psycho-social stress following abortion.* Kansas City, MO: Sheed & Reed.

Spector, M., & Kitsuse, J. I. (1977). *Constructing Social Problems.* Menlo Park, CA: Cummings Publishing Co.

Spitzer, R. J. (1987). Promoting policy theory: revising the arenas of power. *Policy Studies Journal, 15*, 675–689.

Staples, R. (1973). Public policy and the changing status of black families. *Family Coordinator, 22*(3), 345–351.

Staples, R. (1989). Reflections on the black family future: The implications of public policy. *Western Journal of Black Studies, 12*(1), 19–27.

Steinberg, L. (1986). Latchkey children and susceptibility to peer pressure: An ecological analysis. *Developmental Psychology, 22*, 433–439.

Steinberg, L. (1988). Simple solutions to a complex problem: A response to Rodman, Pratto, and Nelson (1988). *Developmental Psychology, 24*, 295–296.

Steiner, G. (1981). *The futility of family policy.* Washington, DC: The Brookings Institute.

Steinman, S. (1981). The experience of children in a joint-custody arrangement: A report of a study. *American Journal of Orthopsychiatry, 51*, 403–414.

Steinman, S. B., Zemmelman, S. E., & Knoblauch, T. M. (1985). A study of parents who sought joint custody following divorce: Who reaches agreement and sustains joint custody and who returns to court. *Journal of the American Academy of Child Psychiatry, 24*, 554–562.

Steinmetz, S. K. (1988). *Duty bound elder abuse and family care.* Newbury Park, CA: Sage Publications.

Stevens, W. K. (1988, 20 October). Welfare bill: Historic scope but gradual impact. *New York Times*, p. 20.

Stipek, D., & McCrosky, J. (1989). Investing in children: Government and workplace policies for parents. *American Psychologist, 44*(2), 416–423.

Stolcke, V. (1981). Women's labours: The naturalization of social inequality and women's subordination. In K. Young (Ed.), *Of marriage and the market* (pp. 30–48). London: CSE.

Stone, C. E. (1985). Efficiency versus social learning: A reconsideration of the implementation process. *Policy Studies Review, 4*(3), 484–490.

Stone, R., Cafferata, G. L., & Sangl, J. (1987). Caregivers of the frail elderly: A national profile. *The Gerontologist, 27*, 616–625.

Sundquist, J. L. (1984). Privatization: No panacea for what ails government. In H. Brooks, L. Liebman, & C. S. Schelling (Eds.), *Public private partnership: New opportunities for meeting social need* (pp. 303–318). Cambridge, MA: Ballinger.

Sussman, M. B. (1985). The family of old people. In R. H. Binstock & E. Shanas

(Eds.), *Handbook of aging and the social sciences* (pp. 415–449). New York: Van Nostrand Reinhold.

Tanaka-Matsumi, J., & Kameoka, V. (1986). Reliabilities and concurrent validities of popular self-report measures of depression, anxiety, and social desirability. *Journal of Consulting and Clinical Psychology, 54,* 328–333.

Tanfer, K. (1987). Patterns of premarital cohabitation among never-married women in the United States. *Journal of Marriage and Family, 49,* 483–498.

Tao, C. (1987, February). Virtuous husbands and good fathers. *Women of China, 2,* 19–20.

Tatalovich, R., & Daynes, B. W. (1984). Moral controversies and the policy-making process: Lowi's framework applied to the abortion issue. *Policy Studies Review, 3,* 207–222.

Thorne, B., & Henley, N. (Eds.). (1975). *Language and sex: Difference and dominance.* Rowley, MA: Newbury House.

Tianjin Ribao. (1984, 26 October). *Regulations concerning protection of the legitimate rights and interests of the women and children of Tianjin Municipality.*

Tietze, W. (1989, Winter). An international perspective on schooling for 4-year-olds. *Theory into Practice,* pp. 69–77.

Torres, A. (1983). The family planning program and cuts in federal spending: Initial effects on the provision of services. *Family Planning Perspectives, 15*(4), 184–191.

Torres, A., & Forrest, J. (1988). Why do women have abortions? *Family Planning Perspectives, 20*(4), 169–176.

Torres, A., Forrest, J. D., & Eisman, S. (1981). Family planning services in the United States (1978–79). *Family Planning Perspectives, 13*(3), 132–141.

Trader, H. P. (1979). Welfare policies and black families. *Social Work, 24*(6), 548–552.

Trager, B. (1973). *Homemaker/home health aides services in the United States.* Washington, DC: U.S. Government Printing Office.

Treas, J. (1975). Aging and the family. In D. S. Woodruff & J. E. Birren (Eds.), *Aging, Scientific perspectives and social issues* (pp. 92–108). New York: D. Van Nostrand Company.

Troll, L. E., Miller, S., & Atchley, R. (1979). *Families in later life.* Belmont, CA: Wadsworth Publishing Company.

Trotter, R. (1987, December). Project day-care. *Psychology Today,* pp. 32–38.

Trzcinski, E., & Finn-Stevenson, M. (1990). *A response to arguments against mandated parental leave: Findings from the Connecticut survey of parental leave policies.* Unpublished manuscript. New Haven, CT: Bush Center on Child Development and Social Policy.

Turkington, C. (1983, November). Lifetime of fear may be legacy of latchkey children. *APA Monitor,* p. 19.

Turner, R. H. (1985). Unanswered questions in the convergence between structuralist and interactionist role theories. In H. J. Helle & S. N. Eisenstadt (Eds.), *Microsociological Theory, 2* (pp. 23–36). Beverly Hills: Sage.

U.S. Bureau of Labor Statistics. (1987). *Usual weekly earnings of wage and salary workers: Second quarter 1987* (News, USDL 87–327). Washington, DC: U.S. Government Printing Office.

U.S. Bureau of the Census. (1961), (1981). *Statistical Abstract of the United States.* Washington, DC: U.S. Government Printing Office.

U.S. Bureau of the Census. (1976). *Daytime care of children: October, 1974 and February, 1975* (Current Population Reports, Series P-20, No. 298). Washington, DC: U.S. Government Printing Office.

U.S. Bureau of the Census. (1980). *Child support and alimony: 1978 (advance report)* (Current Population Reports, Special Studies, Series P-23, No. 106). Washington, DC: U.S. Government Printing Office.

U.S. Bureau of the Census. (1981). *Child support and alimony: 1978* (Current Population Reports, Special Studies, Series P-23, No. 112). Washington, DC: U.S. Government Printing Office.

U.S. Bureau of the Census. (1982). *Trends in child care arrangements of working mothers: 1977* (Current Population Reports, Series P-23, No. 117). Washington, DC: U.S. Government Printing Office.

U.S. Bureau of the Census. (1983a). *Child care arrangements of working mothers: June 1982* (Current Population Reports, Series P-23, No. 129). Washington, DC: U.S. Government Printing Office.

U.S. Bureau of the Census. (1983b). *County and city data book.* Washington, DC: U.S. Government Printing Office.

U.S. Bureau of the Census. (1983c). *State government finances in 1982.* Washington, DC: U.S. Government Printing Office.

U.S. Bureau of the Census. (1984). *State government finances in 1983.* Washington, DC: U.S. Government Printing Office.

U.S. Bureau of the Census. (1985a). *Child support and alimony: 1983* (Current Population Reports, Series P-23, No. 141). Washington, DC: U.S. Government Printing Office.

U.S. Bureau of the Census. (1985b). *Child support and alimony: 1985* (Current Population Reports, Series P-23, No. 140). Washington, DC: U.S. Government Printing Office.

U.S. Bureau of the Census. (1986a). *School enrollment—social and economic characteristics of students: October, 1985* (Current Population Reports, Series P-20, No. 409). Washington, DC: U.S. Government Printing Office.

U.S. Bureau of the Census. (1986b). *State government finances in 1985.* Washington, DC: U.S. Government Printing Office.

U.S. Bureau of the Census. (1986c). *Statistical abstract of the United States: 1987.* Washington, DC: U.S. Government Printing Office.

U.S. Bureau of the Census. (1987a). *After-school care of school-age children: December 1984* (Current Population Reports, Series P-23, No. 149). Washington, DC: U.S. Government Printing Office.

U.S. Bureau of the Census. (1987b). *Child support and alimony: (1985)* (Advance data from March-April 1986, Current Population Reports, Special Studies, Series P–23, No. 152). Washington, DC: U.S. Government Printing Office.

U.S. Bureau of the Census. (1987c). *Who's minding the kids? Child care arrangements: Winter 1984–85* (Current Population Reports, Series P-70, No. 9). Washington, DC: U.S. Government Printing Office.

U.S. Bureau of the Census. (1988). *Fertility of American women: 1987* (Current Population Reports, Series P-20, No. 427). Washington, DC: U.S. Government Printing Office.

U.S. Bureau of the Census. (1989). *Household and family characteristics: March 1988* (Current Population Reports, Series P-20, No. 437). Washington, DC: U.S. Government Printing Office.

U.S. Department of Commerce. (1981). *Survey of current business.* Washington, DC: U.S. Government Printing Office.

U.S. Department of Commerce. (1987). *Survey of current business.* Washington, DC: U.S. Government Printing Office.

U.S. Department of Commerce. (1989). *Survey of current business.* Washington, DC: U.S. Government Printing Office.

U.S. Department of Health and Human Services. (1980). *Research tables based on characteristics of state plans for AFDC.* Washington, DC: U.S. Government Printing Office.

U.S. Department of Health and Human Services. (1986a). *Research tables based on characteristics of state plans for AFDC.* Washington, DC: U.S. Government Printing Office.

U.S. Department of Health and Human Services. (1986b). *Vital statistics of the United States, 1982,* Vol. III, Marriage and Divorce. Washington, DC: U.S. Government Printing Office.

U.S. Department of Health and Human Serives. (1987a). *Characteristics of state plans for AFDC.* Washington, DC: U.S. Government Printing Office.

U.S. Department of Health and Human Services. (1987b). *Monthly benefit statistics: Summary program data,* No. 5. Washington, DC: U.S. Government Printing Office.

U.S. Department of Health and Human Services. (1989a). *Characteristics of state plans for AFDC.* Washington, DC: U.S. Government Printing Office.

U.S. Department of Health and Human Services. (1989b). *Monthly benefit statistics: Summary program data.* Washington, DC: U.S. Government Printing Office.

U.S. Department of Labor. (1972). *Three budgets for an urban family of four persons, 1969–70: Supplement to bulletin 1570–5.* Washington, DC: U.S. Government Printing Office.

U.S. Department of Labor, Bureau of Labor Statistics. (1988, 15 January). Washington, DC: U.S. Government Printing Office.

U.S. Department of Labor, Women's Bureau. (1983). *Time of change: 1983 handbook on women workers.* Washington, DC: U.S. Government Printing Office.

U.S. Executive Office of the President. (1986). *The family: Preserving America's future—A report of the working group on the family.* Washington, DC: Domestic Policy Council.

U.S. General Accounting Office. (1987). *Work and welfare: Current AFDC work programs and their implications for federal policy.* Washington, DC: U.S. Government Printing Office.

U.S. House of Representatives, Committee on Ways and Means. (1987). *Background material and data on programs within the jurisdiction of the Committee on Ways and Means.* Washington, DC: U.S. Government Printing Office.

U.S. House of Representatives, Committee on Ways and Means. (1988). *Background material and data on programs within the jurisdiction of the Committee on Ways and Means.* Washington, DC: U.S. Government Printing Office.

U.S. House of Representatives, Committee on Ways and Means. (1989). *Back-*

ground material and data on programs within the jurisdiction of the Committee on Ways and Means. Washington, DC: U.S. Government Printing Office.

U.S. National Center for Health Statistics. (1988). *Vital statistics of the United States*, Vol. 1, Natality. Washington, DC: U.S. Government Printing Office.

U.S. Social Security Administration. (1969). *Social security bulletin*. Washington, DC: U.S. Government Printing Office.

U.S. Social Security Administration. (1973). *Social security bulletin*. Washington, DC: U.S. Government Printing Office.

Vandell, D. L., & Corasaniti, M. A. (1988). The relation between third graders' after-school care and social, academic, and emotional functioning. *Child Development, 59*, 868–875.

Victor, K. (1987). Not praying together. *National Journal, 19*(41), 2546–2551.

Vladeck, B. C. (1980). *Unloving care*. New York: Basic Books.

Vogel, R. J., & Palmer, H. C. (1985). *Long-term care—Perspectives from research and demonstrations*. Rockville, MD: Aspen Publication.

Waerness, K. (1984). Caring as women's work in the welfare state. In H. Holter (Ed.), *Patriarchy in a welfare society* (pp. 67–87). Oslo: Universitetsforlaget.

Walker, A. (1981). Towards a political economy of old age. *Aging and society, 1*, 73–94.

Walker, A., & Phillipson, C. (1986). Introduction. In C. Phillipson & A. Walker (Eds.), *Aging and social policy: A critical assessment* (pp. 1–12). London: Gower Publishing Company.

Wallerstein, J. S., & Kelly, J. B. (1980). *Surviving the breakup: How children and parents cope with divorce*. New York: Basic Books.

Walton, R. E. (1979, July-August). Work innovations in the United States. *Harvard Business Review*, pp. 88–98.

Wattenberg, B. (1976). *The statistical history of the United States from colonial times to present*. New York: Basic Books.

Wattleton, F. (1989, 24/31 July). Teenage pregnancy: The case for national action. *The Nation*, pp. 128–141.

Wei, S. (1985, 1 September). Proper image of Chinese women in our time defined. *Fujian Qingnian, 9*, 30–31.

Weinberg, D. (1972). State administration and financing of family planning services. *Family Planning Perspectives, 4*(2), 32–41.

Wei Shu. (1985, 1 September). Proper image of Chinese women in our time defined. *Fujian Qingnian, 9*, 30–31.

Weiss, R. S. (1987). On the current state of the American family. *Journal of Family Issues, 8*, 464–467.

Weitzman, L. J. (1985). *The divorce revolution: The unexpected social and economic consequences for women and children in America*. New York: The Free Press.

Welsh, J. B., & Franklin, R. (1988). *Valuing basic needs in New York State: A methodological proposal*. New York: New York State Department of Social Services.

West, G. (1981). *The national welfare rights movement*. New York: Praeger Publishers.

Westinghouse Learning Corporation. (1969). *The impact of Head Start: An evaluation of the effects of Head Start on children's cognitive and affective development*.

Executive Summary, Ohio University report to the Office of Economic Opportunity. Washington, DC: Clearinghouse for Federal Scientific and Technical Information (ED036321).

Wiggins, C. W., & Browne, W. P. (1986). Interest groups and public policy within a state legislative setting. In M. Gittell (Ed.), *State politics and the new federalism* (pp. 111–120). New York: Longman.

Wilson, J. Q. (1985, Fall). The rediscovery of character: Private virtue and public policy. *The Public Interest, 81,* 3–16.

Windley, P. G. (1982). Environmental dispositions: A theoretical and methodological alternative. In M. P. Lawton, P. G. Windley, & T. O. Byerts (Eds.), *Aging and the environment* (pp. 60–79). New York: Springer.

Wisensale, S. (1989, Spring). Family policy in the state legislature: The Connecticut agenda. *Policy Studies Review, 8*(3), 622–637.

Wisensale, S. (1990). Approaches to family policy in state government: A report on five states. *Family Relations, 39,* 136–140.

Wolf, M. (1972). *Women and family in rural Taiwan.* Stanford, CA: Stanford University Press.

Wolf, M. (1985). *Revolution postponed—Women in contemporary China.* Stanford, CA: Stanford University Press.

Wolfe, A. (1989, Spring). The day-care dilemma: A Scandinavian perspective. *Public Interest, 95,* 14–23.

Woman leader on new marriage law. (1981, 16 March). *Beijing Review,* p. 23.

Women of China. (1985, October). Solving family conflicts, *10,* 1–3.

Women of China. (1985, November). Marriage advertisements in China, and New Wedding Trends, *11,* 13–14.

Women in China. (1987, Feburary). How is property divided on divorce? *2,* 42.

Wood, J., & Estes, C. (1985). Private nonprofit organizations and community-based long-term care. In J. Harrington, et al. (Eds.), *Long-term care of the elderly, public policy issues* (pp. 213–231). Beverly Hills: Sage Publications.

Xian, L. (1987, February). Women and men have their distinct roles. *Women of China* (2), 18–19.

Xinhua. (1980, 7 January). *Guangdong Provincial News Service,* p. P-1.

Xinhua. (1980, 4 September). NPC deputies discuss views on marriage law. Trans. in *FBIS,* p. L-17.

Xinhua. (1980, 7 February). Beijing circular on reform of marriage customs. Trans. in *FBIS,* p. R-2.

Xinhua. (1980, 5 September). CPPCC women's group discusses draft marriage law. Trans. in *FBIS,* p. L-18.

Xinhua. (1980, 25 September). CCPCC issues open letter on population control. Trans. in *FBIS,* p. L-10.

Xinhua. (1980, 5 October). Interview of jurist on marriage law and divorce. Trans. in *FBIS,* p. L-12.

Xinhua. (1981, 8 January). Journal interviews women on new marriage law. Trans. in *FBIS,* p. L-21.

Xinhua. (1981, 10 February). Renmin Ribao editorial urges planned parenthood. Trans. in *FBIS,* p. L-16.

Xinhua. (1984, 8 December). Economic reforms promoting sex equality. Trans. in *JPRS* (CPS-85–012), p. 1.

Xinhua. (1985, 18 February). Trans. in *JPRS* (CPS-85–024, 13 March, pp. 17–18.

Xinhua. (1985, 15 March). Womens' federation proposes law on adultery. Trans. in *JPRS* (CPS-85–033), pp. 36–37.

Xinhua. (1985, 23 March). Survey shows changing trend for women. Trans. in *JPRS* (CPS-85–033), p. 35.

Xinhua. (1985, 5 April). Womens' federation proposes law on adultery. Trans. in *JPRS* (CPS-85–033), pp. 36–37.

Xinhua. (1985, 10 December). Ningxia rural women gain skills through courses. Trans. in *JPRS* (CEA-86–003), p. 57.

Xinhua. (1986, 6 October). Women workers become major force in all fields. Trans. in *JPRS* (CEA-119), pp. 67–68.

Zabin, L. S. (1983, September). The effect of family planning policy on maternal and child health. *Journal of Public Health Policy*, pp. 268–278.

Zabin, L., Hirsch, M., & Emerson, M. (1989). When urban adolescents choose abortion: Effects on education, psychological status, and subsequent pregnancy. *Family Planning Perspective, 21*(6), 248–255.

Zakus, G., & Wilday, S. (1987). Adolescent abortion option. *Social Work in Health Care, 12*(4), 77–91.

Zhao, Z. (1981, 21 December). The present economic situation and the principles for future economic construction. *Beijing Review, 51*, 32.

Zhejiang women's group urges protection of rights. (1980, 11 December). *FBIS*, p. O–4.

Zhongguo Funu. (1985, 6 June).

Zhongguo Xiao Feizhe Bao. (1987, 6 April).

Zigler, E. (1987a, March). Formal schooling for four-year-olds? No. *American Psychologist*, pp. 443–454.

Zigler, E. (1987b). *A solution to the nation's child care crisis: The school in the twenty-first century*. Unpublished manuscript. New Haven, CT: Yale University, Bush Center for Child and Family Policy.

Zigler, E., & Finn-Stevenson, M. (1989). Child care in America: From problem to solution. *Educational Policy, 3*(4), 313–329.

Zimmerman, S. L. (1987a). *State government councils on families and/or children: Form or substance: A report of a survey of the 50 states*. Mimeo. St. Paul: University of Minnesota, Family Social Science.

Zimmerman, S. L. (1987b). States' public welfare expenditures as predictors of state suicide rates. *Suicide and Life Threatening Behavior, 17*, 271–287.

Zimmerman, S. L. (1988). State level public policy and individual and family well-being as measured by state suicide and teen birth rates: A systems view. In S. L. Zimmerman, *Understanding family policy: theoretical approaches* (pp. 126–144). Newbury Park, CA: Sage Publications.

Zimmerman, S. L., & Owens, P. (1989). Comparing the family policies of three states: A content analysis. *Family Relations, 38*, 190–195.

Zinsser, C. (1986). *Day care's unfair burden: How low wages subsidize a public service*. New York: Center for Public Advocacy Research.

Zung, W. (1965). A self-rating depression scale. *Archives of General Psychiatry, 12*, 63–70.

Index

About the Editors and Contributors

ELAINE A. ANDERSON is an associate professor in the department of Family and Community Development, University of Maryland–College Park. She has conducted research on work policy and family development at different life stages, the homeless, and AIDS education. She has contributed chapters to several books on family studies and has published articles in the *Journal of Marriage and the Family*, *Criminology*, and *Journal of Housing for the Elderly*, among others.

RICHARD C. HULA is an associate professor at the Institute for Urban Studies, University of Maryland–College Park. He has written numerous articles, books, and book chapters on privatization, urban public policy, and related issues.

ANDREA H. BELLER is an associate professor in the School of Human Resources and Family Studies, University of Illinois at Urbana-Champaign.

DANIELLE BUSSELL is a doctoral candidate at University of Maryland–College Park.

MARY ANNE CHALKLEY is an assistant professor at the College of St. Thomas.

SEUNG SIN CHUNG is an assistant professor in the department of Home Economics, Keon Kook University, Seoul, Korea.

CLIFTON P. FLYNN is an assistant professor of Sociology, University of South Carolina–Spartanburg.

DORIS E. DINKINS FORD is an associate professor in the department of Political Science, Auburn University.

THERESA FUNICIELLO is codirector of Social Agenda.

PATRICIA GARRETT is a senior investigator at the Frank Porter Graham Child Development Center, University of North Carolina, Chapel Hill.

ROBERT K. LEIK is a professor of Sociology, University of Minnesota.

SALLY LUBECK is an assistant professor in the School of Education, University of Michigan.

DEBORAH R. MCFARLANE is an associate professor in the Division of Public Administration, University of New Mexico.

NANCY J. PETERSON has served as an assistant professor in the department of Sociology, University of Minnesota.

JEAN ROBINSON is an associate professor in the department of Political Science, Indiana University.

HYMAN RODMAN is Excellence Professor in the department of Child Development and Family Relations, University of North Carolina at Greensboro.

JOHN SCANZONI is professor of Sociology at the University of Florida.

SANFORD F. SCHRAM is an associate professor in the department of Political Science, Macalester College.

PATRICIA SPAKES is a professor in the school of Arts and Sciences, University of Arizona State University, West Campus.

BRIAN L. WILCOX is director of public interest legislation for the American Psychological Association.

GREGORY H. WILMOTH is a senior social science analyst with the U.S. General Accounting Office.

STEVEN K. WISENSALE is an associate professor in the School of Family Studies, University of Connecticut.

SHIRLEY L. ZIMMERMAN is a professor in the department of Family Social Science, University of Minnesota.